DATE DUE

Childhood on the Farm

❖ ❖ ❖ ❖ ❖ ❖ ❖ ❖ ❖ ❖ ❖ ❖ ❖ ❖

Childhood on the Farm

WORK, PLAY, AND COMING OF AGE IN THE MIDWEST

Pamela Riney-Kehrberg

UNIVERSITY PRESS OF KANSAS

Published by the University Press of Kansas (Lawrence, Kansas 66049), which was
organized by the Kansas Board of Regents and is operated and funded by Emporia State
University, Fort Hays State University, Kansas State University, Pittsburg State
University, the University of Kansas, and Wichita State University

Library of Congress Cataloging-in-Publication Data

Riney-Kehrberg, Pamela.
Childhood on the farm : work, play, and coming of age in the Midwest /
Pamela Riney-Kehrberg.
p.   cm.
Includes bibliographical references and index.
ISBN 0-7006-1388-9 (cloth : alk. paper)
1. Farm life—Middle West—History. 2. Rural children—Middle West—
Social life and customs. 3. Middle West—Social life and customs. I. Title.

F354.R57   2005
305.23'0977'09034—DC22
2005000911

British Library Cataloguing-in-Publication Data is available.
Printed in the United States of America

2 4 6 8 10 9 7 5 3 1

The paper used in this publication meets the minimum requirements of the American
National Standard for Permanence of Paper for Printed Library Materials Z39.48-1984.

Portions of Chapters 1–3, 5, and the Epilogue appeared originally, in somewhat different
form, in Pamela Riney-Kehrberg, "Women in Wheat Country." Kansas History: A Jour-
nal of the Central Plains 23, 1–2 (2000): 56–71; Pamela Riney-Kehrberg, "Helping Ma and
Helping Pa: Iowa's Turn-of-the-Century Farm Children." Annals of Iowa 59, 2 (2000):
115–140; Pamela Riney-Kehrberg, "'But What Kind of Work Do the Rest of You Do?' Child
Labor on Nebraska's Farms, 1870–1920." Nebraska History 82, 1 (2001): 2–10; Pamela
Riney-Kehrberg, "The Limits of Policy: Rural Children and Work in the United States and
New Zealand, 1870–1920." The History of the Family 6 (2001): 51–67; and Pamela Riney-
Kehrberg, "Growing Up in Kansas." Kansas History: A Journal of the Central Plains 26,
(2003): 50–65.

For Rick,

just because.

Contents

❖   ❖   ❖   ❖   ❖   ❖   ❖

Contents

Acknowledgments

Any project this long and involved requires many, many acknowledgments. This book began as an idea in 1997, when I was at Illinois State University. The manuscript came to completion in 2004, at Iowa State University. Between those two points have been many helpful people, organizations, and institutions that have made the project possible.

For funding and research leave, I thank the following: for a University Research Grant and sabbatical leave, Illinois State University; for two Humanities Summer Salary Grants, a Publication Grant from the Center for the Arts and Humanities, a College of Liberal Arts and Sciences Small Grant, as well as research leave, Iowa State University; the Minnesota Historical Society, a Visiting Scholar Grant; the State Historical Society of Iowa, a Historical Research Grant; the Nebraska State Historical Society, a Historical Research Grant. Deserving special mention is the J. William Fulbright Foreign Scholarship Board Senior Scholar Program, at the Alexander Turnbull Library, in Wellington, New Zealand. Although I researched farm childhood in New Zealand while I was there, what I learned was invaluable in my continued work on American farm childhood.

I would like to thank the publishers of *Annals of Iowa, History of the Family, Kansas History,* and *Nebraska History* for allowing me to make use of portions of the following articles, albeit in somewhat different form, in this book: "'But What Kind of Work Do the Rest of You Do?' Child Labor on Nebraska's Farms, 1870–1920," *Nebraska History* 82, no. 1 (spring 2001): 2–10 (Chapter 2); "Growing Up in Kansas," *Kansas History: A Journal of the Central Plains* 26 (spring 2003): 50–65 (Epilogue); "Helping Ma and Helping Pa: Iowa's Turn-of-the-Century Farm Children," *Annals of Iowa* 59, no. 2 (spring 2000): 115–40 (Chapters 2, 3, and 5 and Epilogue); "The Limits of Policy: Rural Children and Work in the United States and New Zealand, 1870–1920," *History of the Family* 6 (2001): 51–67 (Chapters 1 and 3); "Women in

Wheat Country," *Kansas History: A Journal of the Central Plains* 23, no. 1–2 (spring–summer 2000): 56–71 (Chapter 2).

The archivists and staffs at the following research locations were enormously helpful. Without them, I could not have completed this project: the Kansas State Historical Society; the Nebraska State Historical Society; the Illinois Historical Society; the many branches of the Wisconsin Historical Society; the Minnesota Historical Society; the State Historical Society of Iowa (particularly the Iowa City branch); Special Collections, Parks Library, Iowa State University; the Iowa Women's Archives, Iowa City; the McLean County Historical Society, Bloomington, Illinois; and the archives of Winona State University Library, Winona State University, Winona, Minnesota. To those of you who have not yet worked at the Kansas State Historical Society, I recommend it as a particularly fine research facility.

I also highly recommend the helpful people at the University Press of Kansas, particularly Nancy Scott Jackson, acquisitions editor extraordinaire. My thanks, too, to the anonymous reviewers who read and commented on my work, as well as the generous Paula Petrik, a not-so-anonymous reviewer.

A resounding thanks to the many people who allowed me to camp out in their guest bedrooms or on their couches during my many research travels: Karen Hiller and family, Ginette Aley, Micheline Turner, Sue Kehrberg, and Nancy Kehrberg. And many thanks to friends in Madison who fed and entertained me in the weeks I spent there.

A number of scholars have given generously of their time, reading a chapter or chapters for me while the book was in progress: Allan G. Bogue, Andrejs Plakans, David Danbom, Kathy Jellison, Brian Cannon, and Roberta Trites. Any remaining misinterpretations, misspellings, typos, and other errors of fact or interpretation are not theirs, but mine. I am also very grateful to those who had patience with my musings at one stage of this project or another, but particularly the members of the History Departments at Illinois State and Iowa State University. I am especially grateful to the graduate students at Iowa State University for their patience with my "kids." Friends and colleagues in New Zealand were particularly helpful at the book's formative stage. I wish to thank Kate Hunter, Jeanine Graham, and Claire Toynbee for their insights. And for sending me to collections in Wisconsin absolutely vital to this book, I thank Joan Jensen. All of the members of the Rural Women's Studies Association are due great thanks for encouraging me to pursue this project and providing an ongoing forum for the examination of rural history.

Acknowledgments

I can't help but think that my decision to write on this topic stemmed from two different influences: my teachers and my family. I was the happy recipient of excellent teaching throughout my education, much of it provided by rural children who grew up to be highly influential teachers. I am thinking particularly of Diane Ritzdorf, Dalton Holsteen, Ruth and T. K. Barton, and Allan G. Bogue. Their stories and example have been an enormous influence in my life. My family, too, was full of children who left the farm and then told their stories around the kitchen table as adults. Each of my grandparents—Elsie May Swafford Riney, James Harvey Riney, Wesley Alexander Thompson, and Margaret Jane Collier Thompson Barnes—was a farm child who chose, as an adult, to leave the land. Their stories of childhoods lived on the land, and my Grandma Riney's regular admonishments that the "good old days" were not good at all, left me wondering about their lives and wanting to know more. Even though all four are gone now, I feel as if I know them, and their lives, much better. My mother also bears a certain responsibility for the topic of this book, having introduced me at age eight to Laura Ingalls Wilder's Little House books, one of my earliest sources of historical inspiration.

My deepest debts of gratitude are to my most immediate family. My parents, Mary and Norm Riney, continue to provide enormous emotional support, as does my brother, Scott Riney. My son, Richard Frank Kehrberg, born in the middle of this project, has taught me more about family and family history than I ever thought possible. He is a joy and my inspiration, and I am a better historian because of him. Richard F. Kehrberg, my husband, partner, and best friend, has been my most important source of support for nearly twenty years. I dedicate this book to him, just because.

Introduction

I picked potatoes all week. Monday we washed. . . . Lizzie and Evert doesn't go to school either they have to help pick. Friday we picked a load of corn for the pigs and after we got through picking the potatoes.
—Mary Van Zante, age thirteen, near Pella, Iowa, 1889

I hauled a load of feed home. I went fishing with Lewis this afternoon but did not catch any. 36 eggs. I milked 6 cows. Jessie & the children came down. We played croquet.
—Ralph Wood, age fourteen, Trempealeau County, Wisconsin, 1893

Burned corn which I hauled from the field. The chickens had their combs frozen last night. They got feed only once today. Cleaned the stables of snow and had the horses outside a while. Had to open the well again. . . . I went hunting. . . . I determined to go to school, but did not I studied some at home, in general, a very bad day.
—Hermann Benke, age fifteen, Barton County, Kansas, 1886

Mary Van Zante, Ralph Wood, and Hermann Benke were all late nineteenth-century farm children and residents of midwestern states. Despite their origins in Dutch, native-born, and German families and their residence in communities separated by hundreds of miles, they lived in a common world of hard work, grammar-school education, and limited recreation. Although their world and words would have seemed very familiar to many late nineteenth- and early twentieth-century Americans, it was a world and a way of life that was disappearing as they lived it. Between 1870 and 1920, the people of the United States transformed their nation from one that was rural and agricultural to one that was urban and industrial. In ever-increasing numbers, the children of America's farming families left the countryside and joined with millions of immigrants flooding into the nation's cities. By 1920, the Census Bureau could say with numerical certainty that the United States had ceased to be what it had been since its founding: a nation of rural families.

Farm children, however, continued to make up a large proportion of the midwest's population. Although the nation was urbanizing, this process was working much more slowly in the heartland. In 1900, Chicago, with its population in excess of a million and its plethora of downstate urban industrial communities such as Peoria and Decatur, pushed Illinois into the predominantly urban category, but states such as Iowa, Kansas, Minnesota, Nebraska, and Wisconsin remained predominantly rural, with 64, 65, 56, 69, and 53 percent of their populations, respectively, living on farms and in communities of less than 2,500 people.[1]

In the rural midwest, family farming remained an important way of life and continued to shape the prospects of many children.[2] The circumstances of their lives provide a sharp contrast to the idealized childhood of their day. From the early nineteenth century forward, middle-class urban Americans increasingly defined childhood as a time of education and play, excluding labor. By the late nineteenth century, these understandings were beginning to affect law, with the advent of compulsory schooling and child labor laws in many states. The law, however, treated farm children differently from others. Farm children's family labor remained entirely unregulated, and the application of mandatory education laws to farm children was uneven. By 1920, nearly all states had some restrictions on child labor in manufacturing, mining, and retail occupations, yet none regulated the hours of children's labor on their parents' farms. Additionally, many states, such as Nebraska, allowed rural schools to offer a shorter school term than urban schools, and all states allowed farm children to be excused from instruction to aid their parents in farm labor. Although there were exceptions, most farm children lived with age-old traditions of family life and labor that intimately connected the success of the family enterprise with the willingness of all to work.

It is this traditional world, persisting in spite of urbanization, industrialization, and changing familial expectations, that I explore in this book. I examine the lives of midwestern farm children in the years between 1870 and 1920. This time span has been chosen for several reasons. First, it avoids the upheavals the Civil War caused in northern farming communities. Although the war was fought largely in the south, northern families contributed large numbers of men to the conflict, disrupting the fabric of everyday life in many ways. To avoid these disruptions, I have chosen 1870 as my starting date. I have also chosen 1920 as an ending date because of upheavals occurring in the years that followed. Although families began purchasing automobiles and tractors before 1920, these new technologies became increasingly important in midwestern farming communities after this date. The revolution that internal combustion engines brought to farming and farm families holds stories for another time and another place. After 1920, the radio, too, brought far-reaching change to the countryside. Even more importantly, 1920 represents the beginning of twenty years of severe depression in midwestern agricultural communities. The prosperity of World War I gave way to the despair of depressed markets and falling incomes. The impact of these events in farm children's lives is also a story better left to another time and place.

Many changes occurred between 1870 and 1920, with farm mechanization proceeding rapidly, the rural to urban flow of population accelerating, and the agricultural economy moving through a series of peaks and valleys. Nevertheless, much remained the same. Family labor continued to be the primary mode of maintaining midwestern farms, and children continued to be integral to the economic health of their families' enterprises. Midwestern rural children continued to receive most of their education in one- and two-room country schools, with relatively few achieving a secondary or college education. The consumer revolution sweeping the cities had yet to change the fact that most rural families grew much of their own food and manufactured much of their own clothing. In a world where urban youngsters increasingly partook of commercial amusements and played with manufactured toys, fun in the countryside continued, for the most part, to be homemade. In many ways, the essential pattern of rural life was the same in 1920 as it had been in 1870.[3]

In this book, the midwest is defined as Illinois, Wisconsin, Minnesota, Iowa, and the eastern half of Nebraska and Kansas. Although the term *midwest* can be defined in many ways, I have chosen these states because of their geographic proximity and similarity to each other and the similarity of the populations that settled within them. I have not included areas farther to the west because of the special environmental strains imposed on families settling in the semiarid Great Plains. Farming families settled many plains communities in the early twentieth century, and they found conditions that were significantly more harsh than those in better-watered lands to the east.

I have chosen to write about childhood in broad terms because it cannot be defined with any precision in the context of turn-of-the-century rural communities. The term *teenager* had yet to be invented, and many young people well into their teens and early twenties, physically mature and no longer in school, remained at home, working for their parents. Although relationships between parents and children were changing, many farm parents still believed that a youngster's first obligation should be to the family enterprise, defined as the farm, their parents, and their siblings. In that context, a child is best defined as any dependent son or daughter, generally twenty-one or younger, regardless of physical maturity, who remained subject to his or her parents' authority on the farm and in the home. Youngsters who lived away from home periodically, but who were still expected to contribute their wages to the family and return home to labor as necessary, are also defined as children. Their experience provides a contrast to most maturing young people in urban areas who may have remained subject to their parents' authority, but who increasingly worked, played, and pursued an education at a significant distance from the family home.[4]

This is also the story of children of European descent, reflecting the ethnic composition of the midwest. Native-born whites composed between 75 and 85 percent of the population of the states chosen for this study. Wisconsin was the least "native," and Kansas was the most. African Americans made up no more than 4 percent of the population of any of these states, and the Native American population accounted for less than 1 percent. Throughout this portion of the midwest, the largest immigrant group by far was the Germans, and they predominated in each of these states. Swedes made up the second largest immigrant group; and the Irish, Norwegians, and English also formed a substantial portion of the population.[5] The available sources also reflect this distribution of population. I have tried, wherever possible, to make use of diaries, letters, and reminiscences in translation and in English from children from as many different communities as possible, including both native-born and immigrant communities. As a result, in addition to native-born children, those of Swedish, Norwegian, Danish, German, Swiss, and Dutch backgrounds are represented, as well as those descended from English, Irish, Welsh, Cornish, and Scottish ancestors. Where ethnicity made a significant difference in the fabric of children's lives, such as in the work roles of girls, I have noted these distinctions.

This book begins with a discussion of the place of farm children in the late nineteenth and early twentieth centuries. For many Americans, especially reformers concerned with child welfare, this was a complex issue. Although middle-class urban Americans increasingly thought of work and childhood as an antithetical combination, children and agricultural labor were intimately linked. Family farms, as most were at the turn of the last century, struggled to exist without the liberal application of child labor. But while most late nineteenth- and early twentieth-century advocates for children deplored child labor in factories, they were much less sure about the detrimental effects of children working in a family setting, under the supervision of their parents. They were also much less insistent about the application of mandatory education laws to farm children, and they were far less worried about the wholesomeness of their play relative to that of urban children. In their labor, schooling, and recreation, farm children seemed to fall outside of the realm of most people's concerns. They were an integral part of the agrarian ideal of industry, thrift, and independence that many feared was disappearing from the nation. Acceptance of a child's place on the farm as a different place from the urban ideal was part and parcel of maintaining the United States as an agricultural nation, if on a shrinking scale.

Within these parameters, I will discuss a number of issues central to the lives of farm children. First, of course, comes work. Children's work might hold different meanings in different families and at different times, ranging from being a pure matter of survival, to vocational education, to punishment. Although the meaning and exact nature of a child's work would be affected by factors such as a farm's location, the stage of development of the farming operation, and the wealth of the farming family, the contours of children's working lives were remarkably similar across communities and across time. Within a framework of age and gender, mediated by ethnic differences, a fairly comprehensive picture of children's work can be developed. My perspective on work is somewhat different than that presented in a number of recent histories of childhood. Taking my cues from the children, as well as the new perspectives in recent Scandinavian scholarship on child labor, I believe that work could be a self-affirming and positive experience for children, not just one of exploitation.[6]

After work came school. School, too, could hold different meanings for the community, parents, and children but will be described largely from the perspective of the children who attended the midwest's rural schools in the fifty years after the Civil War. School provided not only basic education and discipline, but also companionship and entertainment to young people. For many children, the social function of schooling was as important—or even more important—than learning reading, writing, and arithmetic. As explored in the next chapter, many of those farm children would become teachers, experiencing yet another facet of the rural school. While urban schools increasingly professionalized their staffs, many rural schools operated under the direction of youngsters of no more than sixteen or seventeen. Several extraordinary diaries such as those of Rhoda Emery of Olmsted County, Minnesota, and Hermann Benke, of Barton County, Kansas, make it possible to examine the transition from scholar to teacher and the effect of their work on their students, their families, and their own lives.

A chapter on play complements those on work and the various facets of school. Although parents might value their children's work efforts above all others, children relished their opportunities for play. Toys, games, and books played an important part in farm children's lives, as did the many opportunities for diversion present within the countryside. Children turned farm fields and farm structures into playgrounds and farm animals into pets. Children themselves typically wrote the script for their activities, resisting the prevalent progressive impulse to control and confine children in their recreational pursuits. The combination of toys and games, informal leisure activities, and more structured events available in many communities presented youngsters of varying ages with a far richer variety of diversions than a focus on children's work and school might suggest.

This story, however, would be incomplete if it only focused on the relatively positive tales of work, school, and play emanating from children's letters and diaries. An examination of the well-being of farm children as a group requires study of those who did not write their own stories and who only made their way into the historical record by way of their relationships, and their parents' relationships, to local and state government. Poor families and families beset by various forms of misfortune and dysfunction might come into contact with these bodies by way of courts, poor commissioners, and state welfare agencies. An examination of the relationship of children to these mechanisms within the state of Wisconsin, and especially an examination of Wisconsin's State Public School, opens a window into children's experiences outside of what we think of as the farm and rural norm of intact, functioning nuclear families.[7] Theirs was often a world of more work and less school and play. Many faced the world without the advantage of parents intimately concerned with their plans and futures.

No matter their circumstances, farm youngsters, like their urban counterparts, struggled with the difficult task of maturation and becoming adults. Just like their urban counterparts, they assumed new responsibilities, asserted their independence, and explored their sexual natures.

Parental strictures and claims of authority complicated this transition from child to adult, although for some more than others. One of the most crucial decisions young people faced was whether or not to remain in the countryside, a decision that largely determined their economic futures as adults. Many chose to forgo life in agriculture in favor of what they presumed would be an easier, less uncertain adulthood in America's growing urban areas. This, however, was not a foregone conclusion, and other youngsters, although a minority, turned their back on the cities in favor of the farm.

Although children's immediate experiences are at the heart of this research, the memories of farm-raised adults about their childhoods are also important. In those memories, translated into print, they identified the portions of that experience that most clearly defined who they were and what they valued. In their writings, these autobiographers tried to balance what was positive about their childhood experiences on the farm with what was damaging and hurtful. Both types of memories figure prominently in their descriptions of a world that, for the most part, no longer exists. Ultimately, in their reflections on the precarious and difficult nature of midwestern family farming, they helped to explain why, in the late nineteenth and early twentieth centuries, more and more people left farms in order to raise their own families in towns, cities, and suburbs.

In the late nineteenth and early twentieth centuries, children in the United States lived in many worlds, not just the single, idealized world of middle-class urban America. This book will provide the opportunity to see midwestern farm childhood from the perspectives of work, education, and play, and to see the world through the eyes of youngsters living within a framework of tradition that most in urban areas no longer experienced. It will also provide the opportunity to steer a path between two mythic and historical understandings of the place of farm life in the history of the American child. The experience of farm childhood is often either idealized as the "best" possible childhood, filled with wholesome entertainment and close, nurturing contact with parents, or demonized as a way of life that robbed generations of children of their opportunity to experience a full, happy, and relatively carefree youth. From the perspective of the midwestern children who lived it, farms could provide both or neither of these. Certainly, the potential existed for farm childhoods that were the best possible developmental and social experience, full of warmth, love, and support, but the potential also existed for the worst. But that was true for working-class children on Chicago's

South Side, as well as middle-class children growing up in Saint Paul, Minnesota, or Topeka, Kansas. It is important to see both the best and the worst that farm childhood had to offer the midwest's youth.

❖ ❖ ❖

A NOTE ON SOURCES

I have tried, as much as possible, to tell this story from the perspective of farm children. This has required an examination of a number different types of sources. My most important sources of information have been children's diaries, written in surprisingly large numbers and collected in historical societies and archives across the midwest. The diarists whose writings inform this work range in age from ten to twenty-one, with most being twelve to seventeen. I have also had the great good fortune to make use of several family diaries, such as that of the Nortons of Barton County, Kansas, which include entries written by a number of family members over many years. In the case of the Norton family, the writers ranged from seven-year-old Lucy (an infant at the diary's beginning) to her middle-aged parents. Children's manuscript letters, generally written to aunts, uncles, cousins, and grandparents, also figure into this study, although in fewer numbers. Another highly useful source are children's letters written to and published by farm journals. Periodicals such as the *Nebraska Farmer* encouraged children to share their experiences with facets of farm life, including work, play, school, and pets. Although the potential existed for exaggeration and fictionalization, I believe that most of these letters show enough consistency with other sources to suggest their general authenticity and usefulness as a source of children's own thoughts and words.[8]

Memoirs and oral histories also have their place in this work. Although researchers must be vigilant in the use of these materials, I believe they can be extremely useful sources of information. Reflecting on childhood from a great distance may lead individuals to sugarcoat or distort some memories and fabricate others or omit important facts. Nevertheless, in researching the lives of children, who often did not generate the kind of documents as children that would assist scholars in recreating their stories, it becomes necessary to make use of what is available. Oral histories and reminiscences, when read carefully for recurring patterns and material that corresponds to evidence from diaries and letters, can be useful. They also help the researcher discover what adults believed was important about their past as farm children—information that helps us understand the place of rural childhood in our national mythology.

I have supplemented these children's accounts with other sources. Parents' diaries, which often included extensive notations on children's work and parental expectations, also form an important part of my research. Teachers, too, often kept useful records and diaries. Government documents, such as census records, school reports, coroner's records, court and poor records, and Children's Bureau investigations, provided much needed details. This is particularly true in telling the story of farm children who may have been impoverished, neglected, and abused. Unlike the well-educated and well-cared-for children who were more likely to leave letters and diaries, these children were almost invisible, except in the public record. Among the most useful government documents have been the records of the Wisconsin State Public School, an institution to which the state committed neglected and dependent children, which then indentured them to farm families throughout the state. Some of these children grew up on farms; others were farm children only for the duration of their indentures. Advice literature, reformers' tracts, and fiction have provided supplemental information and have often told me what people believed should be—but often was not—characteristic of farm children's lives. Although this combination of sources could not tell me everything I wanted to know (information about sexuality, for example, was meager), it has provided a window into the lives of the youngsters who worked, played, learned, and lived so long ago.

1

"I Would Rather Live in the Country"

A Child's Place

❖ ❖ ❖ ❖ ❖ ❖ ❖ ❖ ❖ ❖ ❖ ❖ ❖ ❖ ❖ ❖

I would rather live in the country. . . . You can have all the room you want to skate and coast. You can raise corn out in the country and you can not in the city. You can raise your own fuel in the country and you have to buy it in the city. If it was not for the farmer the town jake would starve. The farmer raises everything the town jake eats.
—Twelve-year-old boy, 1902, "What Some Children Think About Living in the Country," Kansas Farmer, February 6, 1902

Over the course of the nineteenth century, in western countries and the United States, conceptions of child life and its purposes changed radically. Americans and Europeans raised fundamental questions about the proper place of children: city or country, field or factory, workplace or school.* By the last decades of the nineteenth century, many reformers had come to the conclusion that the school and the home were a child's place: work, and especially industrial labor, were not.[1] By 1912, when the U.S. Congress passed the legislation creating the Children's Bureau, reformers were proclaiming a "right to childhood," a phrase encompassing any number of personal rights, including education, freedom from manual labor, and attention to a child's health and well-being. As sociologist Viviana Zelizer has aptly put it, educational and social reformers, as well as many middle-class Americans, had come to believe that "properly loved children, regardless of social class, belonged in a domesticated, non-productive world of lessons, games, and token money."[2] But although the change in the status of American children was evident, particularly in law, what was less evident was the application of these changes (and laws) to all American children. In the late nineteenth and early twentieth centuries, farm children provided a particular example of a group experiencing a much different sort of childhood than the kind of childhood that the reformers strived for. For farm children, the issue of place remained problematic and often contrary to the perceived ideal.

Central to the changing place of the child was the changing shape of the nineteenth-century family. The assumption throughout much of human history had been that the family was a working unit. Within that unit, parents and children labored together to provide for the needs of all. Traditional agriculture, without the benefit of extensive mechanization, required the work of an entire family, or easy and inexpensive access to hired labor, in order to produce enough to support a household for a year. Even the wages afforded most industrial laborers required the efforts of an entire household in order to provide everyone food, clothing, and shelter. Rare indeed was the job that paid an adult male well enough to provide support for four, five, or more individuals. Consequently, the idea of the child as a worker was common in this earlier world. Local governments, for example, did not generally maintain poor and orphaned children over the age of seven but bound them out as apprentices, expecting them to work for their daily bread.[3]

The early nineteenth century, however, saw the beginnings of a small but influential urban middle class in America. Within that urban middle class, men engaged in professions that provided a comfortable living for an entire family. From this privileged position, the urban middle class developed new ideas about how the family should be ordered. They conceived of a family in which only fathers ventured into the world of work, while mothers remained in the home, caring for their children, and parents together sheltered children from the harsh realities of life. These new children would be emotionally priceless, one might even say "sacred," but economically useless.[4] In this new vision, education was to be the center of a child's life. The educated child would benefit from the opportunity for social and economic advancement, and the nation would benefit from the existence of an enlightened, skilled population of young people.[5] Historians have argued that in the last decades of the nineteenth century midwestern middle-class families moved from a corporate understanding of family life, which emphasized the economic health of the group over the desires of the individual, to the companionate family, where because of relatively greater economic resources, emotional obligations took greater precedence over the simple physical support of the family.[6]

Although only a few families were economically able to exercise this new understanding of appropriate family life, post–Civil War social change encouraged the transformation of at least portions of these ideals into policy. In the years after the Civil War, increases in the number of divorces and decreases in the birthrate among the native-born middle class, combined with mass immigration from Europe, encouraged reformers to begin to regulate children's lives in an attempt to control the nation's fate. The future could not be left in the hands of a mass of uneducated, unassimilated immigrants and the equally uneducated urban poor. As historian Richard Bremner so aptly described the late nineteenth-century reforming attitude, "The state must protect itself against the menace of hordes of young people allowed to grow up in ignorance and without respect for others."[7] Charles Loring Brace, founder of the New York Children's Aid Society and one of the nation's best-known philanthropists, encouraged Americans to think in these terms. Impoverished immigrant boys, he wrote, "cannot read; they do not go to school or attend a church. Many of them have never seen the Bible. Every cunning faculty is intensely stimulated. They are shrewd and old in vice . . . Few influences which are kind and good ever reach the vagrant boy." The situation among the girls was equally grim. "They traverse the low, vile streets alone, and live without mother or friends, or any share in what we should call a *home.* They also know little of God or Christ, except by name. They grow up passionate, ungoverned, with no love or kindness ever to soften the heart. We all know their short wild life—and the sad end." The damage, however, was not to their lives alone, but to the social fabric. "These boys and girls, it should be remembered, will soon form the great lower class of our city. They will influence elections; they may shape the policy of the city; they will, assuredly, if unreclaimed, poison society all around them. They will help to form the great multitude of robbers, thieves, vagrants and prostitutes who are now such a burden on the law-respecting community."[8] Brace, and others like him, argued that such children—uneducated, untrained, unloved—would seriously undermine the nation's future.

These conditions "encouraged the conclusion that a proper childhood must be imposed if it was not voluntarily embraced."[9] Throughout the nineteenth century, states began instituting child labor laws. Massachusetts and Connecticut were the first states to regulate child labor and in 1842 limited the number of hours children under twelve could work to ten per day. In

1887, Alabama passed legislation limiting children under fourteen to an eight-hour day, but then repealed the legislation in 1894.[10] By 1890, the legislatures of eighteen U.S. states had enacted labor laws limiting children's hours of work, the age at which they could work, or the hours of day at which children could work. Although legislation was rare in 1900, by 1920 the state legislatures of all forty-eight states and the District of Columbia had enacted some form of child labor law. In New Mexico and Utah, these laws were minimal, applying only to youngsters employed in the mining industry.[11] Other states enacted much more comprehensive laws that limited the occupations, hours of work, and ages of young persons allowed to work in stores, factories, and other industries. For example, laws in Illinois prohibited children under fourteen from "any gainful occupation in or in connection with factories, canneries, stores, etc., at any time, or in any work for compensation during the school term." California legislated a minimum age of fifteen for any work in "factories, stores, etc., or 'any other place of labor.'" Exemptions might be granted in some cases: in Alabama for children over twelve during school vacations; in Illinois for children doing voluntary work. Other states allowed exemptions for children over twelve during school holidays, children working in establishments owned by their parents, or those whose families would face economic hardship without their wages. Although legislation did not cause child labor to disappear, the number of children gainfully employed, upon which the economic fate of their family rested, decreased significantly across the first half of the twentieth century.[12] Increasingly, the control over who within a family would work lay not with parents but with the state.

Legislating children out of the workplace was only the first part of the reform equation. The second part was to ensure that children received an adequate education by requiring parents to send their children to school. Massachusetts passed the first compulsory education law in 1852, and other states followed.[13] Again, the content of state laws varied considerably, but by 1920, all forty-eight states and the District of Columbia required at least some school attendance. Alabama, for example, required children under fourteen or who had completed the elementary grades to attend school. The state allowed three exemptions: physical or mental illness of the child, the child living at too great a distance from the school unless transportation was provided, or the inability of the parent to provide clothing or books, in which case the child might become a ward of the state. Illinois law required children fourteen and younger to attend unless a child had graduated from the eighth grade. The state allowed exemptions for physical and mental illness. Temporary absences could be allowed for religious instruction or "for cause," if excused by a principal or teacher. California required children to attend until age sixteen, or until they obtained certain permits that were not allowed until a child was fourteen or older. Physical or mental illness or living long distances from school were also allowable exemptions. The state of Virginia adopted the most lax school law, requiring attendance only from ages eight to twelve and allowing exemptions "for cause" and once a child had achieved literacy.[14] By 1930, most states required children to remain in school until they were fourteen, and many required children to attend until age sixteen. As historian Michael Grossberg has commented, "Making school mandatory was justified along with other measures intended to separate out childhood as a distinct phase of life and to define children as individuals with special needs and interests."[15]

What legislators' formulations had failed to take into account, however, was that another set of realities existed side by side with those of this new, modern, industrial America. Although most middle-class Americans had removed their children from the workforce, farm parents had not—and for the most part, could not. Labor throughout much of the United States was scarce and expensive, so only the most firmly established farming families could afford hired hands. Instead of hiring laborers, families trained their children from an early age to assume the work of the farm. They eased their parents' burdens, and they helped the family to become a "highly flexible production unit," capable of accomplishing many and varied tasks.[16] A Department of Agriculture study made in the 1920s confirmed the wisdom of the principles farm families had operated on for centuries: because of their contributions to the family coffers, having many children resulted in a higher standard of living for the farm family. Older children were particularly useful.[17] For a child on a farm, early rising, long hours of chores, and high levels of responsibility from a young age were the rule rather than the exception.

Most farm children lived with age-old traditions and financial constraints that intimately connected the success of the family enterprise with the willingness of all to work. They lived in a world of mutual obligations that required them to work for the good of their parents and the farm, and often for their siblings as well. Each contributed to the larger success of the family farm and the family as a whole, even if that meant that older siblings had to defer their plans and dreams in order to meet the needs of the younger sib-

*Farm families continued to do many things for themselves. Jacob Gabelmann is
pictured cutting Ludwig Gablemann's hair, Clarksville, Iowa, circa 1920.
Gablemann Collection. By permission of the State Historical Society of Iowa.*

lings. Most would grow up with parental expectations that work and commitments to family came first; schooling and play were secondary considerations. As Mary Neth has described in her study of midwestern farms,
those families had expectations of their children that were often far different from those of the growing urban middle class. Parents expected their
children to work and to contribute to the good of the family. Their children,
in turn, understood their contributions to the family and accepted them as
part of their obligation to the larger enterprise.[18] Jon Gjerde, in his study of
the rural midwest, found the same preindustrial "family morality" in action
but argued that many youngsters, in fact, felt coerced by this family system
that compelled them to work for the family good into early adulthood. Although these strictures were loosening in some Yankee families, Gjerde argued, they remained tight among immigrant parents.[19] But whatever the interpretation, Neth and Gjerde agree that the agricultural economy rested
upon a foundation of family cooperation. Sociologist Claire Toynbee, in her
work on family and community in New Zealand, argued that the term *use-*

ful was the most important descriptor for women and children on the farm. Without "independent, self-reliant, and useful" family members, the farm could not be expected to succeed. And being useful, of course, meant being a worker.[20]

A working rural child as such thus failed to live up to modern western notions—the reformers' notions—of an acceptable childhood. He or she worked far more than many considered appropriate, and that work often impinged upon the child's ability to gain an education. Farm children in the United States labored long hours before and after school, or instead of going to school. As a result, school attendance figures for rural children were often low, and farm children were generally far behind their urban peers in total years of education and made much slower progress through the school curriculum than was considered appropriate. Observing this situation, one might have expected legislators to work especially hard to protect farm children through child labor and compulsory education laws. This, however, was not the case; they left enormous leeway for the economic concerns of farm parents.

Child labor laws never applied to children working on the family farm, even though a 1920 government report indicated that 61 percent of all working children aged ten to fifteen were working in agriculture, and 88 percent of those were working on their parents' farms. The Department of Labor in its own publications acknowledged that children's "work in agricultural pursuits . . . is not included" in state or federal legislation.[21] Legislators attempted to encourage farm parents to limit their children's hours of work by requiring them to send their children to school, but the law was lenient in that regard as well. Laws mandating compulsory schooling left a great deal of leeway for farm families. States could, and often did, allow a shorter school year in rural areas. In some states, such as Nebraska, that year was dramatically shorter. Children could also be excused from attendance "for cause," a loose term that school officials often stretched to fit the economic needs of the agricultural year.[22]

The enacted laws reflected in reality the nation's preoccupation with urban, rather than rural, children. Urban children, and especially those of immigrant parents, were much more visible than those on farms. They often lived in crowded neighborhoods and spilled into the streets, unlike farm children, who lived in a dispersed pattern along country roads, much further from prying eyes. Urban immigrant children were visible, and middle-class Americans often perceived them as a threat to American culture and

THE
NEBRASKA FARMER

Nebraska's Real Farm Paper

ESTABLISHED 1859   MAY 19, 1915   VOL. 57. NO. 20

HELPING WITH THE CHORES

Nebraska Farmer Company, Lincoln, Nebraska

In a 1915 frontispiece, the Nebraska Farmer *emphasized the importance of farm chores for children. From the Collections of the Nebraska State Historical Society, by permission of the* Nebraska Farmer.

the nation's way of life. Without education or regulation, they were likely to remain ignorant and improperly assimilated into the values and work habits of middle America.[23] Although the children of urban immigrants presented a challenge to the dominant values of the nation, farm children seemed to provide an affirmation of the value of hard work and discipline. The legal treatment of the interests of farm children represented a basic trust, whether well-founded or not, in the intentions and parenting practices of the nation's farmers.

These legislative choices also represented a philosophical uncertainty about the nature of farm life and its value to children. Reformers were uncertain how to evaluate work and its effect on youngsters. Those concerned with child labor often criticized urban children for their lack of industry. As sociologist John Gillette commented in 1912, "It is one of the recognized defects of city life that there is nothing at which to set the boys outside of school hours and in vacation periods. Idleness and idle habits, bad associations, and irregular wayward tendencies are the familiar fruits of the situation." On the other hand, reformers often castigated rural children, or rather their parents, for being too industrious, to the detriment of education and play. Reformers like Gillette were faced with a dilemma: was work good or bad for children, or was a combination of both ideal? Although Gillette did not approve of parents who worked their twelve-year-old sons as if they were grown men, he could see the moral value of a reasonable amount of farm work for children.[24] Because many shared Gillette's uncertainty, reformers and legislators were not sure that the law should apply to farm children. Even serious critics of child labor believed that some agricultural pursuits could be healthful for a child. When in 1906 Senator Albert J. Beveridge of Indiana condemned child labor in industry, he embraced child labor on the farm as excellent training for life. In a speech in favor of Senate Resolution 6562, "A Bill to Prevent the Employment of Children in Factories and Mines," he stated: *"This bill does not strike at the employment of children engaged in agriculture.* I do not for a moment pretend that working children on the farm is bad for them. I think it is the universal experience that where children are employed within their strength and in the open air there can be no better training" (italics in original).[25] Most Americans embraced industriousness and hard work as character-building. Farm work, with its implied self-sufficiency, family orientation, and educational components, represented an ideal, not a form of child abuse.[26]

THE
NEBRASKA FARMER

Nebraska's Real Farm Paper

ESTABLISHED 1859   DECEMBER 9, 1914   VOL. 56 NO. 49

LEARNING TO LEAD

Nebraska Farmer Company, Lincoln, Nebraska

This 1914 frontispiece from the Nebraska Farmer *celebrated the educational qualities of agricultural work, even for very small children. From the Collections of the Nebraska State Historical Society, by permission of the* Nebraska Farmer.

This 1872 illustration from the Kansas Farmer *recognized and romanticized children's contributions to the farming effort.* Kansas Farmer, *October 1, 1872. By permission of the Kansas State Historical Society, Topeka, Kansas.*

Richard C. Barrett, Iowa's turn-of-the-century superintendent of schools, echoed many of the same sentiments. In his opinion, the farm itself was, in many ways, a school. "Nowhere on earth has a child such advantages for elementary education as upon a good farm, where he is trained to love work and to put his brains to work. The best taught school in a densely populated city can never equal in educative value the life upon a good farm intelligently managed."[27]

Farm work trained the body and the brain, but more importantly, it improved the character of the child. "The child on the farm is made responsible for something, for some work, for some care-taking, and out of this responsibility grow trustworthiness, habits of work, and a feeling of personal power in all the essential elements of character."[28] If Barrett was to be believed, agriculture trained children to be, in all important ways, good citizens. He had very few reservations about the quality of a child's life on Iowa's farms, and he asserted that those few reservations could be easily remedied by properly managed rural schools. In turn, Barrett believed that those properly managed rural schools would keep Iowa's children on the farm and away from the evils of the growing cities.

Superintendent Barrett was not the only educator who believed in the importance of rural values and training to proper child development. Evidence from throughout the nation indicates that many educators were either ambivalent or hostile toward the effects of urbanization and believed instead in the educational value of the countryside.[29] Charles Eliot, a former president of Harvard University, claimed that "a roaming child brought up on the farm, learns from nature what it is almost impossible to impart to a city child." Farm children, he believed, learned from nature "spontaneous, intense, self-directed use of their faculties," something that could not be replicated in a city classroom.[30] Educators also feared the loss of such qualities as industry, thrift, and appreciation for the natural world. In the name of preserving the values of the country in an urban setting, educational reformers advocated new programs, such as nature study, school gardens, and manual training.[31] Preston Willis Search, the superintendent in 1895 of Los Angeles' public schools, even suggested that the form of the one-room rural school, in a farmlike setting, should be recreated in urban locations. He argued, "The losses from reversion from the rural life to that of the city would be partially overcome. The farm, with its many lessons from Nature and its many trades and occupations would be rich in instructive exercises. The gardens would bring back the forgotten touch with the soil, and the delights of animal life would awaken new human interest."[32] Leading educational theorist and reformer John Dewey emphasized learning by doing and incorporating vocational aims into a child's education. When he looked for an ideal historical moment at which a child's working life complemented his or her educational life, he pointed to "pioneer times," when "outside occupations gave a definite and valuable intellectual and moral training." A farm child's work informed that child's life, whereas an urban child's outside occupations were decidedly "anti-educational" and needed to be restricted under child labor laws.[33] For late nineteenth- and early twentieth-century educators, it was easier to see the virtues of farm life than the virtues of the city.

The United States Children's Bureau found many of the same values in child life on the farm. Although the bureau generally condemned urban child labor and some types of child labor on farms (such as hired work in beet fields and truck gardens), it also applauded the values learned through appropriate levels of agricultural child labor. "Children who do a reasonable amount of farm work, suited to their years and under the supervision

*Just as children could be little farmers, they could be little
gardeners, too. Kansas Farmer, June 15, 1872. By permission of
the Kansas State Historical Society, Topeka, Kansas.*

of their parents, are fortunate. Such work inculcates habits of industry and
develops family solidarity, both desirable objectives in any system of child
training."[34] Farm life, unlike most urban occupations, allowed parents and
children to work together as a single economic unit. In the best cases, this
might provide a real sense of belonging and accomplishment to all family
members.

Some commentators went further and whole-heartedly endorsed child
labor on farms. Charles Galpin, professor of Agricultural Economics at the

University of Wisconsin, provided a positively rosy description of the social value of a rural childhood. As a burgeoning rural sociologist, deeply interested in the preservation of rural communities, he was particularly interested in farm children. In them, he saw the salvation of rural areas. Children would bring new ideas and new direction to the family, farm, and community. Galpin believed that child labor on the farm trained youngsters for their all-important role as conservators of the nation's heritage.[35]

> The labor of the child on the farm in America, with some few localized exceptions, has about it a minimum of child-labor features dangerous to the child and to society. Work in the fresh open air, attended with great variety of movement both from place to place and task to task, has none of the hazards of mines and factories to the growing body and soul. . . . The open country is a large mold, and the child's nature fits the mold. . . . The farm-bred child . . . is the contribution of rural life to the human stock of society.[36]

From Galpin's point of view, work could either be defined as healthy or unhealthy, and farm labor clearly fell into the healthy category; it was safe and life-affirming, for both the child and the nation.

Not only that, but the working farm child helped to strengthen the home and the family. "The child, as an economic asset to the farm family, is a premium which nature seems to have offered in order to bolster up the institution of the family. Where the child is a constant liability, as in many an urban home, we may see the effect of weakened home ties."[37] Children with a true economic value, who made a positive contribution to family life, were the key to the continuation of strong traditional families, argued Galpin. Although few were as enthusiastic about the benefits of farm labor as he, few were completely opposed to it either. The key to the matter was to define how much work was too much, something that reformers found very difficult to do. When the reviews were so mixed, it was hard to take a firm stand against what was common practice on hundreds of thousands of the nation's farms. This uncertainty would not just have an impact on late nineteenth- and early twentieth-century legislation; when in 1938 the Fair Labor Standards Act codified national child labor standards, agriculture was exempt. In 1974, legislators included the first standards for agriculture, but left them far looser than for any other industry. The minimum age for agricultural workers is twelve; for hazardous work, the age is sixteen.[38]

Reformers, both in the Children's Bureau and educational institutions, were tapping into a deep well of sentiment that stressed the value of rural childhood over urban childhood, particularly for American boys. Historian Richard Wohl has argued that, according to many late nineteenth-century Americans, the country boy, unlike the "slum boy and the immigrant lad recently arrived from Europe," embodied all of the physical health and moral virtues in which Americans believed. "The country boy seemed healthier, and his pink cheeks, bright eyes, and broad biceps soon became the trademark of his mythical counterpart. Real country boys might be rude and crude, but they were engagingly ebullient and brisk, vigorous and enterprising; all these were the hallmarks of a sound boy in a culture which worshiped work and energy. They seemed unspoiled, full of pent-up hope and brimming with optimism."[39] A "Country Boy's Creed," found in the Young Men's Christian Association publication *Rural Manhood*, outlined the essential virtues of American farm boy and rural life:

> I believe that the Country which God made is more beautiful than the city which man made; that life out-of-doors and in touch with the earth is the natural life of man. I believe that work is work wherever we find it, but that work with Nature is more inspiring than work with the most intricate machinery. I believe . . . that my success depends not upon my location, but upon myself—not upon my dreams, but upon what I actually do, not upon luck, but upon pluck. I believe in working when you work and in playing when you play and in giving and demanding a square deal in every act of life.[40]

This vitality stood in sharp contrast to the supposed impact of urbanization on the American male.

Urbanization, often equated with civilization, threatened to rob the American boy, and the American male, of his very masculinity. President Theodore Roosevelt, for example, feared that the American people were becoming too cultured, refined, and soft to maintain their position as leaders among the world's people.[41] He, and many other Americans, feared that a too-civilized life was making American citizens unfit for the struggle to maintain their place in a competitive world.[42] An important part of the solution to this problem was for young men to live a "strenuous life" and for parents to inculcate into boys the importance of a life of "toil and effort, of labor and strife."[43] There was no doubt that farm youth embodied those virtues. Prominent psychologist and educator G. Stanley Hall believed similarly that boys, not allowed to be adequately "savage" or uncivilized as small children, would grow into weak, neurasthenic men, unable to function adequately in physical, sexual, professional, or in any other way.[44] The prescription for the overly civilized adolescent boy, according to Hall, was immersion in undomesticated nature.[45]

The founders of boys' and young men's organizations, such as the Boy Scouts of America and the Young Men's Christian Association, decried the effect of the city in degrading the morals and health of American boys and recommended the healing power of country pursuits. In fact, both organizations were slow to organize any activities for rural youth because "they saw little need for character building among lads whose pastoral virtues served as a foil for city vices."[46] As late as 1910, the YMCA did "country work" in only sixteen states, and in those states, only a very few county organizations existed. In only four Iowa counties, for example, could young men in the country join the YMCA. In Wisconsin and Illinois, there were no rural clubs.[47] A general lack of concern for farm children, and especially for farm boys, stemmed from a lack of anxiety about the wholesomeness of their circumstances. (The even greater unconcern over farm girls derived from a belief that boys, more than girls, were the inheritors of the nation and the family farm.) Farm children lived vigorous lives at a distance from the perceived vices and pollution of America's cities. Urban children, on the other hand, lived in a much-diminished atmosphere, and reformers devoted enormous energy in trying to reintroduce rural virtues into the lives of deprived city youth. Reformers had little time to be concerned with the deficiencies of a rural childhood, except to prescribe nature study and agricultural education as a means of keeping youngsters on the farm and away from the influence of the cities.[48]

The power of people's belief in the virtues of agricultural labor are evident in one of the nineteenth and early twentieth centuries' best-known experiments in child welfare. Reformers' affinity for the positive moral values of farm childhood and appropriate work for children led to a more-than-seventy-year experiment in relocating children from congested urban areas to the supposedly more healthful (both physically and morally) countryside. Charles Loring Brace, founder of the New York Children's Aid Society, investigated the city's slums, finding countless children who were illiterate, unchurched, and unemployed. Hoping to save children who "seemed to be as much beyond the reach of society at large as they were beyond the control of their own parents," Brace formulated a plan.[49] Between 1853 and 1924, the New York Children's Aid Society sent more than 100,000 youngsters from the city streets to homes in rural communities, hoping to reform

and educate them by way of life and work in a farming family. Brace justified the plan, writing,

> The United States have the enormous advantage over all other countries, in the
> treatment of difficult questions of pauperism and reform, that they possess a
> practically unlimited area of arable land. The demand for labor on this land is
> beyond any present supply. Moreover, the cultivators of the soil are in America
> our most solid and intelligent class. . . . It is, accordingly, of the utmost impor-
> tance to them to train up children who shall aid in their work and be associates
> of their own children.[50]

For more than seventy years, the Children's Aid Society distributed children
throughout the nation, largely to farming families. The programs' end in
1924 stemmed from several factors. Child welfare agencies had begun to
question the wisdom and humanity of sending children by the trainload
into rural communities and into largely unsupervised placements. A 1926
Children's Bureau report characterized the Children's Aid Society's methods as "unspeakably careless and cruel."[51] Additionally, beginning with
Michigan in 1887, state legislatures began to restrict the movement of dependent children from state to state. By 1924, twenty-eight states had some
sort of provision against placing children from out of state in foster homes,
or made the procedure so cumbersome and expensive as to be prohibitive.[52]
By that time, however, many other organizations, both public and private,
such as Nebraska's Home for Dependent Children or Wisconsin's State Public School for Dependent and Neglected Children, had followed the same
model as the Children's Aid Society and sent hundreds of children to small
towns and farms within their states. In the fifty years after the Civil War, in
an urbanizing nation, where youngsters more often voluntarily moved from
farm to city, those active in child welfare believed that the best future for the
poor and unwanted child was in the countryside, where he or she would
breathe clean air imbued with the virtue of hard work. Reformers hoped to
provide what was best for the child while meeting the need for laborers in
the agricultural midwest and west.[53]

By the 1920s, children's work and education were subject to increasing
governmental regulation in every state of the union, although with varying levels of commitment by state—and with varying levels of commitment
to different classes of children. Another aspect of a child's place in the world,
however, remained relatively unregulated. That aspect of child life was play.
Although playing was certainly not a right that ever would be legislated, it

*Children worked both inside and outside the home, as this
illustration, "The Little Washerwoman," acknowledged.*
Kansas Farmer, *July 15, 1872. By permission of the Kansas
State Historical Society, Topeka, Kansas.*

was a right that concerned early twentieth-century child advocates. The opportunity to play in many ways represented what it was to *be* a child: to run,
to laugh, to exercise the imagination, and to be free of adult cares and responsibilities. By the late nineteenth century, social scientists had "discovered" children's play and had begun to analyze it, coming to the conclusion
that play had an "important role in socialization and education, especially
since other instruments for these processes—the churches, the family, and
the schools—seemed to be failing."[54] In urban areas, the impulse to provide

a venue for children's play led to the creation of parks and playgrounds, areas set aside for children's recreational pursuits. Others, however, argued that the effort should extend farther than this, and that play should be part of every child's birthright. In fact, in a 1922 National Child Labor Committee report on rural child welfare, the organization argued that every youngster should have a recognized claim to recreation. The authors of the report declared, "Above all, let them play; for play is the means to growth and refreshment. This is both creative and recreative." The committee made four specific recommendations for reform in this area. First, adults should encourage "wholesome play and recreation," by way of the home, school, church, and community. Second, children should have access to public facilities for play, such as parks, playgrounds, swimming pools, and libraries, and should have opportunities provided by clubs, lectures, and athletic events. Third, trained leaders should promote and oversee children's play. And fourth, public authorities should regulate and supervise "commercial amusements and public gatherings," presumably places such as dance halls and theaters.[55] In the early 1930s, even the president took up the issue of play, with the White House Conference on Child Health and Protection declaring it a right of childhood.[56]

This promotion of a right to play represented at least two different impulses on the part of reformers, one of which has been discussed already: a desire to move children out of the workplace and into activities that the educated middle classes considered more appropriate. The other impulse was one to "civilize" and control children's play, making it more safe and less violent.[57] Note the National Child Labor Committee's emphasis on recreation that is both wholesome and publicly regulated. The committee envisioned a world where experts developed and monitored children's recreational activities, leaving little to chance. These recommendations emanated from a growing knowledge—and horror—of the ways in which unsupervised urban children played. In their unscientific observations of urban children, reformers had discovered children entertaining themselves with destructive and even criminal activities. Charles Loring Brace found "roving boys" drinking, gambling, and demonstrating their "constitutional love for smashing windows and pilfering apple-stands."[58] Jacob Riis observed "street Arabs" playing craps "with all the absorbing concern of hardened gamblers."[59] Scholarly research reinforced these reformers' observations. In a 1913 study of the activities of Cleveland children involved in unsupervised play, researchers found a large percentage of them were either "doing noth-

ing" or "just fooling," categories that included "breaking windows, de-
stroying houses, chalking suggestive words on buildings, throwing mud
at street cars, touching girls, looking at pictures of women in tights on bill-
boards, wearing suggestive buttons, stealing, gambling, and drinking."[60] Although many children's advocates decried a world in which children were
too "civilized," they also believed that some children's activities, particularly those found in cities, needed to be curbed in favor of more wholesome
forms of recreation, such as crafts and nature study. Although reformers did
not envision a world in which parent-organized play groups and play dates,
sports practices, and scripted activities such as meetings of Boy and Girl
Scouts consumed most of a child's free time, a twenty-first-century description of such activities is far closer to reformers' understanding of the
ideal than the anarchic world of disorganized play in which many children
indulged.[61]

In the countryside, both reformers and parents were beginning to become
concerned about a child's need for play. Although rural reformers were not
quite as adamant as the National Child Labor Committee about the child's
right to play, they did believe that more play (but not too much) could have
positive effects, and that children's play did need greater parental and
community supervision. By the early twentieth century, Country Life reformers who were concerned about farm youngsters leaving agriculture and
the countryside for the cities increasingly came to see the encouragement of
play as one of the solutions to this problem. If farm youngsters found occasional freedom and wholesome entertainment in the farm home and its environs, then they would be far less likely to leave that home for the city, or
so adult reasoning went. Reformers suggested enlisting the schools, the
grange, and the churches in fostering "native instincts" to play. "Plays,
dances, folk music, pageants, festivals that spring directly from the soil of
the rural community, should be fostered, organized and given the finish-
ing touches of the artist."[62]

Although the Country Life Commission made a few rather abstract suggestions about the need to improve the quality and increase the amount of
play, recreation, and games in rural areas, those writing to and for publications such as the *Nebraska Farmer* and the *Farmer's Wife* offered a number of
concrete suggestions to be implemented by farm parents.[63] A correspondent
with the *Nebraska Farmer* commented, "If there is one thing I dislike to see
it is a farmer making regular field hands of little children." To do so, in his
opinion, was "a crime against children." Little boys "should have the time

to be a boy. . . . Let us give the little fellows a play-time during their early years and make their boyhood one to be fondly remembered instead of something akin to a nightmare."[64] Another writer encouraged parents to think of play and holidays as times to which "every boy has a divine right." "Work, work, work all the time" would only have the effect of driving youngsters from the home.[65] Fathers were encouraged to allow their children, and especially boys, time to play, while mothers were encouraged to read to their children, to sing to them, and to provide them with enjoyable, but also enriching, playthings.[66]

Beyond allowing youngsters designated playtime and a few well-chosen toys and books, others suggested that parents should plan "country gatherings" in order to give youngsters a directed social life. One author reasoned that "young people are bound to seek pleasure and entertainment somewhere," and that the somewhere should be within the confines and chaperonage of parents.[67] Another writer was even more explicit: if youngsters were left to their own devices, they would "probably . . . go to the pool hall to play or visit or go to an unsuitable picture show." By providing "music, a phonograph, books and games and a place to visit with friends," parents could keep their children in the wholesome atmosphere of rural neighborhoods and "away from smoke-filled pool halls and the many evil environments that go with it."[68] Active churches equipped as social centers and homes stocked with books and music provided necessary entertainment and relief from the tedium of work.[69] But others warned, too, of the dangers of allowing farm youth too much leisure. Girls would grow up dissatisfied with life in the countryside, and boys "will always find something to do. If we set no tasks for him, Satan will have cigarettes to be smoked, melon patches to be raided and naughty stories to be heard and told."[70] The results for rural neighborhoods, such arguments implied, could be catastrophic.

Manufacturers attempting to create a farm market for their products jumped on this same bandwagon, exploiting parental fears about wandering children and dissatisfied farm women. The makers of the Crown Combinola Player Piano were hardly subtle in their appeal: "Mr. Farmer, are you robbing your family of the things they ought to have, just to make more money out of your farm? Will the boys jump at the first chance to leave home, or will they want to stay on the farm and make your old age pleasant? Will the girls be glad when marriage takes them away from your roof, or will they be sorry? Have you given your wife everything she needs to

Advertisers encouraged farm parents to make home purchases to keep their children on the farm, and happy. From the Nebraska Farmer, *January 4, 1912. From the Collections of the Nebraska State Historical Society, by permission of the* Nebraska Farmer.

make a real home for you and your family?" Familial dissatisfaction might be ameliorated by the purchase of a player piano, which would bring "all the beautiful music of the world," hymns, "old-time songs," popular music, and classical masterpieces into the farm home, "and you or any member of your family can play them without practice."[71] A world of refinement and leisure was within the reach of all and would guarantee the greater happiness of the farm family, something that was essential to securing the future of that family as well as the larger rural society.

An important point to note about these pleas for children's play emanating from the countryside (and from advertising as well) was that they promoted children's play not for its own sake, or even for the greater good of the child, but for the good of the farm and the rural community. By providing youngsters with toys, games, and other diversions, and the opportunity to enjoy them, farm parents would be ensuring the continuation of the family farm. Properly entertained children would perceive the farm environment as a pleasant one, conducive to a happy, fulfilled life. As in the case of the commitment to work and somewhat weaker commitment to education, the most important guiding force was family survival, in both the short and long run, with personal fulfillment a much less important goal.

Even as the larger society was reformulating a child's world, rural children in many ways remained a separate category, operating under different rules and expectations. What are we, then, to make of this farm child's world, so different from that which we have come to think of as ideal and correct? Because our reactions are often so quick and so negative, it is rare for scholars to think very creatively or deeply about the meaning of work in children's lives. Historians often present children's work, especially in industry, as evidence of adults' insensitivity and callousness toward children and their needs. The editors of *Industrious Children: Work and Childhood in the Nordic Countries, 1850–1900,* summarized this position well: "Among historians of child labour there is a general tendency to describe . . . children . . . as the victims of adults' ignorance, whether they were profiteering capitalists or irresponsible parents, who had failed to understand that it was better for their children to attend school."[72] The same tendency is apparent in the scant literature examining the history of rural children and their work. Elizabeth Hampsten, author of *Settlers' Children: Growing Up on the Great Plains,* argued that children and their needs "had to wait" while the family accomplished the work of farm building, much to the detriment of the children.[73] Historians' concerns mirror societal attitudes that had been developing since the early nineteenth century. A child's place, at least theoretically, had been radically reconfigured. But the theoretical aspect of this rethinking of ideas about childhood should be emphasized. No matter what reformers thought, no matter what modern Americans believe to be the proper place of children, many turn-of-the-century children and their families continued to live outside of those definitions and in a rather different place. Although some children, and maybe even all at given moments, may have believed themselves oppressed by their role within the family, many also found meaning and enjoyment in the traditional world they occupied. Work could be a matter of pride, and even in a world where parents exercised strong control over children's lives, youngsters developed a high degree of autonomy and individuality. Although their lives were clearly different from the norm, different should not imply inferior.

As the differences between urban and rural children's lives become apparent, it should also be apparent that there was considerable potential for wide variations among the contours of individual farm children's lives. Just as there was no single "child's place" in the larger culture, a child's place in an agricultural context was modified by a number of different considerations. Economic factors were very important in defining a child's place. The children of poor and struggling families would most likely be forced to work harder than those of middling and prosperous farming families. They might miss more days of school, shoulder heavier burdens, and have less access to leisure and entertainment. The same might very well be true of children raised on farms in their first stages of development. The work of developing a new farm, such as breaking sod, felling trees, and building shelter imposed additional burdens beyond those inherent in life on an established farm. Other factors beyond the purely economic also shaped children's lives. Youngsters who fell outside the racial and ethnic norms of the community might face discrimination. Their parents might also raise them with different expectations regarding work, school, and leisure than those of the dominant culture. For example, within many ethnic groups, such as the Germans and Scandinavians, it was not uncommon for girls and women to work in the fields, a practice many native-born Americans disapproved of. Gender, too, in many ways, shaped a youngster's place and expectations. Boys and girls generally, but not always, did different work. They might receive more or less schooling based on gendered expectations. Their leisure activities might be controlled more or less by their parents, based on parental desires to protect their daughters' virtue more than that of their sons. Birth order could create situations that were radically different between the oldest children in a family and the youngest. Oldest children, raised on struggling new farms, might grow up in a much different world than younger children, born more than twenty years later on established farms with large workforces of older, laboring siblings. Conversely, if a family's fortunes declined, or if parents became infirm over time, younger children might face hardships that their older siblings escaped by virtue of age. Birth order could even throw the gender division of labor into disarray. In a family with all girls, or girls born first, those girls could very well become their fathers' "right hands," or "hired hands," contributing as much outdoor labor to the farm as a son might. A middle or younger son born into a family with no daughters, or no daughters of a sufficient age, might be drafted into doing women's work. Any and all of this, however, could be mitigated by parental values and expectations of children that might place as heavy burdens on a middle-class child as a poor one, based on a commitment to the value of hard work, or lighter burdens on a poorer child, based upon an unusually large dedication to education and related activities.

Some children faced even higher levels of stress as parents died, became ill, or were incarcerated. Others had parents who abandoned or abused them. Unfortunately, because of the upheaval in their lives, the voices of these children are rarely found in diaries and letters. Instead, they are found in court records, such as divorce files, and the records of state agencies such as the Wisconsin State Public School for Dependent and Neglected Children. Fortunately, their numbers seem to be small relative to the total number of farm children. Although between 1886 and 1913 the State Public School investigated nearly four thousand children for admission, only slightly more than 5 percent of those youngsters were identified as the children of farmers and farm laborers.[74] The need for labor in rural communities meant that even if a child's parents died or became incapacitated, there would likely be relatives or neighbors who would take the child into their home. Economic realities encouraged the operation of informal networks of support in the countryside.

Despite all of these qualifications, however, it is safe to generalize that a core group of values and needs shaped most farm children's lives. Their families relied on and expected their efforts as laborers, placing necessary work above all other children's activities. The commitment to education was more variable, with school accommodating itself to the needs of the agricultural year. Play, although a distant third in parents' calculations, was extremely important to children themselves and was carried out in a vigorous and largely unscripted fashion. As Brian Sutton-Smith has discovered in his research on rural children's play in New Zealand, their activities "call our attention to children's self-reliance and their capacity for innovation in their rural environment." Of necessity, they became enterprising, often in ways that urban children were not.[75] Children, although acted on by familial circumstances beyond their control, were also active in the creation of the kind of world in which they wished to live. They took pride in their work, and they found purpose in their education and freedom in the world of play they fashioned from the farms and fields around them. The place farm children inhabited was far different from that of the idealized child of the day, but that difference did not imply a life without opportunity, adventure, and growth. Although not every child would agree, there were many who would echo the assertion that began this chapter: "I would rather live in the country."

2

"But What Kind of Work Do the Rest of You Do?"

Farm Children as Laborers

❖ ❖ ❖ ❖ ❖ ❖ ❖ ❖ ❖ ❖ ❖ ❖ ❖ ❖ ❖

Of course we all play but what kind of work do the rest of you do? I have a sister fourteen years old and a brother twelve years old. They husk corn and I herd cows in the stalks. We have eighteen cows.
—*Margaret Carr, age eight, 1907, "Work and Play Club,"* Nebraska Farmer, *January 2, 1907*

Although there were many facets to farm children's lives, it is most appropriate to begin with a discussion of children's work. Although farm children generally attended school at least part of the year and played just as any child might play, work was at the center of their lives. Any discussion of children and work, however, requires the writer to think long and hard about the meaning of work within the context of the child laborer and his or her family. From the early twentieth century onward, the immediate emotional reaction of many relatively affluent and educated Americans to the idea of child workers has been essentially negative. According to middle-class urban sensibilities, children and work simply do not belong together. A child with a paper route, a few lawns to mow, or an occasional baby-sitting job seems acceptable. Doing a few hours of chores per week in order to share in family responsibilities or to learn housekeeping skills is deemed appropriate. A child working long hours in the hot sun or over a hot stove in order to feed and clothe his or her family, however, seems neither right nor fair to the child, who should, according to modern notions of children's lives, be either in school or at play.

Farm children, however, lived in a world where everyone's work was essential. From a child's earliest moments, work shaped his or her life. Because women's work was so essential on many cash-strapped farms, babies and their care had to be integrated into their mothers' working schedules as quickly after birth as possible. In 1919, Children's Bureau researchers studying maternity and infant care in Wisconsin recorded stories about women kneading biscuit dough in bed, the day after delivery. Within two weeks of delivery, more than half of all mothers were washing and ironing, which the researchers defined as heavy housework; they resumed cooking and light housework even earlier. They kept one eye on the baby and one eye on their work. In many families, especially those of immigrant origin, women with infants were not exempt from field labor. Small nursing babies might go along into the fields, or be left in the care of other small children, to be visited by their mothers at feeding time. Two months after childbirth, investigators found a Polish mother "in the heart of the winter . . . cutting brush and wood in the forest, leaving the baby and a 2 year-old-child in the care of their 8-year-old sister."[1] Work affected children's lives well before they were able to contribute their efforts to the family enterprise.

As children matured, a child's willingness and ability to work often meant survival for his or her family. In the late nineteenth and early twentieth centuries, farm families dealt with the uncertainties of the market by relying heavily on the labors of women and children. Although farm families rarely faced actual starvation (although during very hard times, such as droughts and grasshopper plagues, this remained a possibility), poor decisions, low prices, and bad weather might result in the loss of a farm or financial hardship. In order to combat this ever-present possibility, farm families produced most of what they consumed and employed all of their members in order to produce both for the market and for home consumption.[2] As a result, across the midwest, the contours of farm youths' lives were very similar. Although crop mix and family circumstances might shape an individual son's or daughter's duties, expectations would have been quite similar from state to state and across farms. As a rule, parents expected that their children would be useful. Usefulness began the moment a child was old enough to contribute to the family's efforts, usually at age four or five, and continued until that child left the family farm, generally at marriage or after the age of twenty-one. For some children, usefulness even extended beyond their life on the farm, as they sent home the funds from outside employment in order to support their cash-poor parents. Age helped to determine a child's level of usefulness. Very small children participated in the simplest of chores: carrying kindling, wiping dishes, and generally helping their mothers around the house and barnyard.[3] An innovative farm mother found that with the aid of his wagon, her three-year-old son could bring wood into the house, and also haul the laundry as she hung it on the line. She commented of his industriousness, "It saves me bending over every time and he is so proud."[4] Small hands might be used to hull hickory nuts and walnuts, or to gather corncobs to burn.[5] At this age, boys and girls generally shared the same types of chores; differentiation between girls' and boys' tasks came with greater age.[6]

Given their individual family situations, and sometimes their own preferences, daughters might spend their time working indoors or out, or more likely in a combination of both. Girls' work, more than boys', was shaped by the weekly rhythm of their mothers' tasks. Farm women generally followed a schedule, washing on Monday and ironing on Tuesday, and then assigning churning, baking, cleaning, and mending to their own days according to personal preference.[7] Girls either helped their mothers with these regular tasks or attended to those that might be neglected as a result of the pressures of the weekly round of duties. Many girls, for example, tended infants and toddlers while their mothers did Monday's washing, a dangerous task that often included open flames, harsh chemicals, boiling water, and hand-crushing wringers. A young Iowan, Sarah Gillespie, may have described a girl's lot best when she wrote on November 6, 1879, "Help ma! help ma!! help ma!!! all day."[8] "Helping ma," generally defined as sewing, cleaning, and gardening, circumscribed most days for most midwestern farm girls, but it did not preclude them from going into the fields when necessary to "help pa." For Gillespie, helping her father might include chopping and stacking firewood, shelling corn, or herding the cattle.[9]

In the late nineteenth and early twentieth centuries, the suitability of field work for girls was a subject of debate. Many believed there were boundaries beyond which farm daughters' work should not go. After two young women wrote to the editor of the *Kansas Farmer* asserting their ability to do all varieties of agricultural work, one of them further arguing that it was preferable to stereotypical women's work, a youngster calling himself "Yankee Boy" wrote to chastise them. Although he acknowledged their abilities,

Even tiny children could take their wagon to the yard and feed the chickens. By permission of the State Historical Society of Iowa.

writing, "I have seen women do work that would astonish even this pair of young heroines," he argued that girls should balance their labors between the home and the field. "I . . . believe they should learn all the mysteries of housekeeping. It might come handy to them some time, if they should suddenly conclude to marry some young man that did not know how to cook and wash and bake." Clearly, "Yankee Boy" placed the value of domesticity to husbands above the value and pleasure of outdoor work to young women and their families.[10] Popular culture reflected this disdain for women working in the fields, with writers such as Hamlin Garland criticizing the practice in his short stories "Among the Corn Rows" and "The Creamery Man." In his tales, only the deprived daughters of the foreign born worked in the fields. The daughters of the native born, adhering to proper gender roles, did not.[11]

A powerful early twentieth-century indictment of daughters doing what was properly sons' work came from Martha Foote Crow, a Country Life reformer and author. In her 1915 analysis of the lives of farm daughters, *The American Country Girl,* Crow chastised as un-American any male who would put the women in his family to "outside farm labor." Crow wrote, "The truth is that it has never been the custom in this country that the women should enter into the heavier farm work; from the beginning women were held so sacred that nothing must be risked that could injure their permanent strength. The men rolled in the logs of wood for the big fireplaces and did all the heavier work of the place, answering without a moment's demure the request of the women for help."[12] The idea of "foreigners . . . coming across the wide seas to find homes in our farming regions" and putting their womenfolk to work in the fields "is abhorrent to the institutions of our country; the men of the republic, not to say the women, will not tolerate it."[13] Notwithstanding Crow's apparent historical inaccuracy, her words represented the sentiments of many native-born Americans, who truly believed that a woman's place, and even a very young farm woman's place, was in the house, the garden, and hen house, and not the fields.

The diaries of native-born farm mothers, such as Helen Emery of Olmsted County, Minnesota, reflected this disdain but also the reality of many farm families' lives. Although Emery lamented her daughters' performing field labor so taxing that it made them "most sick" and was "sorry they have to work so," she also knew that they were essential to crop production. Her husband was in his sixties, and "it is hard for the poor old man to get along without them." The absence of her older son, as well as the relative youth of the younger, complicated the situation. In spite of her prejudices, Helen Emery's daughters, like many others, would work in the fields.[14]

As the Emery family's case illustrates, even if many observers found field work unsuitable for girls, families had to make do with the hands that were available to them. The high labor demands of corn planting and the corn harvest, in particular, took girls into the fields, and the sexual division of labor generally crumbled in the face of necessity.[15] If a family had daughters but no sons of working age, girls might continue to work regularly in their parents' fields. At times when labor demands were particularly high, such as planting and harvest, parents often sent their daughters into the fields, viewing them as surplus labor. Lottie Norton, living and working with her family in Barton County, Kansas, was probably typical of many young women out of their teens who continued to reside on their families' farms. Her most important task was to aid her mother in managing a household of twelve. She cooked, sewed, quilted, and gardened and did the washing for her own family, as well as for soldiers at Fort Larned, contributing most of her income from washing to the family coffers. However, in addition to these tasks typically considered women's work, she also helped her father plant both corn and sorghum.[16] Lottie Norton's activities exhibited a flexibility common to most young women, although the larger portion of her labors were completed within the home and garden. Had the Norton household not included five small children, and had it not benefited from the efforts of four sons over the age of ten, both Lottie and her mother might have been compelled to spend more of their time working in the fields. Her labors within her parents' home ceased in 1880 when she married and began to keep her own farm home in Illinois.

Other daughters divided their time differently. Twenty-one-year-old Agnes Schulz, living in a German community in central Kansas, often worked beside men in the fields. Although her father noted frequently that she washed, scrubbed, made soap, and did other "women's" work, she also participated in the production of the family's primary crop, wheat. Agnes weeded the fields along with her other siblings, and she regularly cooked for the men during harvest, but she also shocked. In his diary, her father noted Agnes' hard work: "Harvesting upon Morrell's farm, Agnes preparing [sic] dinner there & helping in the field, her nose bleeding several times, caused from the hot weather."[17] That Agnes Schulz's family was German may very well have influenced her level of participation in field work; women of German and Scandinavian descent more often worked in the fields than those of English ancestry.[18]

Other girls, not German or Scandinavian in background, also worked in the fields as needed, acting as their parents' reserve force of labor.[19] Corn, in particular, demanded that girls go into the fields. Just like Lottie Norton, many girls helped their fathers or other male family members plant corn.[20] Picking and husking corn were enormously time-consuming tasks that often could not be accomplished without the aid of the whole family, girls included.[21] Mary Peet, of Jones County, Iowa, picked and husked so much corn that she sprained her wrist, but she kept working anyway, commenting, "My wrist is swelled tonight, and is awful lame."[22] Haying, too, demanded all hands, with girls driving teams and pitching hay. When small Mollie Harbold, not yet a teenager, wanted to play with two visiting girls rather than attend to her tasks as a driver, her father refused, saying, "No, that would hold up haying." As Harbold later remembered, "It was my first lesson in responsibility." She was also paid twenty-five cents a day, a fact that made a great impression on her.[23] These girls' diaries and reminiscences regularly noted their movement in and out of the fields as family circumstances required, regardless of their ethnicity.

Issues such as birth order and the gender distribution of children within families, as well as individual preferences, affected girls' work roles. Girls

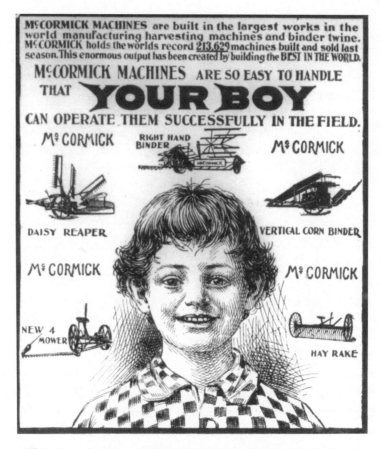

This 1900 advertisement for McCormick implements emphasized an important selling factor: they were so easy to handle that "YOUR BOY can operate them successfully in the field." Kansas Farmer, *February 8, 1900. By permission of the Kansas State Historical Society, Topeka, Kansas.*

who were the oldest children in the home might very well find themselves assigned the role of "father's boy" or "father's hired hand." Fathers without sons might choose a daughter to teach the skills of farming. Sometimes, as in the case of Carrie Dean Pruyn, an Iowa farm girl, this was a fortunate situation. Working out of doors became her preference as she learned to enjoy working with animals and tending crops.[24]

Boys experienced a different set of familial expectations. Oscar Hallam, who grew up near Dodgeville, Wisconsin, aptly described the difference between the lives of small boys, who worked in and around their mothers' spheres of occupation, and older boys, who had graduated into their fathers' orbits. Hallam wrote, "The small boy might have some time for play, but in general, he had things to do. His tasks were sometimes boresome, principally because they were 'little boy' tasks." The little boy planted seeds, weeded the garden, picked berries, and gathered eggs. At the end of the day, he brought the cows home. "He envied the big boys in their bigger work." The big boys, on the other hand, would "'take a team' and plow, harrow, plant, roll or cultivate for the yearly crop, and cut, rake and stack the hay, and in the harvest cut, bind, shock, load, stack grain, dig things underground and husk and crib corn. There was no time for the big boys to play until night." This was the work they owed their parents, "the 'keep' and parental care which he had all his life received, was ample advance payment for all the services he rendered and a day off for . . . the Fourth of July, the Fair and perhaps Cole's or Burr Robbins' circus was all that he had reason to expect."[25] A big boy's work was never done.

It was generally fathers who decided when their sons were ready to make the transition from little boys' to big boys' work. As soon as a father judged his son to be old enough and strong enough, he would usually go into the fields. Boys as young as twelve might be considered mature enough to take a man's place behind a plow. The experiences of Lottie Norton's younger brothers illustrated a full range of typical boys' chores. In the late 1870s, Will, John, Curtie, and Henry, all between the ages of ten and twenty, devoted themselves to any number of tasks, herding their family's cattle, hauling manure for the garden, plowing, and gathering buffalo bones to sell for fertilizer. The value of this last task should not be underestimated. A merchant in Larned paid $6 per ton, and in the first three months of 1879, the boys traded 1,500 pounds they had gathered for a barrel of salt and twelve pounds of nails.[26] For a cash-strapped family, this was a not insignificant sum. In an 1877 entry, John Norton described the way in which he and his brother Curt shared their labors. "Herded today. . . . We are shucking corn now. When it is my day to herd Curt shucks and I do the same when he does."[27] Although herding might give the boys the time and opportunity to explore the area surrounding their family's farm, it could also become tedious as the months wore on. John Norton noted, "The cattle went away on the 5th of December. Curt and I leaped for joy."[28] That did not mean, however, that the boys had time to rest. Instead, John hired out to work for a neighbor, the boys chopped up a tree for firewood, picked up and sold more bones, and picked several pounds of wool from a neighbor's dead sheep. Hunting, an activity that also brought food to the family table, was one of their few forms of recreation.[29] John and Curt Norton, like their brothers and thousands of others, contributed substantially to their parents' farm, a situation that they accepted as both normal and necessary, but one that limited their opportunities for both leisure and education.

Although boys typically worked beside their fathers, it was not unthinkable that a boy might cross gender lines and participate in chores that were more common to girls. Although it may not have been perceived as particularly dignified, many males did help with women's work, even if on a limited basis.[30] John Stilson, a Linn County, Iowa, teenager, helped his mother and sister with the washing. Especially heavy items, such as quilts, may very well have required the extra strength.[31] Clifford Drury, also of Iowa, noted that his mother often assigned the tedious task of working the lever on a manual washing machine to a small boy, or to her husband. The tedium was further confirmed by William Graf, who not only agitated the washing machine, but also churned butter. Beating carpets and operating hand-pumped vacuums also appear in boys' descriptions of their labors.[32] What may have motivated these assignments, in addition to a need to complete the family chores, was a mother's desire "to utilize the kinetic energy of the farmer's son."[33]

Although more rare, a son whose regular assignment was domestic labor was not an impossibility. The Wood family, of Trempealeau County, Wisconsin, illustrates this situation. James Wood, born in 1867, was one of the two older boys in the family and regularly carried out traditional boys' work. His diary is filled with notations such as "cleaned out the shed," "corded a little wood today," and "banded bundles" during the wheat harvest.[34] He and his older brother, Archie, were their father's primary help in the fields, although the family seems to have used some hired help as well, allowing James to attend school regularly.[35] Two Wood daughters, Sarah and Alta, were born between James and Ralph, but in October 1877, both died of diphtheria. Ralph was born fifteen months later.[36] Perhaps as a result of this family tragedy, Ralph's working role in the family was different from that of his older brothers. David Wood relied primarily on his two older sons to do field labor and traditional men's chores. Mary Wood lost the two daughters who would, under normal circumstances, have helped her in the house and the barnyard. Ralph Wood, unlike most sons, seems to have been his mother's right hand.

Ralph Wood was an unusual boy in that he participated in a whole range of household chores and was willing to admit to them in his journal. As a ten- and eleven-year-old, he ironed, cared for infants, churned, sewed carpet rags, gathered eggs, and washed clothes.[37] During harvest, he drove teams, carried bundles, and husked corn, as might be expected, but most times, he seems to have been assigned to his mother, sharing a pattern of inside and outside labor that has been described for many older girls.[38] The following 1889 entry illustrates a typical day for Ralph Wood: "I helped Ma today I made a ladder for her. Took care of Elmer [an infant] some. Ma and I picked currents [*sic*] and some beans. I washed and ironed today."[39] What is interesting is that as Ralph grew older, he continued in the same pattern. He noted helping his mother with household chores and gardening. Additionally, he regularly took care of the chickens and collected eggs and began to milk the cows and process the milk.[40] If Ralph Wood was uncomfortable with his role as his mother's helper, he certainly did not mention it in his journal. His discussions of work were quite matter-of-fact, and he showed no signs of embarrassment. The notations in Ralph's journal also indicate that his parents allowed him to keep some, or perhaps all, of the proceeds from his work with the chickens, giving him funds to spend on candy, a pocket knife, marbles, and gifts for young relatives.[41] This may have helped to assuage any insecurity he may have felt about working largely for his mother rather than his father. How Ralph's parents came to this somewhat novel arrangement is a matter for speculation. Whether this was the result of negotiation between David and Mary Wood or a seemingly natural solution based on circumstances and Ralph's inclinations, we do not know. That Ralph's sisters' deaths affected his work assignment seems likely.

In the late nineteenth century, Ralph Wood's experience did not fit easily into the common patterns of boys' and girls' labors on their families' farms. What the following anecdote illustrates seems to have been more generally true. "One day as [Gladys] was helping Daddy throw fodder bundles for the feeding of the livestock, Uncle Perry dropped in and really scolded his brother for letting the hobo sit in the house eating a handout meal while Gladys was doing what should have been the job of the hobo. Gladys also wondered why Kenneth [her brother] was sitting in the house instead of helping. It seems the girls helped with the outdoor work, but the boys didn't help in return."[42] Girls, more often than boys, crossed over into others' domains to aid the family in the completion of its labors.[43] Men's work generated cash for the family, whereas women's often did not, creating a sense of urgency about the completion of men's work that may have been absent for women's.

Whatever the balance of their chores, however, girls and boys and young men and young women spent their early years working, and the farm child who lived a life of leisure was an exception rather than the rule. Although all farm families seem to have expected some work from their children, difficult circumstances forced some families to rely very heavily on their young. In 1880, when Benjamin and Mary Gitchel's family settled in Buffalo County, Nebraska, Gitchel was the primary agricultural laborer. In 1889 or 1890, however, Gitchel became ill and suffered an apparent stroke, causing a progressive paralysis of his right side. The drought and hard economic times of the 1890s compounded the family's already difficult situation, leaving them woefully short of the funds necessary to hire labor. As a result, in 1890, the Gitchel boys, aged eight and ten, became farmers. Their mother, in letters to relatives, proudly told of her sons' labors and the small sums the family needed to expend on hired labor. Still, Ben Gitchel appreciated the sacrifice their work represented, writing to his mother, "They are good boys to work."[44] In spite of their straitened circumstances, Ben Gitchel wanted more for his sons, as well as the benefits that only education could provide. Even though circumstances prevented them from attending school full time, the boys were able to attend school occasionally. Gitchel wrote, "The boys take turns herding the cattle on the prairie and go to school, but that will last only a month longer and whether the feed will carry the stock through or not is to be told."[45] The Gitchel daughters attended school more regularly, much to the family's benefit, since they then had the qualifications to teach school and bring an income into the household. In spite of difficult circumstances, Ben Gitchel had high hopes for his children. "We want to give our children an education if nothing else then they will be better able to compete for a livlihood [sic] in this world of strife and opression [sic]."[46] Eventually, all of the Gitchel children achieved sufficient education to become schoolteachers—quite a feat, given their father's precarious health and disability.

Stories such as the Gitchels' were sad but not unusual. Absent fathers sent many children into positions of great responsibility. When Manzo Swain went west from Wisconsin to become a miner, he left his wife and young son to operate the family farm. His son, Willie Swain, took it upon himself to care for the turkeys, geese, and cattle and to tend the crops, including hay, winter wheat, barley, and corn. He also made a fence and shelter for the hogs and banked the house for the winter. He wrote his father for instructions, but he seems to have done much under his own initiative and to have garnered a neighbor's praise for his "nice and clean and well tended" corn.[47] Even so, the work pressed heavily. As Mary Swain, Willie's mother, wrote to her absent husband in the fall of 1881, "Oh the boys do wish you would come home and see to running the farm. . . . they cant get ready for school when it comenses for it Comenses week after next."[48] In Kansas, in a similar case, drought forced a father to find work farther to the east while his wife and twelve-year-old daughter farmed the land. The youngster's work included planting, weeding, cutting, shocking, and husking corn, gathering and hauling pumpkins, and planting and harvesting castor beans. She and her mother tended and harvested wheat growing two miles from their homestead. Their efforts meant that "we had enough corn and wheat together, to last us all that winter."[49] Emergencies and absences made youngsters responsible for the fields well before their parents, or they, might have wished.

Just as farms could not operate without laborers to work in the fields, farm households could not function without someone to clean and cook, and girls, often at a quite young age, might be asked to stand in for an incapacitated, absent, or dead mother. Given a mother's poor health or the birth of a sibling, girls might expect to remain home from school and give their attention to household chores. In a letter to a children's publication, young Imogene Sorber, of Gowrie, Iowa, explained her situation. "I have been going to school; but it was out yesterday. . . . Ma has been sick, and I have had to stay at home to help her for two weeks."[50] Illness in a family might temporarily increase a girl's workload; a death had the potential to burden her permanently. When Illinois farmer John Campbell Bailey's wife died of complications of childbirth, leaving four children, daughter Lizie, not yet a teenager, took over many of her mother's housekeeping duties. Bailey was notably unsuccessful in finding permanent hired help, and his own mother, although able to assist at times, was unable to do all that was necessary to care for her four grandchildren. Bailey's diary, which had previously noted that "children went to school," began noting that "boys went to school" as Lizie remained at home to work. Typical entries in 1873 stated "Lizie staid [sic] at home to bake & wash," and "Robt. & James is [sic] at school. Lizie is washing. Grandma Bailey come down & helped her & went back." Bailey remarried shortly thereafter, which eased the load on young Lizie, allowing her to attend school more often.[51] Had John Bailey been unable to remarry so quickly, Lizie could have faced years of toil and heavy responsibilities.

All of these examples fall within the realm of necessity. Farm families needed to feed and clothe themselves and generate cash for purchases, and children's labors made that possible. Boys and girls, from the moment they were able, became the family workforce. Hiring adult labor was much too expensive for most families, so they raised and trained their own workers. For some families, the need for child labor was even more pressing when fathers and mothers became ill or died, leaving their tasks to children who were not yet in their teens. Although parents might regret the circumstances that created this necessity, they had no choice but to rely on small workers, who had to sacrifice school and play to the larger needs of the household.

Some children made further contributions to their families, hiring out on either a full- or part-time basis to work in other farm households. In mid-western states in 1870, farm labor was by far the most common type of work that boys performed for wages. Between 80 and 92 percent of boys aged ten to fifteen who worked did so in agriculture. Among girls, agricultural field labor was less common. Instead, "professional and personal services," which included domestic labor in farm households, was much more common.[52] When parents did not need their children at home or needed cash more than they needed extra hands, the solution was to hire them out to neighbors. In some cases, this seems to have been a relatively benign arrangement, beneficial to all. The elderly James and Fannie Ivins, of Barton County, Kansas, hired twenty-year-old Fred Veatch to work for them. At age seventy-six, James was arthritic and unable to maintain the farm fully. Fannie, at sixty-six, had heart problems and may have been an invalid. Fred, then, completed many of the tasks necessary to the farm's maintenance, cutting and hauling sorghum, wheat, and feed, husking corn, plowing, harrowing, listing, and planting. The Ivins seem to have treated Fred as if he were just another youngster in their household, because he participated with their apparent blessing in all of the activities of the neighborhood. He attended debates, parties, and gatherings sponsored by the local literary society. Sometimes these events kept him out late, as Ivins wrote, "Fred over to S[chool] house, Teacher here with Mother & I. Fred out till 11½ O'c. we retired after letting him in." The Ivins paid Fred his wages, and his presence allowed them to maintain their farm until February 1901.[53]

Other youngsters had much more mixed experiences with hired labor. In 1872, Peter Petersen came with his family from Denmark to the United

States. His mother and one brother died in Chicago before the family could settle in rural Nebraska. Petersen's father, not believing in the necessity of education and not needing his son's help at home, hired him out to work for various families in the area. His employers did not pay him wages but were supposed to provide the boy with food, clothing, and shelter. Some of his employers were reasonably good to him. Charles Christiansen, a local bachelor, wanted a twelve-year-old Danish boy to work for him. Christiansen began the process of teaching Peter to read and write and treated him well. He did, however, fail to provide Peter the clothes he was promised as a part of his wages.[54] The next family who employed him, the Goetches, was far less accommodating. Mr. Goetche was kind, but Mrs. Goetche was "very strict, and hard in her ways, at times abusive." Mrs. Goetche required Peter to knit for himself both the socks and mittens that she was supposed to provide to Peter under the terms of his employment, and she fed him bread and lard, while she and her husband ate "bread and butter, meats, jelly, preserves, fruits and other good things." The Goetches provided Peter no bed, and he slept on the floor. Petersen's father finally brought him home, at least in part because he "did not like the idea of the bread and lard diet."[55] In 1875, Peter hired out for wages for the first time, earning $2 per month. None of the other employers were as stingy as the Goetches, and Petersen had few complaints. Between 1875 and 1883, he would rotate between work on his father's farm and hiring out to neighbors, until finally going west with a friend working on the railroad. His father did eventually allow him to attend some school, but Petersen spent most of his childhood and youth either bringing wages home to his father or working on his father's farm. This pattern may have been somewhat more common for the children of immigrants than for the children of the native born, since "putting out" children to work remained a common training strategy for the young in European countries.[56]

Potentially most difficult was to be a hired child without any real protection from the family with whom he or she was placed. This was the situation of thousands of children placed by various "child-saving" institutions on farms throughout the midwest. Although organizations attempted to find good homes for children, and many children certainly had supportive and kind foster parents, that was not always the case. Floyd Miles's father sent five of his children to the Child Saving Institute in Omaha, Nebraska, after his wife died of tuberculosis. The institute parceled out Floyd, his siblings, and other children like them to farmers throughout the state who promised to provide them homes in exchange for a reasonable amount of work. Although the first family with whom Floyd lived provided a warm and loving home, the second, the Westerlings, did not. Roy Eiker, the farmer who took in Floyd's brother, Leslie, discovered that the Westerlings were abusing seven-year-old Floyd. The Westerlings often worked Floyd long hours and allowed him to go to school only sporadically. When he went to school, his lunch pail contained only cold biscuits and lard or jelly. Floyd hid during lunch, rather than allow the other children to see his meager meal. Mr. Westerling beat Floyd three or four times a week. Eiker confronted Westerling, threatened him with a beating if he hit the child again, and made arrangements with the Child Saving Institute to remove Floyd and send him to another foster home. Fortunately, within four months, the Institute placed him with a couple who would provide him with a loving and secure, if slightly impoverished, home for the rest of his childhood.[57]

Although these examples illustrate boys' work as hired laborers, girls worked for wages too. Given the rigorous nature of women's work on the farm and the demands childbearing placed on married women, numerous opportunities existed for girls to hire out as cooks, housekeepers, and providers of all sorts of necessary female labor. Families obtaining children as helpers from the Wisconsin State Public School appear to have requested girls as often as boys.[58] And as the example of the Bailey family shows, finding good female help could be difficult indeed, forcing families to shift the burden of labor onto their own daughters.

Clearly, the hired child was subject to a wide range of working experiences. Some worked for wages, and others worked for room, board, and clothing. Some found reasonable employers who treated them like members of the family. Others found that they were second-class members of the household, or worse. Those children who fared the best as hired laborers had parents who kept in close touch with them, monitored their situation, and had the wherewithal to bring them back home if their employers became abusive. If a child only did day labor away from his or her parents' farm, then the family would know on a daily basis whether the working conditions were reasonable for the child. Like dividing work by age or gender, hiring out was a family strategy, meant to make the most of family resources or deal with family emergencies or shortfalls. It had the potential to resolve difficult financial situations by either relieving parents of the burden of one too many mouths to feed or by bringing cash into the family coffers. Young men, given the approval of their fathers, used hired labor as an opportunity to build nest eggs, to be applied to furthering education, starting a career, or buying land. Hiring out, despite its sometimes painful results, served a definite economic purpose within farming families.

The group that we, unfortunately, know the least about are those youngsters who left home and embarked on careers as independent agricultural laborers, either with or without the blessing of their parents. Hugh Orchard, in his autobiography, indicated that four of his brothers ran away from home before reaching the age of twenty-one, in order to escape their father's tyranny. How they fared, and how common their experience was, we do not know.[59] Jon Gjerde has written that farm children were cast as employees, but employees with little choice but to work in the family business: "Adolescents, unlike hired hands, did not have the option to leave home for higher wages."[60] Apparently this was not true in all cases. Older boys, in particular, could and did leave home to work elsewhere. The cost might be high, in terms of alienation from their families.

Work had yet another function within the family; it trained children for the life in agriculture that many parents expected them to have. As historian Mary Neth has noted, a child's work not only aided in the support of the family, but also had many educational purposes. It socialized them into men's and women's work roles, taught them the skills necessary to a life in agriculture, and also involved them in the most essential of tasks: the survival of the family. "Work gave children a sense of responsibility to the farm and family, because they knew that their work was necessary, not superfluous."[61]

Farm childhood was a time of training, and youngsters worked beside their parents until they were able to perform necessary farm tasks without supervision.[62] The care of animals was an important agricultural chore that children assumed at an early age. Parents honed children's skills by giving them small, weak animals to raise that might otherwise have died. In this way, parents trained youngsters in the care of livestock without risking anything more than some time and the life of an animal that was otherwise uneconomical to keep. The story of young Katie Classen, of Gage County, Nebraska, was typical. To the *Nebraska Farmer* she wrote: "We have some sheep and last summer we had some little lambs. Papa gave me one which had been sick and he didn't think it would live but it did and when it was big I sold it."[63] The implication was that Katie's father rewarded her efforts by allowing her to keep the proceeds of her work. This was sometimes, but not always, the case, and would have taught Katie the value of hard work and

Caring for calves and other small animals was often a farm child's chore. Alden Family Papers. By permission of Special Collections, Parks Library, Iowa State University, Ames, Iowa.

responsibility, not to mention training her in the care of lambs. In addition to caring for small and orphaned animals, children often learned to care for larger animals as herders. Many families could not afford adequate fencing, and they substituted children's time and efforts for wire and posts. Some, on the other hand, may have forgone the purchase of fencing simply because child labor was available. In either case, it became a primary childhood responsibility. Ten-year-old Myrtle Jordan and her sister herded 750 sheep. Other boys and girls, such as Viola Pospeshill, of Venus, Nebraska, herded cattle. The thirteen-year-old wrote, "When we first came to our ranch we had to herd cattle to keep them away from the stacks of hay. I always rode a white horse named Daisy."[64]

It was this additional, educational function of agricultural labor that made it difficult for many late nineteenth- and early twentieth-century reformers to outright condemn agricultural labor for children. In a fashion typical of many agricultural publications, the *Nebraska Farmer* described the farm—and in this case, the dairy farm—as a training school for farm youngsters. There, they learned the importance of cleanliness, orderliness, and methodical habits, the "foundations for a sterling character to be developed in later years." They learned to "think for themselves" and to develop "those qualities of mind and body which are found in our best citizens."

In the best of cases, shared work could be the glue that held the family together, creating bonds of love and respect between parent and child. Although many urban children watched their fathers leave home to go to work each day, rural children often found themselves working side by side with their fathers and mothers. As historian Steven Hoffbeck has noted about his mid-twentieth-century childhood on a Minnesota dairy farm, work was all he and his father had time to do together, but those labors, generally completed in silence, spoke volumes about a shared work ethic and commitment to and love for the family.[65] Henry C. Taylor, who grew up on an Iowa farm and eventually became a professor at Iowa State College (now Iowa State University), had much to say in his memoirs about the value of a farm childhood. For him, the compensations most importantly came in the form of time spent at his father's side, learning the art and craft of agriculture. This education began at an early age.

> My first memory of his training was when I was two years old. He took me with him to the field and had me stand and watch him at work while he was making some repairs on a reaping machine. He always seemed to like to have me with him, even when I was too small to help, and I have no memory of his ever indicating that I was in his way. If he were making a repair at night, he would have me hold the lantern for him and would say, 'You hold the lantern so that you can see, then I can see.'[66]

From the age of two onward, Henry Taylor's father taught him the family business, from fixing machines, to plowing fields, to shearing sheep. He was experiencing what reformers feared urban children would rarely enjoy: a practical education gained by working side by side with a parent through the seasons and the years. For Henry Taylor, it was a valuable education not only in agriculture but also in life skills. His father was his first, and best, teacher, and the one he emulated in later life.

It should not be assumed, however, that parents and children always worked side by side. Many children's tasks, such as herding, left them alone, or in the company of other children, for hours on end. Parents might assign children tasks, such as tending the baby, in order to free them for work in another part of the home or farm. Manzo Swain's father left his family to go west, and Manzo worked at a man's task without his father's assistance. Economically distressed fathers migrated away from home in search of work; others regularly went to town to attend to family business. Historian Stephen Frank has commented that "while this heightened availability of rural fathers did exist, it was frequently disrupted." On the other hand, he found that agrarian work rhythms and the slack times of the year did allow opportunities for greater involvement of fathers with their children's lives.[67]

Beyond meeting the needs of the family and providing necessary socialization, work might meet other needs of children as well. If a child was allowed to profit from his or her own labors (not all were, as a child's wages and person legally belonged to the parent until he or she reached the age of twenty-one), he or she might be able to apply the proceeds to the pursuit of personal goals. In 1872, Oliver Perry Myers was a teenager working on his father's Iowa farm. Although it is clear that he was an active participant in the family economy, he also had the time and opportunity to pursue his own interests. Oliver Myers planted, plowed, and harvested crops, hauled manure, dug drains, set out trees, and generally made himself useful to his parents. Myers, however, also worked for himself. He owned his own livestock and sometimes sold and traded animals with his father. His father gave him his own fruit trees to plant and tend. He trapped prairie chickens for sale, and he also hired out his labors to neighbors. Oliver Myers was not only a participant in the family enterprise, he was also a young entrepreneur. On July 31, 1872, he wrote: "I have Earned $7.25 this harvest working from home I made a hand all this harvest. . . . I had a small patch of oats this year. I got 23 shocks on it. My hogs are doing fine though all the pigs died."[68] Unlike some parents, Myers's father allowed him to keep his earnings. Although Myers did not note the use to which he put his hard-earned funds, they may very well have helped to pay for the education he eventually pursued at the University of Iowa.

Girls might also engage in profitable enterprises. Mary Peet, of Jones County, Iowa, for example, combined family labor with personal gain. Peet was an avid gardener who raised vegetables as well as a wide variety of flowers, particularly geraniums. She also found herself milking and caring for chickens. The chickens, however, served a specific lucrative purpose. She wrote, "I am going to take care of the little chickens this year. I commenced saving eggs to get me a new dress with."[69] Louisa Sophia Gelhorn Boyland's father gave her the runt of a litter of pigs and told her that if she could raise it, the proceeds would be hers. The fattened pig brought $1.25 at market, "paper money" that bought the fabric for a dress and a hair ribbon and twenty-five cents' worth of savings.[70]

Children's accounts of their own labors also carried undertones of pride in accomplishment that made it clear that work was not simply drudgery, but a matter of gaining skills, responsibility, and maturity.[71] In a letter to the *Nebraska Farmer*, eleven-year-old Ruth Landwehr, of Columbus, Nebraska, described her work in a matter-of-fact tone, commenting, "When my mamma was sick of course I had to do the housework." For Ruth, this entailed scrubbing and cooking, neither of which she found too objectionable. The scrubbing, she asserted, was even "fun." Her proudest accomplishment was making soup for her mother. "My papa killed a chicken and I dressed it and made mamma chicken soup. Mamma said it tasted good. She said I was doing pretty well."[72] Ruth's mother had successfully prepared her to perform household duties, and she relished the opportunity to demonstrate her skills. In fact, many girls wrote to the children's editor of the *Nebraska Farmer*, proud of their ability to meet adult responsibilities. Agnes Adelle Stewart, of Friend, Nebraska, took over for her father when he attended the livestock sales. This included the care of twelve horses. Although Agnes "had to start at three o'clock and got done at five o'clock," she fed the horses daily, in addition to completing the other barnyard chores.[73] Perhaps it was because most people considered these tasks to be "boy's work" that Agnes Stewart felt such a sense of accomplishment.

Aside from the satisfaction of a job well done, labor might carry with it other pleasures as well. Working with animals brought some children great satisfaction, as did submerging themselves in the sights and sounds of nature.[74] Although descriptions of work as play are rare in children's diaries and letters, memoirs of farm youth discuss the many ways in which the pain of toil could be lessened. Elma Bamberg, who grew up on a Kansas farm, explained the way in which she and her brother made work into play: "Call it play or call it sport, we had to mix play with work. There had to be some contest or competition going on, or boredom over took you. You had to be a winner, at least for part of the time; get the most done, play the most pranks; or even eat the most radishes for dinner." Contests could make work into play, and creative parents might find ways to do so as well. Frances Olsen Day's parents eased the tedium of shelling corn or sewing carpet rags by reading aloud as the work progressed. As the children learned to read, they would read to the family too.[75]

The sheer excitement of some events, such as threshing with steam power, helped to relieve the oppression of work. No farm implement inspired awe like the steam engines that powered threshing machines. They fascinated, thrilled, and alarmed boys with their "belching smoke" and "smell of hot grease and coal smoke." Also, being included in men's work might exhaust a boy, but it brought its share of pride and enjoyment in being included in male camaraderie. Milo Pitcher of Story County, Iowa, recalled the periodic lulls in a day's work. "As the men sat around frequently they would get to telling stories. Whenever that happened I always managed to be there. I just couldn't bear the thought of missing out on any of those stories."[76] Although time may have done much to soften memories of work, that work did carry the potential for enriching a child's life, teaching skills, creating common bonds with parents, and leaving a lasting impression of time well spent. And at the most basic level, it filled their stomachs, clothed their limbs, and put a roof over their heads.

None of this, however, denies the fact that farm work was hard and often tedious. The days of the week, with their chores indoors and out, continued relentlessly. The seasons of the year, each with their specific tasks, followed one after another. Some tasks were merely routine; others were extremely unpleasant. In 1870, farmer John Inman of Benton County, Iowa, was father to four sons. While he was often away on business as a county supervisor, the four boys, all fifteen and under, toiled away at the farm work and were even hired out to thresh for their neighbors. When they broke gears on the threshing machine two days running, they repented the third with a day's labor hauling manure, one of the most odious of farm chores.[77] Although we do not know the ultimate fate of the Inman boys, they must have thought long and hard about their work, and its weight, on that long September day.

A further measure of the weight of children's work was in its sheer danger and capacity to hurt, cripple, or even kill young workers. No matter what work meant in terms of its contributions to family life, it posed concrete dangers to the children involved. Farm life was dangerous, and children were not immune to its hazards. Youngsters were not always as careful as parents would have wished, and sometimes they were overtaken by circumstances beyond their control. Animals could be threatening, as horses, cows, sheep, and pigs were generally much larger than children, and children often came into close contact with them. In 1905, a serious accident occurred when six-year-old Norman McClary, of Lewellyn, Nebraska, passed too closely by a cow in the barn. The cow swung her head around, "striking him squarely in the mouth—loosening 6 teeth, breaking three of them off—up inside the gums." "Poor boy," his father wrote, "he is certainly worked

The large size of the horses and the log emphasize the small size of the working boy. Heiber family farm, Black Hawk County, Iowa, circa 1900. By permission of the State Historical Society of Iowa.

up over it *and so am I.*"[78] Simply walking through a barn exposed children to risk. Everyday actions and normal activities carried the possibility of injury.

Farm implements were every bit as dangerous as animals. Clarence Jacobson slipped while driving a hay rake, falling in front of the rake but in back of the horses. One of the horses kicked him in the head, and both started to run, dragging him a considerable distance. He survived, but with a fractured skull, a broken lower jaw, and facial cuts requiring stitches. He learned a valuable lesson: "a rake is a dangerous implement with frisky horses and a twelve-year old 'kid.' "[79] Harrows could do damage as well, an unfortunate fact that the Story family discovered. On March 5, 1880, while working with his grandfather, young Leouis Story tangled with the harrow, and "one of the harrow teeth had penetrated his side below his heart and entered the dear little fellows lungs." His father described his condition as "critical," and it may well have been, because valuable, hard-working Leouis did not return to the fields until April 30.[80] A disc accident took the life of fifteen-year-old Carl Beck of Viola Township, Audubon County, Iowa. His horses, frightened by an automobile, ran away; the lines tied around his back dragged him to the ground and under the disc.[81] Farm implements, farm animals, and farm work offered infinite possibilities for serious, even fatal, injury.

Household tasks also offered many opportunities for mishaps, especially because many chores involved fire. Before World War II, most farm families cooked, washed, and ironed with fire. It did not take much to demonstrate to a child that fire could be dangerous. When Edithe Lundstrom's parents left her at home alone with her three brothers, the children decided to make themselves a hot dinner and left a kettle of water and meat on the stove. While the children were in the barn attending to other chores, the fire nearly went out. One of Edithe's brothers, deciding to remedy the situation as quickly as possible, added kerosene to the smoldering corncobs and applied a match. Predictably, "the fire blazed up and blew the stovepipe down and lifted a lid from the stove. It made everything in the room black with soot and also the cellar." Fortunately, no one was injured. The children hoped to avoid telling their parents, but they arrived home sooner than expected to a filthy house. As Edithe wrote, "Mamma found the whole house was covered with soot and she was frightened. . . . I was so frightened that I will never forget it."[82] It would be instructive to know what actions the Lundstrom parents took in this situation, but Edithe ended her story with their arrival at home. No doubt punishment of some sort followed, given their parents' knowledge of the real danger of their actions. The results of their folly could have been far worse. In 1915, two small Maiden Rock, Wisconsin, girls burned to death, unable to escape the house after they poured kerosene on the coals in the kitchen stove.[83] Then, as now, the home was a dangerous place, and accidents were a common cause of injury and death.

Other parents exposed their children to danger in ways that fly in the face of modern notions of child protection and parental responsibilities. Few early twenty-first-century parents would expect their young children to be able to kill rattlesnakes, but such was the case of Charles Turner, raised in Nebraska. In a matter-of-fact tone, Turner related the following tale about his childhood working experiences. While his father broke prairie, he expected Charles to "plant a garden of melons, squashes, pumpkins and citrons by cutting a gash in a sod and hand dropping the seeds and tamping the gash together with the back of the axe." Rattlesnakes impeded Charles's progress, and "every little while I would call my father to come and kill a rattlesnake. He was killing one very often by stamping them to death with his heavy high topped boots." Charles's father eventually lost patience with this procedure and told his son, "'If I was a boy ten years old and had an axe I'd never call any one to come and kill a rattlesnake for me.' Well the next one I met I very carefully reached and killed him and before we finished breaking that little patch I had killed 10 rattlesnakes and he must have killed over fifteen on about an acre of land."[84] And so, at the tender age of ten, Charles Turner mastered the art of rattlesnake slaying. His work in the garden was his own responsibility, and if that included clearing poisonous snakes from his path, so be it. The work, both his and his father's, had to be done. And despite the dangers, most children, including Charles Turner, lived to tell their tales of work and its hazards in later life.

Although there is little statistical information about the levels of accident, injury, and death that farm children experienced, the anecdotal evidence suggests that the number of injuries and near misses was quite high. Even so, farm children's experiences need to be put into perspective with those of all children in their time. In 1900, the Census Bureau collected information from those states registering deaths (not all did) and found that, in general, the urban environment was more unhealthy than the rural environment. For infants under the age of one, in cities, there were 165.8 deaths per 1,000 births; in rural areas, the number was 108.7. For children under the age of five, 343 died per 1,000 in cities, while only 218.1 died per 1,000 in rural areas. The overall death rate in urban areas was 18.6 per 1,000 of population, while in rural areas it was 15.4 per 1,000.[85] Infectious diseases, such as tuberculosis, were particularly virulent in cramped urban environments.[86] And although children in urban areas rarely came into contact with discs and harrows, they faced many other hazards. Horses, and their attendant dangers, remained common in urban areas. Children also crossed the paths of trolleys, streetcars, and trains. Poorer families continued to cook and clean over fires. Electricity, too, was not without its hazards. Turn-of-the-century cities, which combined poor sanitation with crowded conditions, were hardly safe places to live. Childhood, urban or rural, was lived in inherently dangerous environs.

Childhoods spent working long and arduous hours were not uncommon in the nineteenth and early twentieth centuries. Hundreds of thousands of farm children shared similar burdens. Additionally, many poor urban children toiled in factories, earning wages that would allow their families and themselves food, clothing, and shelter. In most cases, children's wages and children's efforts contributed to the well-being of the family as a whole, and not to the individual savings and spending of children. Legally, a child's wages and efforts belonged to his or her parents until he or she was twenty-one, and few farm families—or working-class families, for that matter—could afford to grant children the right to any significant portion of their wages. Youngsters might be liberated or sent off to high school or college by a relatively well-to-do or indulgent parent, or a child might liberate himself or herself by taking leave of the family homestead, but in the traditional household, leave-taking had to wait until marriage or until the age of twenty-one. As Isaac Haycraft explained about his own Minnesota family, "Father followed the same rule with all three boys. When Em[il] was twenty-one, he was told that his time was his own but that there was always a bed and a place at the table for him until he wanted to strike out for himself."[87] Even so, for many young people, their relationship to their family's farm continued as they contributed their labor or their wages to the family enterprise, even as they began more independent lives. Work was the foundation of the farm family's life, and children played a vital role in ensuring the strength of that foundation.

3

"We Have Splendid Times at School"

Farm Children and Education

❖ ❖ ❖ ❖ ❖ ❖ ❖ ❖ ❖ ❖ ❖ ❖ ❖ ❖ ❖

I am going to school now. Susie Moore is Teacher. We have splendid times at school. We play blackman and ring and charades and ball and every thing else almost every day. I study Reading, Grammar, Geography, Physiology, Arithmetic and Writing.
—*Rosa Armentrout (later Dr. Rosa Armentrout Butterfield), age fifteen, diary, February 4, 1877*

In terms of the time involved, school was the second most important factor in midwestern farm children's lives, after work. In terms of devotion to school, education could be an element of little importance to a youngster, or of utmost importance, as it was for young Rosa Armentrout, who grew up near Wilton, Iowa. But whether a farm child loved school or loathed it, education was quickly becoming a requirement in most children's lives, with state laws mandating a minimum number of hours of instruction over the course of a somewhat limited school year. This legislation, however, accommodated the needs of the agricultural family by allowing the educational calendar to be shaped by the demands of planting and harvesting and also allowing families to remove their children from school when necessary. Work was the most important competing force education had to contend with, but there were others. Reformers charged that the rural school itself was an impediment to education, with its worn-out buildings and books, limited curriculum, and often poorly prepared teachers. Beyond the school and its curriculum, the weather often interrupted school attendance, as did epidemic disease. Other less predictable intrusions might also impede education's progress, such as the so-called boy problem in rural schools. Older boys, often on the verge of leaving school for full-time employment, tended to be a disruptive force in the classroom, sometimes even driving teachers out of their schools. Parents, too, could range from supportive to hostile. A rural education could be a hard-won experience, in every sense of the word.

Schools, the school day, and the academic year varied from location to location but had enough similar characteristics that good generalizations can be made. Most midwestern farm children attended one- and two-room country schools. These schools were usually simple structures, often with separate doors for boys and girls. They were usually lighted by rows of windows on one or two walls, with a blackboard covering one wall. Smaller desks for younger scholars were at the front of the room, with larger ones for older students at the back. Schools might house as few as two or three students, or as many as fifty or more.[1] Scholars might range in age from toddlers, deposited there by parents who perceived the teacher as a glorified babysitter, to young men and women of up to twenty-one years of age.[2] A stove heated most schools, and a well or pump provided water for a bucket, from which students drank with a common dipper. Students did their work at the blackboard and on slates. Students brought their own books to school, and a multitude of texts of varying authors, ages, and quality might be used by students in the same grade.[3]

Although many state boards of education argued for improved conditions, progress was slow. In 1916, for example, the Kansas State Board of Education established the requirements for a "Standard Rural School," as well as "Superior Rural Schools." Included were suggestions for adequate classroom proportions, proper lighting, modern heating and ventilation systems, and a sanitary privy, as well as instructions to purchase such items as decorative and instructive artwork, maps, a globe, and a dictionary. These, however, were suggestions rather than the law, and improvements had to be made within the context of local budgets, conditions, and attitudes. Many school districts moved slowly. A 1922 survey indicated that six years after the program's inception, fifteen of the state's counties lacked a single school meeting the board's standards, and only a handful of counties had as many as ten schools meeting the standards. Improving conditions was a slow process, achieved most often in districts that had consolidated their schools and therefore their resources.[4]

Children who lived at a great distance from school might drive a cart, in this case pulled by a donkey, to school. These youngsters lived near Agenda, Kansas. By permission of Mary Thompson Riney.

Students assembled at the school in the morning, coming from near and far. Parents sometimes brought their children to school, but most arrived on foot or on horseback. Classes generally began at 9:00 AM and continued to 4:00 in the afternoon, although dismissal times were negotiable at some schools. Teachers might opt for a short noon hour or short recesses so that students could return home by daylight during the winter months. Parents might push for a short noon hour and early dismissal, while their children lobbied for a long noon hour that would give them more time for skating, sledding, or other pursuits.[5] The standard subjects a rural student learned were reading, arithmetic, spelling, grammar, and history or geography. Nature study might be included in some schools. Students learned these subjects through a combination of independent study at their desks and recitations at the front of the class. Teachers sometimes called upon older students to help the smaller ones with their subjects. Early twentieth-century studies in Wisconsin indicated that many teachers heard between twenty-four and thirty different subjects recited during the day.[6] The repetition could be wearing on students and teachers. Fifteen-year-old Mary Pascoe, attending school in Hazel Green, Wisconsin, noted its sameness in her journal. "I have been to school that is the same thing over and over again day after day."[7] Others used the spare time to good effect. As soon as she finished her lessons, Theresa Baughman Rickett turned to the school library for entertainment. "I read practically every book in it each season."[8]

A creative and well-educated teacher might alleviate this sameness with the introduction of subjects not normally in the curriculum. New classes appeared according to the ability and interests of the teacher. Oliver Perry Myers, who grew up in Washington County, Iowa, studied algebra in addition to the usual subjects, and his teacher sometimes ventured into other advanced topics, such as physiology. Before he went off to Iowa City to pursue a secondary and college education, he had "got to Africa in geography I got to the 228 page in Algebra Through the principle past in grammar To History—Reading & Spelling in proportion."[9]

The thoroughness with which teachers were able to cover the necessary subjects was often determined by the length of the school year. As dictated by state law, the school year varied in length from location to location and between states in the midwest. School districts might enroll children for fall, winter, spring, and summer terms of up to eight weeks each. Schools that enrolled students for only twelve weeks per year were generally in session only during fall and winter or winter and spring terms. Because schools often had new teachers each term, or after two or three terms, there could be a lack of consistency in coverage.

Teachers enlivened the school week and school year with special events. Students looked forward to Fridays because the last hour of the afternoon, or even the whole afternoon, might be devoted to spelling bees, math contests, or "speaking," when students had the opportunity to present pieces they had memorized. May Crowder, who grew up on an Iowa farm, remembered a special Friday afternoon song that preceded spelling contests. The students sang:

> Oh, dear! Oh, dear! I shall never learn to spell;
> I shall always be a dunce, I know very well.
> For the letters get mixed up in such a queer way
> That I never can tell what they mean to say.[10]

Students might even visit a neighboring school, and the schools would compete against each other to see which students were best at spelling or ciphering.[11] It was an opportunity for the school to shine, or to be embarrassed. Frances Olsen Day, who grew up near Dixon, Iowa, remembered a competition with a neighboring school that reflected very badly on her own. The teacher, "inordinately lazy" with "no respect for his job or pupils," had allowed the school to become "filthy dirty a[n]d disorderly." The sight of a sled of students on their way for an afternoon's entertainment forced the teacher into swift action. He "begged the kids to help tidy up. There wasn't much time but we did what we could. . . . tidying really accomplished wonders."[12] Students also tidied and prepared their classrooms for end-of-term exercises. After they had taken their exams and completed their studies, they and their teachers would plan a day's worth of events. At the end of a spring term, this might include a maypole, spoken exercises, and a dinner or picnic, either in the schoolhouse or on the grounds.[13] It was an opportunity for scholars, and their teacher, to demonstrate what had been learned throughout the term. In this very tangible way, parents discovered what their children had accomplished during their time away from the family farm. Public exhibitions helped to build community support for education.

The majority of midwestern children learned their reading, writing, and arithmetic in these locally controlled one- and two-room schools. It was a relatively simple education, and one that varied considerably in quality from location to location. By the late years of the nineteenth century, rural educators were beginning to wonder about the efficacy of that education and were negatively assessing the health of their schools. Fred Lacey, an Iowa farm boy turned superintendent of the North Des Moines, Iowa, schools, noted their weaknesses in an 1898 report. He bemoaned the individuality of that education, especially in that the textbooks the students presented were often the sole determinant of their curriculum. Because students came with such a variety of textbooks, "the multiplicity of classes made it impossible for the teacher to give sufficient time to any class to enable his pupils to accomplish anything of real value." Too often, students learned by rote.[14]

By the early years of the twentieth century, concerns such as Lacey's were coming to the attention of the nation. When Theodore Roosevelt's Country Life Commission made its report in 1912, one of its chief concerns was the deficiencies of the rural public schools and the educational problems they posed for the nation's children, enormous numbers of whom attended these small, often one- and two-room grammar schools. In fact, education came to be the centerpiece of the Country Life Commission's concerns about rural America. As the report stated, "In every part of the United States there seems to be one mind, on the part of those capable of judging, on the ne-

SCHOOL
CENSUS
————————
5 1 6 . 4 0 0

RURAL
55%

CITIES OF
3D CLASS
18%

CITIES OF
2D CLASS
14%

CITIES OF
1ST CLASS
13%

In teaching and in school equipment does the country boy get a square deal?

As this 1911 editorial cartoon from the Kansas Farmer *implied, children in rural schools may have been the majority, but they did not necessarily receive an education equivalent to that of children in urban areas.* Kansas Farmer, *October 21, 1911. By permission of the Kansas State Historical Society, Topeka, Kansas.*

cessity of redirecting the rural schools. There is no such unanimity on any other subject."[15] According to the report, as well as educational reformers, the problems of the schools were numerous. They were often old, poorly built, and unsanitary. Little money was expended on their upkeep, and attending school within their walls could be demoralizing and a threat to health. The schools had an old-fashioned curriculum, largely dependent on rote learning, and the subjects often had little relevance to the lives of farm children.[16] The teachers were one of the biggest concerns. Reports charged that they were the youngest, least experienced, and most poorly educated of all of the nation's teachers, and yet they had one of the most difficult tasks: with the barest of resources, they taught large numbers of children spread among multiple grades, all at the same time. In 1908, Kansas' State Superintendent of Public Instruction noted that the age of teachers in rural schools was declining and commented that "too often the old-time 'good teacher' has gone to the city. The ambitious scholar follows him, often taking the family with him."[17] The statistics in the state's next report on education showed that nearly 30 percent of the teachers in the state's one-room schools were in their first year of teaching.[18] Conditions such as these were high on Country Lifers' lists of problems to be remedied. Because of this host of problems, they believed that rural schools were highly inefficient and entirely incapable of fostering the kind of change necessary to promote a healthy and sustainable countryside.[19]

The relative merits of these charges were debated hotly in the early twentieth century and continue even today to be a matter of debate among historians of education.[20] As might be expected, there was some truth to these accusations, but reformers also missed some of the more positive facets of rural education. Many schools were old and in disrepair, but some communities boasted schools that were models of cleanliness and efficiency. The curriculum did often rely on rote memorization, but it also encouraged cooperation and learning among students of different ages and abilities. As one woman remembered of her education in a one-room Kansas school, "the pupils developed a spirit of sharing with older students looking after the younger ones. Each of the older girls sort of adopted one of the first graders and looked after him or her, helping with wraps, boots, etc."[21] Many country schoolteachers were young and inexperienced, but some brought a wealth of energy and enthusiasm to the task. And as the years progressed, more resources, such as summer teachers' institutes, were available for and catered to the needs of rural teachers. A rural school education might provide a very poor educational experience for some students, but for others it provided an excellent foundation for further study in secondary schools, normal schools, colleges, and universities. The same may be said of suburban and urban schools of a hundred years ago and today. Unfortunately, however, the average conditions and standards of rural schools tended to be low, and they were too dependent on the strengths or weaknesses of a single, generally very young and minimally trained teacher.

The limitations of rural schools aside, farm children found their educational prospects constrained by any number of forces competing for their time and energy. This, of course, was contrary to the wishes of reformers who were endeavoring to move children out of employment and into regular school attendance. Reformers discovered that this was an easier goal to achieve in urban than in rural areas. Children working in industrial and service occupations in the cities were relatively visible. Their work often took them into the public eye and into public places where authorities felt comfortable intervening.[22] By the turn of the century, those who worked under sweatshop conditions in their own homes were also becoming more visible, in part because of the journalistic efforts of reformers such as Jacob Riis.[23] A poor urban child's work was just as important to his family as a farm child's work, but because the location of that work was often outside the family home, authorities did not view prohibiting that labor as an intervention into the private life of the family. Limiting child labor on farms was another matter altogether. Intervention meant an intrusion into the home and the family—an intrusion into what was perceived as thoroughly private space. Farming was a family enterprise, and reformers often classified children's work on farms as beneficial, having social and familial value that industrial labor did not. Iowa's child labor laws, for example, addressed the industrial workplace rather than the farm. By 1920, the state had placed restrictions on children working in factories, stores, businesses, and service establishments operating during school hours and had prohibited children from working at night, but they had made no provisions for children working on their parents' farms.[24] A 1914 state publication investigating child labor in Iowa essentially dismissed the necessity for such legislation, commenting that "much work in which children are engaged is beneficial—especially that which is performed around the home and in the open air," a definition that encompassed nearly all of farm children's labors.[25] Faced with these considerations, legislators generally used laws governing school attendance to attempt to force farm children out of the fields and into the classroom.

The midwestern states varied considerably in their commitment to guaranteeing an education to their states' children, and the timing of that commitment also varied. Kansas made an early effort to legislate compulsory education. The state's first compulsory education law came in 1874 and was modeled on Michigan's 1871 law. The state required parents or guardians to send children aged eight to fourteen to twelve weeks of school per year, six weeks of which were required to be consecutive. A number of exceptions to the law, however, existed. Parents who could not afford to clothe their children adequately were excused from the law's provisions, as were those instructing their children at home or those living more than two miles from the nearest road. Parents violating the law were guilty of a misdemeanor and subject to fines of up to $20 for multiple offenses. In spite of Kansas's early action on this issue, the degree to which the law was enforced was questionable. An 1890 survey of country superintendents by the state superintendent of schools revealed that 70 percent of the county superintendents believed that the law was ineffective, or "a dead letter." The other 30 percent believed it had increased attendance somewhat. The primary problem with the law appeared to have been a lack of collective will to enforce it. "There are few persons, comparatively, that possess sufficient educational enthusiasm to incur a neighbor's displeasure by attempting enforcement of the law."[26]

When the Kansas State Superintendent of Public Instruction surveyed county superintendents nearly twenty years later, the results were somewhat more positive, but still mixed. Over half of the county superintendents reported that they had good levels of compliance with the state's truancy law. The superintendent in Allen County reported that "many were kept in school through fear of the law." Chase County reported "better attendance and evener, more uniform work, especially in the country districts," and the superintendent in Harvey County noted that attendance had increased from roughly 60 percent of affected youngsters to 80 percent. In Hodgeman County, the law offered an opportunity to educate farming parents, particularly those of immigrant origins. "Poor, hard-working foreigners will come to the county superintendent to get permission to have the child help in field a day or two, and get a brief lecture on the need of education and regular attendance at school." In spite of this improvement, however, problems persisted. Several county superintendents reported that there were too few truant officers to enforce the law properly and that it was hard to get convictions. In the case of Allen County, the county attorney refused to prosecute truancy cases. Transporting small children to far-distant schools remained a problem in Scott County. Perhaps most seriously, the compulsory attendance law resulted in the shortening of the school year in farming communities. Several county superintendents noted this problem. Rather than maintain long terms of school that would force some students into truancy, rural districts simply shortened their terms in order to avoid conflicts during critical planting and harvesting seasons.[27] Despite ongoing problems, the law continued to be strengthened, and by 1920, Kansas children aged eight to sixteen were required to attend school, although families could remove their literate fourteen-year-old children in "extreme cases of emergency or domestic necessity."[28]

Wisconsin was also early to incorporate compulsory schooling into state law. In 1879, the state legislature voted to require all children between the ages of seven and fifteen to attend school at least twelve weeks per year.

This, however, did not affect youngsters living more than two miles distant from school by the nearest traveled road.[29] According to the state superintendent of schools, one of the primary goals of the legislation was to direct public attention to the one-third of the state's children whose parents were not sending them to schools, rather than to compel attendance.[30] By 1905, the legislature mandated special inspections for rural schools, and attempts at consolidation began in 1909.[31] But even in 1920, discrepancies remained between educational expectations in rural and urban areas. Whereas school years of eight and nine months were common in cities, a school year of only six months was allowable in smaller locales.[32]

In 1883, compulsory education became a fact of a child's life in Illinois. In that year, the state legislature mandated that all children between the ages of eight and fourteen be required to attend school for no fewer than twelve weeks of the year. Parents might be excused from sending their children to school for a number of reasons, including the home instruction of their children or the lack of schools within two miles of a family's residence. The loopholes in the law encouraged a number of modifications over the years, and by 1920, Illinois law generally required attendance by all youngsters seven to sixteen years of age, although children could be excused "for cause," a term not provided a specific meaning.[33]

In 1885, Minnesota adopted the provisions of the Kansas law but extended the age of attendance to sixteen, rather than fourteen. And like Kansas, the state had trouble enforcing the law because of the unwillingness of residents to enforce its provisions on their neighbors.[34] Over the years, the law also maintained characteristics peculiar to a farm state. Although Minnesota's laws did not specifically indicate that farm children could be excused from school, its provisions made this possible in at least some seasons. In 1920, the law required children in urban areas to attend the whole academic year, whereas those fourteen and older in rural areas whose parents required their help might be excused from school from April 1 to November 1 each year, leaving a school year of only six months. These dates encompassed both the spring planting and fall harvest seasons.[35] And because localities set their own requirements for teachers, those in rural schools generally had only an eighth-grade education, whereas in urban areas, such as Rochester, the school boards required teachers to have a normal school degree.[36]

By the early years of the twentieth century, Nebraska's school laws were perhaps the most lenient of any in the midwest. Although education became mandatory in 1887, there was very little will to enforce the law, even on the part of the state superintendent, George B. Lane. In 1890 he wrote, "I am not in favor of any rigid enforcement of the law. It can not be of much service if enforced by external authority. I am in favor of the law as far as it can be carried out by means of supervision, encouragement, and moral support."[37] Perhaps as a result of this attitude, Nebraska's school law for rural districts changed little between its inception and the early years of the twentieth century. As late as 1920, the state allowed for a school year of only twelve weeks in rural districts, as compared with nine months in Nebraska's urban counties, Lancaster and Douglas. During those twelve weeks, the law required only that a youngster attend for eight hours per week, and it allowed exemptions essential to the support of their families. The state's preponderantly rural population meant that four-fifths of the state's children lived in communities where the law compelled only the barest minimum of instruction.[38] Major changes, however, were soon to come. By 1922, the attendance requirement in rural school districts became six months, but it was still three months less than the term required in Omaha and Lincoln.[39]

In Iowa, mandatory school attendance was a long time in coming. The state did not pass mandatory attendance laws until 1902, and then largely because of concerns for urban, rather than rural, children. In the last two decades of the nineteenth century, Iowa began to urbanize, a situation that caused legislators great concern. As early as 1888, city children who did not attend school had become a concern of the state superintendent of schools.[40] These apparently idle urban youth were highly visible, and they worried legislators in ways that rural children did not, prompting turn-of-the-century lawmakers to grapple with the issue of compulsory school attendance.[41] Not surprisingly, the law, when enacted, more strictly enforced school attendance in urban than in rural locations. The school year in most rural locations was substantially shorter than that in urban areas, and the state only required twenty-four weeks of instruction. Estimates placed the total months of education for urban children at sixty-six, compared with twenty-six for children in the country.[42] The law did not compel attendance for rural children in the same way that it did for those in urban areas, as it only provided for truant officers in cities of twenty thousand inhabitants or more. It also allowed to be excused from attendance children whose "distance from school makes attendance undue hardship."[43] Lawmakers appear to have believed that nonattendance was a less important issue in rural communities.

As the history of school law in the midwest suggests, legislators generally left the enforcement of the law to local authorities, and local authorities were highly reluctant to take their friends and neighbors to court. Sociologist John Gillette, examining this problem in North Dakota, alleged, "I have heard county superintendents advise rural school directors that the compulsory attendance laws would be leniently executed. Since the farmers' vote is responsible for the incumbency of superintendents it is readily seen why they must be cautious in exercising their duties in this direction."[44] Elected officials could not help but be aware of the potential cost of enforcing school attendance laws. Access to education remained a problem for farm children, and one that received far less attention than in urban settings.

The reasons for lax enforcement were complex. First, legislators realized that farming families desperately needed their children's labor and were reluctant to threaten the health of the farming economy. And as John Gillette suggested, to do so might threaten their continued careers as public officials as well. Also, as I argued in Chapter 1, legislators and reformers had highly ambivalent feelings about the effect of a farm childhood on the nation's children. Most Americans embraced industry and hard work as character-building. Could farm work, then, be completely wrong? Although the law increasingly compelled farm youngsters to attend school, the compulsion was never as great as that applied to city children.

Need dictated the balance among work, school, and leisure. For the sons and daughters whose lives are described here, work was at the center of their existence. The farm, with its animals, crops, and daily chores, was with them every day. School, be it half a mile down the road, or six, existed at a distance. This distance was greater for some children than for others. Although some children rarely missed school, others rarely attended. In many farm families, parents perceived education as a luxury and work as a necessity, and they sacrificed their children's educations to the demands of the farm. In 1889, only 75 percent of Iowa's school-age children enrolled in school, and only 47 percent actually attended.[45] May Crowder grew up on a Palo Alto County farm, and her brothers were a part of that half of all Iowa children who did not attend school. Crowder wrote, "The children had their work to do as soon as it was possible for them to work. Brother Fred took a man's place from the time he was ten years old and Frank followed suit though he did have a little better chance for schooling since he attended a few spring terms."[46] Children in families such as this might begin school at age seven or eight or older, end their formal schooling long before completing grammar school, and have spotty attendance records due to bad weather, long distances, and the ever-present demands of work.[47]

Although all farm children were susceptible to pressures that might limit their schooling, boys seem to have suffered particularly. In the spring and the fall, many parents kept their sons at home to help with the planting and the harvesting. The diaries of a Wisconsin brother and sister demonstrated this very pattern: William Converse often worked while his sister Effie attended school. On March 25, 1883, William wrote, "I dragged and planted in the forenoon and plowed in the afternoon. . . . Effie went to school." On May 4, he commented, "We [he and his father] drawed manure. Effie went to school."[48] The records of the North Liberty School, in Iowa Township, Cedar County, show a pattern of attendance that was typical of country schools. In the spring of 1877, thirty-nine children attended. Of those, only twelve were boys, and only three of those boys were over the age of ten. None of the three teenaged boys, John Roberts, Charles Roberts, or Charles Russell, attended more than fourteen days out of a three-month term. On the other hand, ten girls over the age of ten were enrolled and generally had strong attendance records. During the winter term, 1887–1888, twenty boys and twelve girls attended the school. During the spring, when planting and cultivating were primary concerns, the boys virtually disappeared from school, with three boys and seventeen girls attending. The same was true, although to a lesser extent, for the fall corn harvest: eight boys and fifteen girls attended. By the beginning of the winter term, the numbers of boys and girls were almost even: twelve boys and eleven girls. In the course of the academic year, only one child, a girl, was neither absent nor tardy.[49] Boys who had been kept out of school regularly for planting and harvest often fell behind the other students, with disastrous consequences for their education. Unable to complete a year's lessons in the time their work obligations allowed, they often needed to repeat grades. This could be both disheartening and embarrassing. As one former teacher commented, "Boys become ashamed to stand with little girls and they leave school before the eighth grade is completed."[50] Of course, the same could happen to girls as well when circumstances at home caused them to miss school and embarrassment over their lack of progress led them to abandon their education altogether.[51] What these comments do not take into account were youngsters' preferences. Some may very well have preferred to work rather than attend school, especially if they had fallen behind in their studies, or they may have found the curriculum in the rural schools boring or irrelevant to their plans for their lives.

Although the demands of farm labor limited many a child's education, it was not the only force working against school attendance. Youngsters writing about themselves to children's publications, such as *American Young Folks,* described their work, their play, and their family lives. They also explained the reasons for their absences from school. Given the high disease rates of the late nineteenth and early twentieth centuries, it is not surprising that many children lost weeks or months of school to illness. Ella F. Campbell, of Lucas County, Iowa, was one of those children. She wrote, "My sister Susie died this winter of diphtheria and lung fever, and I had it very bad at the same time, so that I could not go to the funeral. I am going to school now. I did not go this winter on account of my sickness."[52] Some children sacrificed school not to their own illnesses, but to the illnesses of others. Young Imogene Sorber, of Gowrie, Iowa, explained her situation. "I have been going to school; but it was out yesterday. . . . Ma has been sick, and I have had to stay at home to help her for two weeks."[53]

Sanitary conditions in schoolhouses often left much to be desired, with students working in small, poorly ventilated spaces, sharing common water dippers, and using less-than-sanitary privies. Catching whatever bugs were going around was distressingly easy. Mollie Krutza, who attended a one-room school in Appanoose County, Iowa, had vivid memories of one such occasion. She sat in her seat at school, in back of a younger girl. "I watched the lice run up and down her braids. Yes, I caught them! . . . It seemed a long time before I was rid of them."[54] Other conditions were just as easily communicable. As a result, epidemics, or the threat of epidemics, closed schools for extended periods, with potentially fatal diseases such as scarlet fever, diphtheria, and measles being some of the more common culprits. Even a rumor of diphtheria in a neighborhood could set a teacher to speculating about the possibility of her school closing. In the spring of 1893, Wisconsin teacher Louise Bailey expected school to be canceled on account of the disease. She wrote, "Am quite alarmed about diphtheria. Little Esther Pigg, one of my scholars, has it and I won't be a bit surprised if the school is closed." Fortunately, it was a false alarm, and school proceeded uninterrupted. "Have heard nothing about closing the school, my alarm was probably needless."[55] Young Ralph Wood, of Trempealeau County, Wisconsin, noted the effects of a threatened scarlet fever epidemic on the neighborhood school. On Monday, January 7, 1889, he wrote, "No school this week on account of scarlet fever. Three of Mr. Hansons children have it but not very hard." A week later the problem persisted, and the school board decided to

This January 1879 illustration from the children's paper, American Young Folks, *recognized the lengths to which farm children often had to go to attend school. By permission of the Kansas State Historical Society, Topeka, Kansas.*

take stronger action. "There will be no more school till next spring on the account of the scarlet fever." Students would have lost a whole term, but the affected youngsters recovered more quickly than expected, and classes resumed at the end of the month.[56] It would not have been unusual, however, for school to be dismissed until March or April. Given the difficulties of containing disease once it had infected a few of a school's scholars, and given the high mortality rates of the time, it was more important to try to maintain children's health than to press for perfect attendance records.

In an era before all-weather roads, central heating, and easy access to automobiles, weather might also prove an immovable obstacle to school attendance. Both rainy weather and the spring thaw might render roads impassable, and parents often did not send students to school in the rain because there was no way to keep them dry, or to get them dry when they arrived. Very cold weather also forced students who lived at too great a distance from school to remain at home and teachers to cancel classes. Cold weather was a serious threat to life and limb, as teacher Louise Bailey noted one frigid December morning: "It was so cold this morning that one of the boys froze one of his feet coming to school."[57] When classes did continue in very cold weather, it was sometimes too uncomfortable for students to sit in their seats. Instead, they clustered around the stove, trying to keep warm.[58] Given these conditions, temperatures in the range of ten to twenty below zero seem to have been sufficient for parents and teachers to cancel school.[59] Excessive heat, on the other hand, does not seem to have been a critical issue, and students and teachers alike sweated through long, hot summer terms. As Louise Bailey commented one June day, "This has been the hottest day we have had yet. I never taught in a school room that was as uncomfortably warm as this one is." Uncomfortable though it was, excess heat did not seem to threaten student health, so classes continued.[60] Had the students been at home and working, the heat would have been comparable, or perhaps even worse.

Not all of the forces obstructing quality education were outside of the control of farm children. One obstacle to education, the "boy problem," was the students' creation, or at least the creation of older male students. Descriptions of rural schools are full of commentary about older boys and the havoc they could wreak against organized education. As the *Wisconsin Journal of Education* reported in 1892, "The overgrown bully, who goes to school for the purpose of making trouble, who seems utterly devoid of all gentlemanly instincts, and bent upon defying authority unless the person in whom it is vested is able to cope with him physically and overcome him, is unfortunately by no means uncommon in rural districts."[61] School boards that hired young women in the spring and fall terms sometimes preferred to hire male teachers during the winter term, when more older boys came to school. As one farm-raised woman remembered her school days, "in the summer we had a lady teacher and . . . in the winter a man teacher. They needed a man to handle the big bad boys who went to school in winter. And they were bad.

Once Fred Manning and Charlie Hoyt got into a fight and Charlie drew his jack knife to stab him but was checked by the teacher. Both boys were dismissed from school for a week, but reinstated and were very good friends after." Incidents such as this convinced some school boards that only men could provide the discipline necessary to control rowdy boys who might be eighteen, nineteen, and twenty and coming to school only to cause trouble.[62]

Teachers, who were often quite young and minimally trained, might be unprepared to handle many of the discipline problems they faced in the classroom. Although educational theorists encouraged them to "engage" the older boys and to provide them "a practical knowledge of what will be essential to him" in life after school, they were not always able to do so.[63] Their lack of training and unruly charges might lead, as one youngster wrote, to "fearful disorder" and "confusion worse confounded."[64] Iowan Sarah Gillespie Huftalen noted that her teacher did not have many problems with the girls in her school, but the boys were another matter altogether. Fourteen-year-old Huftalen observed that her teacher kept two whips in her desk in order to control her charges. Even so, the classroom could get out of hand. The school's "very bad boys," as Huftalen described them, would run away when the teacher called them for class, put small boys' hats down the privy, and disrupt lessons. When the teacher attempted to restore discipline with a wholesale whipping of the bad boys, a student's mother intervened "& called the teacher out on the stoop & had a real talk with her & when the teacher came in the schoolroom she was crying." The result was more bad behavior on the part of the particular student, "& the teacher didn't say a word to him only once or the rest of the boys either."[65] In Effie Elsie Converse's Wisconsin classroom, the boys also created problems for the girls during the winter term. To her diary she confided, "I wish the boys and school would be more gentle to us girls, so we could be called quite a nice school." Later, she elaborated more fully, "I dred the noon and recesses because the boys plague us so bad."[66]

Given the tensions inherent in such a situation, it is no small wonder that discipline occasionally got out of hand and strayed into outright abuse. George Van Horne, a Nebraska teacher who often confided to his diary his general bewilderment with teaching, was sometimes rough with students without even seeming to try. On one January day, he wrote, "The general character of the school was somewhat rougher than yesterday. I jerked one boy rather hard on the spur of the moment." On another occasion he commented, "I used a little boy somewhat roughly—jerked him was all."[67] In an attempt to maintain the little control that they had, some teachers were brutal, venturing considerably beyond a jerk or a shake.[68] In a memoir, one woman described two of her male teachers as "regular bears. . . . They would twist the boys ears kick them and when they whipped them with a big hickory stick the whole school would turn pale with fright."[69] In Vernon County, Wisconsin, a male teacher, facing a classroom of obstreperous young men, used a rod of ironwood to defend himself, fracturing a student's skull and killing him. Commenting on this occurrence, the *Wisconsin Journal of Education* not only criticized the teacher for his lack of restraint in resorting to severe corporal punishment, but also took to task the school board for failing to protect the teacher against unruly, bullying students.[70]

How disputes in the classroom were resolved depended on the students, teacher, and school board involved. Ongoing conflict in a rural Grundy County, Iowa, school resulted in the dismissal of both a student and a teacher. "Two boys refused to comply with the rules of the school, and after several weeks' deliberation and much trouble, the board of directors came this morning and expelled the older one and the teacher from the school." Evidently, the student was at fault for failing to follow the rules and the teacher for failing to maintain discipline. The student reporting the incident was relieved that greater order was in the offing: "Hope we will get along peacably [sic] now."[71] Rhoda Emery, a Minnesota farm daughter turned schoolteacher, faced her own "boy problem" in her first year teaching in a rural school. In 1889, she was seventeen and largely untrained. She managed her classroom through trial and error. In the fall of 1889, she experienced continuing troubles with the young men in her school. Laughter and disobedience were regular problems, but much more seriously, several boys persisted in fighting. Giving the boys "a talking to" did not dissuade them, and after a day of endless struggle, Emery was "so tired and discouraged and blue generally this noon that I couldn't eat a bit of dinner; and I don't feel much better now." To her diary she lamented, "This has been such a long, dark lonesome day, I do hope I may be able to do better to-morrow."

When the morrow came, more trouble threatened, and "I had determined that if those boys made any more trouble I should threaten to turn them out; but I was not sure that I had the authority to do it or that the board would uphold me." That morning, she announced that she would expel any scholar who fought. An adult visitor to the schoolhouse, armed with a whip, informed Emery that the boys were planning a fight for the noon hour, and that the school board would support her in any disciplinary measures necessary to stop the fighting. Emery wrote, "I felt jubilant then." She intercepted the boys on their way to the fight, interrogated the most serious offenders, and used her ultimatum, backed by the school board, to force them to come to an agreement. If they could not get along, they could not attend school. Because at least one of the troublesome young men was determined to gain an education, this tactic appears to have worked, and "peace was declared."[72] Emery's resolve, backed by the school board, averted more serious problems. And on the whole, this was the most serious discipline problem she faced in her first five years of teaching. Boys continued to cause problems, throwing ink, leaving the premises without permission, and bringing guns to school, for example, but Emery was able to deal with these problems without sacrificing either discipline in the school or her own dignity.[73]

It is the rare rural teacher's or student's account that does not mention at least a few problems with discipline, although in some schools it seems that order was very important to students. As May Crowder wrote about her own school days, "We were looking forward to a time when we could leave the farm and do something else, preferably in a town or city, so there was a good deal of speculation the first day of school as to how much help the teacher was likely to be as a stepping stone to our ambition." When attitudes such as this reigned, "there was little or no insubordination in our school."[74] In most locations, however, if a teacher was to remain effective and to provide a reasonable education to her or his students, a degree of cooperation between the teacher, students, parents, and the school board was required.

When determining which children would attend school and which would not, and the effectiveness of schools within communities, the most important part of the equation was the parents, their attitudes, and their economic prospects. Parents who valued education generally made it possible for their children to attend school. Parents in dire economic straits may have had a hard time supporting the concept of education when debt and hunger loomed. Those who attempted to limit their children's schooling sometimes had concerns that went beyond economics; they feared education's consequences. They believed that a higher education would make their children unfit for a life in agriculture. A writer to the *Nebraska Farmer* railed against the results of indulging farm girls' desires for a high school education. "Not one thing do these girls learn in the whole time that will be of practical value to them as homemakers and child-trainers . . . and at the end of their school life they come home with exaggerated opinions of their ability and importance, and are forever dissatisfied with the farm and all it represents."[75] The writer envisioned a world where unprepared women populated the farms, or worse yet, left the farm altogether. This, in fact, may have been what some parents intended, as they sent their daughters to school to prepare them for alternatives to life as a farm wife. Others found this prospect frightening.

These parental fears, in some cases, may have been well founded. The lives of the Ise children, growing up before the turn of the century in rural central Kansas, are instructive. Henry and Rosie Ise had twelve children, eleven of whom lived to adulthood. Their offspring had, for that day, what could be considered a good childhood. The Ises loved their children and provided them the best lives they could afford. This included medical care, a decent home, and education. By the turn of the century, the Ise family farm was quite large and prosperous, allowing a very high standard of living for their time and place. One of the best indications of this is that out of the eleven surviving Ise children, nine attended at least some college, and five went on to graduate or professional school. John Ise, who wrote his family's story in *Sod and Stubble: The Story of a Kansas Farm*, earned a doctorate in economics and taught for many years at the University of Kansas.

The Ise children, however, chose not to become farmers. Out of the surviving eleven, only one wanted to pursue agriculture as an adult. Interestingly enough, the son who wanted to farm did not take over the family operation when the others moved to town, a mystery that Ise's chronicle left unexplained. The rest followed paths that led away from the land, pursuing careers in education, the law, and other professional fields. Indeed, the family left the farm as the youngest Ise child graduated from high school. The children urged their widowed mother to sell the family's belongings, rent the land, and move to town, something she reluctantly did. The experience of the Ise family raises the all-important question: Why would the children of a successful farming couple choose to walk away from the farm?

The answer to that question has several parts. First, Rosie and Henry Ise raised their children on a pioneer farm. The Ise children saw grasshopper plagues, droughts, and prairie fires. They knew life on the farm was hard, because they saw it in their parents' prematurely old faces. They also experienced it firsthand, working long hours in the fields in addition to their hours of school. They experienced disease and accident as a result of the conditions of their childhood. But they also gained an education. Their mother, who had only attended school half a day in her entire childhood, sent all of her children to grammar and then high school. For those who desired it, she helped them to gain a college education. Rosie Ise provided her sons and daughters the education that allowed them to teach school themselves, and to see that there were other possibilities that required less sweat and uncertainty. She educated them out of wanting the farm themselves.[76]

As some parents feared, education opened doors to other opportunities, and farm children took them, knowing the hardships and uncertainties that their parents had experienced raising them. Parents who believed that education might lead their children away from the farm and into the city might very well have been correct. Children with educations could, and often did, leave the farm in search of different, if not better, lives in other locations. Some parents were able to accept and cope with that possibility. Some welcomed that outcome.[77] Others resisted the school system's encroachment because they feared education's results.[78] In either case, parents often gave very little time or attention to the business of education because work was often pressing. A teacher, frustrated by this lack of attention, composed the following:

> Oh, dear! What can the matter be?
> Oh, dear! What can the matter be?
> Oh, dear! What can the matter be?
> Parents don't visit the schools.
> They care for their houses, they care for their dollars,
> They care for their laces and ribbons and collars,
> But little we think they care for their scholars.
> Now why don't they visit the schools?[79]

Another writer, addressing the readers of the *Nebraska Farmer*, also chastised farm parents for their half-hearted concern with education. "Wake up, parents, wake up! Take as much interest in your children and their education as you do in your stock! . . . You profess an interest, and blame the teacher for everything short of what you expect."[80] Parents sent, or did not send, their children off to school, sometimes voted in school board elections, and sometimes served on school boards, but much of the business of educating children, and its success or failure, was left to teachers and their young charges.

In analyzing farm children's education, however, it is important to recognize that those children often saw education through different eyes than the adults around them. Although parents and teachers may have perceived instruction in reading, writing, and arithmetic, or even learning self-discipline, as the most important objects of schooling, children often had different ideas. According to many farm children, it was the entertainment value of school that made attendance worthwhile. Morning and afternoon recesses, as well as lunch hours, were the only regularly scheduled, reliable times for play that farm children had. As nine-year-old Fred H. Jones, of Knox County, Nebraska, bluntly put it, "I like to go to school because when recess comes I can slide down hill."[81]

In the morning before school, parents generally required their children to complete chores. Long walks to school followed. The day's lessons would conclude, and children would return home to evening chores. Given this strenuous schedule, time allotted to play was a rare commodity.[82] As Iowan May Crowder recalled in later life, "Most of the year meant drudgery on the farms, and school was a relief from hard work"[83] Depriving children of their time for outdoor play, even if it was because of inclement weather, posed serious problems for the teachers. A rainy May day forced Louise Bailey to keep the students inside, and she lamented her misfortune. "To-day has been unpleasant, the boys had to remain in doors, and it is like housing a volcano I imagine to keep them in."[84] Youngsters approached the prospect of free time with great creativity and vigor and were loathe to relinquish it to anyone or anything.

Students played a number of organized games, many of which are recognizable even from the distance of a century or more. Students played chase-and-capture games, such as Hide and Seek, Prisoner's Base, Fox and Geese, and London Bridge. One former rural school student described Fox and Geese: "When it snowed there was fox and geese played by making a circle in the snow with spokes and a center. A leader was chosen. The children ran around the circle and the leader would try to tag them, and put them out. The last one tagged got to be the new leader."[85] Games such as this required nothing beyond an open area and a group of players. Games that required equipment, such as football and baseball, seem to have been played less frequently. Marbles was a favorite game, involving drawing a circle in the dirt and attempting to knock another's marble out of the ring in order to claim it. Marbles might be played "for fun" or "for keeps," and dedicated players developed a large collection of marbles of various weights, sizes, and materials. Another game of skill, not requiring purchases of equipment, was Duck on a Rock. One player would place a small rock, the duck, on top of a larger rock, while the others threw their own rocks, attempting to knock the duck off of the rock.[86] As historian Elliott West has commented, these games were common to schoolchildren across the country and could serve as a means of entrance into child society as families moved into new neighborhoods and children into new schools.[87]

Youngsters seem to have been equally fond of all types of disorganized fun as well. In winter, those going to schools on or near hills brought sleds and toboggans to school. A school near a pond also allowed ice skating.[88] The possibilities inherent in the schoolyard and surrounding fields were enormous. Although many young scholars wrote about the fun of the schoolyard, perhaps none was more eloquent or forceful than young Lucy Van Voorhis, who grew up in Grundy County, Iowa. As a twelve- and thirteen-year-old, school enriched and enlivened her days. Even though rain offered the possibility of a day at home, she commented, "I would not stay away from school for anything." Her recess adventures included going down to a creek and playing "old witch under the bridge" or wading, telling stories, and playing "Cinderella." She and her classmates also played Drop the Handkerchief and Post Office, but whether in her case these were the kissing games that bear the same names now is impossible to tell. A day-long rain might result in the manufacture of puzzles and games for each other, while a night's rain that left the playground wet might result in a noon of playing in the mud and making mud pies. Students also constructed playhouses in the avenue along the schoolhouse and on top of the coal shed. Although she commented that "we all feel so much better when we have good lessons," it seems to have been equally important to have a good day's play. As she wrote on a May day near the end of the school term, "It seems as though I felt like anything but studying, that is, I felt like playing."[89]

Although it was rarely discussed in diaries, or even later in memoirs, school provided a venue for boys and girls to begin exploring each other as potential sexual partners. Older boys and girls who wanted to get to know each other better attempted to sit together in class. As a former farm boy reminisced, "When our biggest text, a geography book, was draped on the edge of a desk, one might wonder what kind of geography was being studied. When a teacher would suggest that both hands be used to hold the book, both hands where she could see them, I think she wondered what foreign lands were being explored."[90] These explorations might continue onto the playground, with kissing games such as Drop the Handkerchief and Post Office. And the same hills, creeks, and trees that provided a venue for wading and playhouses could provide the opportunity for privacy and close contact.[91] Physical contact was probably also the point of many chase-and-capture games. Adolescent Mary Van Zante, whose parents farmed near Pella, Iowa, commented on the rough-and-tumble games she and her friend, Jessie, played with boys. "This noon we had so much fun with the boys, Jessie and I. They would trip us and throw us down and pinch and hurt us all the time. We would push them back, but they didn't care for that." In the next week, she further wrote about her time spent with the boys: "We had a good deal of fun. We always have when we play with them."[92] Others, however, firmly resisted what were unwanted attentions. When Augusta Thomas "landed" on a boy who wanted to kiss her and "chastized him good," other boys took up the challenge, and "I was very afraid for a while. . . . One evening three of them followed me on the way home, bragging about what they would do. Finally one of them grabbed my cape. I whirled and struck him on the forehead with my ink bottle so hard he cried. I had no more trouble."[93] School and the school grounds provided unparalleled opportunities for young people to meet and interact with each other, away from parents and often with minimal adult supervision. Sometimes the interaction was pleasant; other times it was not.

In the final analysis, the meaning of school in the life of the farm child was highly idiosyncratic. For Oliver Perry Myers, the rural school was an opportunity to exercise his mental faculties and prepare for higher education. For May Crowder, the education she achieved in a country school was a means of escape. Students in her school attended to their lessons and heeded the teacher, knowing that their lessons could lead to an easier life outside of agriculture.[94] Other students left school as quickly as possible. Those who missed many days of school helping their families might find themselves behind in their studies and were too embarrassed to sit in the front rows with the smaller children. Tensions in the classroom over discipline could frighten youngsters. Some did not see the connection between reading, writing, arithmetic, and the lives that they hoped to live as adults. Those for whom education was extremely important often somehow, against the odds, found a way to achieve it, while the others found it a fairly simple matter to conclude their education at age fourteen, or when they completed the eighth grade. For the vast majority, graduation from the eighth grade was the limit of their ambition, or of their family's resources.

The meaning of education in the life of one midwestern farm daughter is illustrative not only of the importance education could have, but also of the barriers that stood between it and many youngsters. Even in families that valued education, achieving it could be difficult. Rosa Armentrout, whose family lived near Wilton, Iowa, grew up to be Dr. Rosa Armentrout Butterfield, but at times she despaired of completing her education. She loved to attend school, writing often in her diary about her fellow students and school activities. School was both an academic and a social occasion. In 1877, at sixteen, she wrote, "I am going to school now. . . . We have splendid times at school. We play blackman and ring and charades and ball and every thing else almost every day. I study Reading, Grammar, Geography, Physiology, Arithmetic and Writing."[95] If the volume and intensity of Rosa's writing is any indication, school and learning were the primary concerns of her young life.

Her love of education, however, could not always overcome the barriers she faced on the way to the schoolhouse door. Like most youngsters, she found that the forces of nature worked against school attendance. Rain and snow often rendered dirt roads and farm fields impossibly, and impassably, muddy. After a night of torrential rain, "the sloughs were so bad that Mother wouldent let me go."[96] The next day the rain continued, and her disappointment was acute: "Oh how I cried, For the laziness of men, Can never be described. No one knows how bad I wanted to go to school today. I couldent keep from crying, because teacher was going to give me her watch this evening, and I was going to teach for her awhile tomorrow . . . but the men were actually too lazy to put the bed on the wagon, so they could take me."[97] Even when the day was bright and she did not need any help to get to school, chores might interfere. Washing was the chief culprit. She wrote, "I did not go to school today. I dident like to stay out but Mother went up to Johns today and I had to stay at home and help wash. I don't like to wash. I know I am pretty lazy but I cant help it."[98] Although a self-proclaimed lazy daughter, Rosa Armentrout often assisted her mother in washing and cleaning, sometimes at the expense of school.

Duty was the most evident force working against Rosa's education, and she feared that she might have to sacrifice school to the needs of her family. When her mother became ill in the summer of 1877, she believed that she had lost her opportunity to pursue a higher education in Iowa City. "Mother is about the same today," she wrote. "If Mother would be able to spare me I would get to go to school the Fall term in the City, but I know Ma will not be well enough to do the work although she says she will."[99] When fall came, however, Mrs. Armentrout had recovered sufficiently to allow Rosa to pursue her education. Although she was now free to study "Arithmetic, Analysis, Physiology History and Penmanship," she still worried about her mother, noting, "I know she is lonesome without me."[100] Undoubtedly Rosa had been her mother's right arm, providing both companionship and invaluable assistance with the many chores required to make a farm home.

Even after she left her home and the one-room schoolhouse behind, Rosa Armentrout's experiences illustrated the difficulties farm-raised youngsters faced when they tried to further their education. Financial difficulties impeded Rosa Armentrout's studies; she was responsible for her own expenses, and she worked to pay the cost of her own room and board in Iowa City. In the first week of school, she explained her predicament: "It is late now and I am not ready to go to bed yet. My studies alone would not keep me so busy but I have the two rooms upstairs to see too. beds to make. sweep out & tidy up in general, and help the hired girl with the dishes every noon and night. that is what takes my study time."[101] In spite of the work and aggravation that her education cost, Rosa Armentrout was indeed lucky. Although her parents allowed her to work for her own benefit and her own education, many farm families preferred, or indeed needed, their daughters and sons to remain at home and contribute to the support of the entire family. That Rosa Armentrout was able to achieve the education she desired was a testament to both herself and her parents.

It is important to acknowledge that Rosa Armentrout was one of a very small minority of midwestern farm children, or the nation's children in general—those who were able to pursue a secondary education. In 1900, only 8 percent of all American youngsters went to high school; even in 1920, less than one-third attended high school.[102] Although it was not at all uncommon for farm children to have completed school through the eighth grade, completing a high school education or going on to postsecondary education was quite unusual. By 1900, most small towns in Iowa, for example, could boast high schools, but very few rural communities had similar facilities. As David R. Reynolds commented in his book, *There Goes the Neighborhood: Rural School Consolidation at the Grass Roots in Early Twentieth-Century Iowa,* "At the turn of the century, the reality of the situation was that Iowa possessed two school systems—a modern one for its almost 800 cities, towns, and villages, and a traditional one for rural children."[103] Parents who wanted their children to have a high school education might move the whole family into town in order for them to have access to a quality and quantity of education unavailable in the country.[104] Other farm youngsters, in order to pursue a high school education, traveled to town to go to school, either on a daily or weekly basis. Those who went on a weekly basis had to board in town, which could be an expensive proposition. These costs were one set of burdens on families, but time was as well. Going to high school represented a sacrifice of a nearly adult child's time and efforts on behalf of the family farm. Even when parents valued education and wanted to send their children to high school, the costs could be prohibitive. Some youngsters, faced with this reality, studied at home or received supplemental instruction in advanced subjects after regular hours in country schools. Some might eventually attend secondary school, but many did not.[105] Because of the expense, parents might require their children to take turns, with one continuing his or her education while others waited. As Justine Norton Johnson, a Cresco, Iowa, farm mother, wrote to her son while he was attending business college, "We are giving you your chance now. . . . [his brother Walt's] will have to come later."[106]

Education was a force that pulled and pushed youngsters in many different directions. It pulled them away from farm labor, and sometimes away from the farm altogether. It pushed them to think about possibilities they might not have previously considered. It could be a force for good or a force that introduced disorder into their lives. Their teachers might offer them the world, or nothing at all. In a world where education was becoming standardized and regularized, the education of farm children remained highly idiosyncratic, based on personal wants and desires and local conditions.

4

"Today Is the First School-Day"

Farm Youth as Rural Teachers: The Stories of

Hermann Benke and Rhoda Emery

❖ ❖ ❖ ❖ ❖ ❖ ❖ ❖ ❖ ❖ ❖ ❖ ❖ ❖ ❖

Today is the first school-day in the new year. I open the school early in the morn-
ing. Have 2 entirely new scholars. . . . In all 9. The day passed very quickly, and I
retire very late.
—Hermann C. Benke, age sixteen, January 3, 1887

I got along nicely-to-day. I did have good order all day. There was another fight
this noon and I made all the fighters come in and take their seats until school
called then kept them and last nights' ruffans after school and gave them a good
talking to. I didn't sit down once to-day from 9 to 12 and not much of any this
after-noon. My back feels as though it would break, so I am going to bed so soon
as possible.
—Rhoda J. Emery, age seventeen, October 30, 1889

For the ambitious farm child, one of the goals of completing eight grades
of grammar school education might be to become a teacher. Rural schools
were constantly in need of teachers, and teaching provided a reasonable, if
somewhat precarious, living. It was also one of the few means of earning a
salary while remaining close to the family home. For farm parents, it was a
way to bring an extra income into the family coffers without relinquishing
a child to the city. Children could work in the neighborhood school, or an-

other within a reasonable radius, and come home either daily or on the weekend to do farm and domestic work. When the school term ended, the youngster would be available to do farm work on a regular basis. What was particularly attractive about placing a daughter as a schoolteacher was that it was a respectable way to make use of the productive energies of girls. If for three or four months of the year a school-teaching daughter could bring home $25 to $35 a month, minus expenses such as her board, that income could considerably ease the economic burdens of the family while retaining her services during times when family labor on the farm was crucial.[1] Teaching sons could generally earn more per month than daughters, but as a result, they might find it more difficult to find a position. School boards sought to pay as little as possible for their teachers, and they often preferred to hire young women as a result. But whether male or female, becoming a wage-earning schoolteacher did not generally remove farm youngsters from their families and make them independent adults; instead, it made them only slightly more independent. They were often an essential element of their families' economic strategies.

Teaching at a rural school did not only involve instructing children in reading, writing, and arithmetic. With the help of their students, teachers were also their schools' janitors, because school boards generally would not pay a salary for employees in addition to a teacher. When the need arose, teachers also served as the school nurse. They were disciplinarians, too, responsible for maintaining order in what could be a chaotic environment. The duties that modern teachers often share with aides, janitors, nurses, counselors, and principals fell on them alone, although some janitorial duties might devolve upon the students. Even then, the teacher would have to supervise the youngsters' work. Teaching was not simply the instruction of children, but the maintenance of the entire school environment.

There were other challenges to the occupation that might concern a teacher even more than the complexities of the labor involved. One was the job's uncertainty. Most districts issued contracts one term at a time, and they often hired new teachers at the beginning of each term. A teacher generally did not know from term to term whether she or he would be employed. School districts that hired young women for the spring and the fall terms sometimes preferred to hire men during the winter term, when more older boys came to school.[2] In addition to the uncertainty of continuing employment, being a country schoolteacher meant accepting living arrangements without privacy: most teachers boarded with either their own families or their students' parents, and tight finances forced them to return to their parents' homes at the end of each term.[3] Even older, experienced rural teachers found boarding to be an emotional strain. As twenty-four-year-old Louise Bailey, a Wisconsin teacher, wrote, "School went as usual, when I got home tonight I found a houseful of babies and people here. . . . It makes me feel homesick to have so many in the family together and I the only odd one."[4] The insecurity and inconvenience of such a life might encourage a young woman to marry simply to avoid teaching another term, or a young man to leave teaching for another, more secure occupation. Rural school teaching was not an easy road to travel, and few considered it a lifetime vocation.

Many farm youngsters made this transition from student to teacher, although an accurate accounting of their numbers is impossible to make. Many taught for only a term or two, leaving their labors for further education, marriage, a job in a city, or a return to the farm. Most of them did so quietly, without leaving much, if any, record of their brief sojourn as teachers. Some, however, left extensive records of their endeavors, making it possible to see how youngsters negotiated the journey from student to teacher and how they dealt with their families after becoming breadwinners outside of the context of the family farm and its labors. This chapter will present the stories of two such youngsters: Hermann Benke, of Barton County, Kansas, and Rhoda Jeanette Emery,[5] of Olmsted County, Minnesota.

❖ ❖ ❖

HERMANN C. BENKE: FARMER'S SON, TEACHER, ARTIST

In the mid-1880s, the Benke family lived in central Kansas, near the aptly named State Center, in Barton County. The farming family was of German extraction, and in 1885, father Charles, age fifty-one, presided over a family of five, including a mother, age forty-two (her name, unfortunately, is illegible in the census), son Hermann, age fifteen, daughter Bertha, age thirteen, and daughter Ida, age eight. The lavishly illustrated diaries left by Hermann and Bertha attest to the fact that this, perhaps, was not the usual farm family. The family invested heavily in the education of its children and allowed them a great deal of leeway to enjoy books, music, and art. Given this family atmosphere, it was not surprising that son Hermann used his education to teach in the area's country schools.

In many ways, the Benke family was typical of midwestern farming families. The children contributed to the operation of the farm by herding, weeding, chopping corn stalks, and aiding their parents with the many tasks required to run both the farm and the home. Despite differences in age and gender, the children worked with each other to accomplish some tasks, such as shocking the corn, while working with their parents to accomplish others, such as sowing the wheat.[6] Like other youngsters, they sometimes stayed home from school to help their parents when work was pressing. While the Benke parents completed the corn harvest, Bertha remained at home to bake the family's bread and to care for the cattle.[7] In other ways, the family seems unusual. The parents allowed their children a great deal of leeway to study and pursue personal interests, such as drawing. On summer days, while their parents worked in the fields, garden, and kitchen, the Benke girls buried themselves in books. As Bertha wrote one August day, "M[other] digged potatoes in morning. . . . Studied all day." While Charles Benke helped the neighbors thresh, Hermann (who was supposed to be ailing), "Plaid music . . . ate lots of melons" and "went on hunting."[8] That same summer, Charles Benke followed the harvest throughout the neighborhood, but Hermann was not working at his side. Instead, on June 30, he and his sister were idle. "I write poetry etc all day—B[ertha] & I draw . . . pictures. . . . I write this page and a poem, 'Is there a God.'" A day later, he was still writing: "I write a poem 'Love's Sad Story.' . . . Fool around most of the time."[9] Although it is unclear why the elder Benkes allowed their children such latitude and excused them from work that would have been expected of others, Charles Benke may have been acknowledging either his son's inclinations or his abilities by allowing Hermann to absent himself from the fields. Bertha Benke also noted the investment her father made in books when he traveled to State Center to purchase *The Rural New Yorker*, *How to Teach Numbers*, "a catalogue of educational books," and *Cyclopaedia of Universal History*.[10] Given the timing of their purchase, the educational books were most likely intended to further Hermann's preparation for teaching.

Young Hermann Benke seems to have had aspirations beyond farming in central Kansas. His diary reflects a love of, and many hours spent pursuing, art, poetry, and music. He filled his diary with intricate illustrations of the world around him, as well as carefully written prose that did—and did not—reflect the difficulties of life on a Barton County farm. For example, on January 2, 1886, he noted the bitter cold that forced the family to burn bed posts for fuel, as well as his efforts at melting snow to water stock, but ended

Fourteen-year-old Bertha Benke drew this depiction of her family home in the front cover of her diary. Bertha Mary Emily Benke diary. By permission of the Kansas State Historical Society, Topeka, Kansas.

with the day's most important labors: "Engaged in light literary work, drawed, wrote & ciphered."[11] In the winter of 1886, his life revolved around farm chores, his studies, hunting, and the weekly "Literary" meetings he attended at the schoolhouse. The literary society in this corner of Barton County was essentially a debating society, and Hermann was an enthusiastic participant. The debates covered a broad range of topics, from "Resolved that the voting of R.R. Bonds to aid in the construction of R.R.s is beneficial to the community," to "Res. That an educated woman has more right to vote than an uneducated man."[12] Hermann greatly enjoyed oratorical events and took every opportunity to make speeches when the occasion arose. He presented the teacher with an album at the end of the school term, took part in "a dozen different things among which 4 songs" at the school exhibition, and visited another school's exhibition, favoring them "with a declamation."[13] When allowed the opportunity, he honed his teaching skills. On January 29, 1886, while still a student, he wrote: "*I taught school after recess.* Had spelling school and recitations. Dismissed at 4:20."[14] Eight months

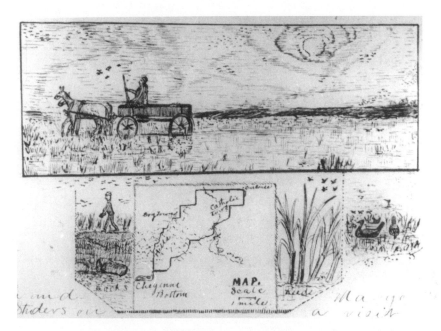

*Hermann Benke sketched a map of Cheyenne Bottoms, its wildlife, and himself
visiting the area. Hermann C. Benke diary, February 28, 1886. By permission of
the Kansas State Historical Society, Topeka, Kansas.*

later, his parents moved him to Great Bend for several weeks to attend what
may have been a teacher training institute, sponsored by a local normal
school. Although Hermann's diary was silent on the matter, Bertha's was
not, and she noted that her parents spent $3.25 a week on his board bill.[15]

The Benke family's investments in time, books, and room and board were
repaid when Hermann found employment in a school near Cheyenne Bottoms, close to Great Bend. After securing his position, he went to State Center and obtained a teaching certificate. In January, he brought his first paycheck, minus the cost of boarding, to his parents, $58.65.[16] He continued his
teaching in the winter of 1887, earning $30 a month, out of which he paid a
board bill of $10 a month.[17] Hermann appears to have contributed his wages
to the family coffers rather than saving the money for himself. He continued to contribute to the family in other ways as well, returning home to
work on weekends and school holidays.

Hermann wrote little about the transition from scholar to teacher. In some
ways, his life as a learner continued. While the students worked, he studied

In this self-portrait, Hermann Benke drew himself addressing the crowd at a school board meeting. Hermann C. Benke diary, January 13, 1887. By permission of the Kansas State Historical Society, Topeka, Kansas.

his own lessons; he may have intended to pursue further education at some point in the future. He still attended the local literary society. He was also a youngster, wanting to play. When the students went outside at recess, he often joined in the fray, on several occasions participating in snowball fights. In other ways, however, it is apparent that Hermann had begun to perceive himself differently. Becoming a teacher and being given authority over a classroom encouraged him to think of himself as an adult. He was no longer just speaking at student-run literary meetings, but at public gatherings. When the school board met, he participated with relish, speaking to the assembled audience. Hermann described the scene: "I am introduced and make a political speech in the German language. Audience cheers. . . . I ap-

In this 1886 sketch, Hermann Benke captured the excitement of the end-of-the-term school exhibition. Hermann C. Benke diary, April 21, 1886. By permission of the Kansas State Historical Society, Topeka, Kansas.

pear again and speak in English. . . . House in high spirits. . . . I was everywhere well received and Mr. Reints says to me 'you had better teach our school.' . . . entirely satisfied with the results of the night."[18] Apparently not everyone present was pleased with his speech. A local man believed that Hermann should have been arrested because he "was a minor" and "had nothing to say." Predictably, this attitude "exasperated" Benke.[19] When the local educational society met, he attended with interest, and then put himself on the program for the next meeting.[20]

Teaching, too, appealed to the dramatic side of Hermann's nature. At the conclusion of the school year, he organized the usual closing day program, including student exercises and gifts for the scholars. In his diary, he recorded the gist of his closing speech. "I make the closing speech. It is full of pathos and I recite it with much feeling. Among passages are the following. 'And now, Lds. and Gtl. it is your sacred duty, to your trust committed by the almighty to see to the education of these little boys & girls.' 'Obedience is the first duty of youth etc. The address closed with 'This is the last of 120 of the brightest happiest and most precious days of my life, . . . [ellipses Benke's] I can do no more let the record Stand as it is; dismissed.' At the signal all rose; and after some parting glances and hand shaking, dispersed."[21] Being a schoolteacher made Benke a public figure in his community, and he enjoyed taking his place on the stage.

Like most rural teachers, Hermann would spend the following summer looking for a new school. At the end of July, his efforts were rewarded; he found a new school, and it paid $40 a month. His efforts that summer also included attending another teachers' institute and applying for a second grade certificate, which would indicate greater qualifications to potential employers. Unfortunately, Hermann Benke's diary, and story, more or less end in the summer of 1887. A little book, tucked into the back of the 1887 diary, detailed a trip taken to the 1893 Chicago World's Fair, where he met up with his mother and Bertha.[22] From where he traveled to meet them remains a mystery. At what job he ultimately worked, and to what degree he was able to pursue further schooling, also remain mysteries.

Additionally, readers of the Benke diaries cannot know everything they might like to know about this family. From a distance of more than a hundred years, we cannot know why Hermann Benke's parents allowed him to spend so much time writing, drawing, and playing the violin while they pursued work in the fields. The elder Benkes also allowed his sisters, Bertha and Ida, some of the same latitude, suggesting a familial love of learning. Other explanations, however, are also possible. Perhaps Hermann was small, uncoordinated, or in poor health. Or perhaps his parents knew that, given his interests, he made a far better schoolmaster than chore boy. In any case, the Benkes allowed their son, even as a teenager, to follow a path that he relished: teaching and becoming a part of the public life of the community.

❖ ❖ ❖

RHODA J. EMERY: DUTIFUL DAUGHTER AND LIFELONG TEACHER

About Rhoda J. Emery, and her life as a school-teaching daughter, we know much more. Rhoda Emery began her lifelong career as a schoolteacher on October 21, 1889. It was not an auspicious beginning. She wrote in her diary, "The first day of school is over and I, for one am not sorry. I got along very well; had fifteen scholars. I like my boarding place first-rate; have a nice room all by myself. I am awful tired. It is not so much fun as it might be."[23]

For a young woman of her era, her story was both a common and an uncommon one. Like many a late nineteenth-century farm daughter, Emery finished her grade school education and became a teacher in the local country schools. Her career in education, however, was far different from the average. Rather than teaching a few terms before marriage, like most young women, she made teaching her lifelong vocation, eventually becoming an elementary school principal in St. Paul, Minnesota. Also unlike most of her fellow country schoolteachers, Rhoda Emery kept diaries of her early work, describing the hours she spent teaching, the dreams that she had for herself, and the hard reality of being an income-producing daughter in a cash-strapped farming family. Her mother also kept a diary, and many family letters survive in the archives of the Minnesota Historical Society. Rhoda Emery's life, diaries, and family records provide an important window into the complexities of being a young adult daughter with midwestern farming origins, striving for independence but tied to a family that could not easily survive without her labor and wages.

Born in 1872, Rhoda J. Emery was the second daughter, and third child, of Oronoco Township, Olmsted County, Minnesota, farmers Caleb Coxe Emery and Helen George Emery. Rhoda Emery's family was among the earliest to settle in the area. Her maternal grandfather, James George, came to the county in 1854, just as it was being settled. He was a veteran of the Mexican War who would later serve in the Civil War as a lieutenant colonel. After the war, he became a prominent local attorney.[24] In 1867, Rhoda's mother, Helen George, married Caleb Coxe Emery, a Civil War veteran and established county resident. They settled down on an eighty-acre Oronoco Township farm and raised six children. Clara, or Clal as her family called her, was born in 1868. James, the eldest son and black sheep of the family, was born in 1870. Rhoda was born in 1872, followed by Mary in 1876 and Helen, or Nell, in 1878. The final child, Robert, was born in 1890. Clara, James, and Rhoda all spent substantial time teaching in the area's country schools.

Rhoda Emery's early years on her parents' farm would have been quite similar to those of most midwestern farm children. Girls like Rhoda worked in the garden, cared for chickens, and milked cows. When their parents needed their help, they also went into the fields to work.[25] Although it was more common for girls from German and Scandinavian families to work regularly in the fields, it was not at all unusual for the daughters of native-born parents to do so as well, especially at busy times such as planting and harvest. Some mothers, such as Helen Emery, did not approve of their girls working in the fields, believing that work to be both too hard and improper. Even so, the Emery daughters did field work, in accordance with family needs.[26] Daughters played a significant role in the continued survival of midwestern family farms, especially those that were small and struggling.

Given her family history, becoming a schoolteacher may have seemed a natural, or even inevitable, course for Rhoda. Her older siblings, Clara and James, both taught school. Their experiences would have told her what to expect, even down to an understanding of the discrepancy in wages between male and female teachers. In 1895, for instance, Clara and James Emery both worked in the same two-room school. Although they had similar education and years of service in the county schools, as well as similar duties, Clara earned only $40 a month to James's $60. In a letter to Rhoda, James wrote, "Clara also seems to take it as a matter of course."[27] School teaching was also a natural choice for Rhoda because of parental expectations. As much as she needed her children's wages, Rhoda's mother believed that domestic labor was socially inappropriate for her daughters.[28] Even when daughter Mary went to aid a neighboring family struggling with illness, Helen disapproved of the idea, writing, "I do not relish the idea of one of my girls doing anyones Kitchen work & will not let her stay more than a week just to give them time to find some one else."[29] If the Emery daughters were going to work, their mother clearly preferred that they do so in a "respectable" occupation. In late nineteenth-century rural Minnesota, that meant teaching.

Rhoda's teaching experience, in terms of the size of her classes and the pay she earned, were typical of turn-of-the-century midwestern schools. The report Rhoda filed for the fall term of 1892, probably while teaching at Pennington School, described a fairly typical term. She taught nineteen youngsters from seven different families for fifty days. On average, fourteen scholars attended daily. Her students ranged in age from five to fifteen. Although she did not record in what grades the children were enrolled, she may very well have taught children in all eight grades at once. As a teacher with limited formal education who had attended no high school, normal school, or college, she earned $30 a month for her labors.[30]

As a seventeen-year-old, Rhoda stepped into a difficult task. Like other teachers, she was instructor, disciplinarian, and janitor. Only a few days into her teaching career, Rhoda herself wondered whether it was worth the work, musing, "I don't know as I shall ever like school-teaching. Perhaps

Miss Perkins was not very far wrong after all when she preferred working out."[31] Although housework and hard physical labor occasionally looked like an excellent alternative to her after a semester of teaching, Rhoda never traded her life as a educator for that of a domestic.

Making the leap from student to teacher could be a difficult process. Emery was just seventeen at the time she began her career, and she described the way in which she, as an essentially untrained adolescent, mastered her fears and educated youngsters who were hardly younger, and sometimes older, than herself. Emery detailed the process by which young people assumed authority, tested their new limits, and became independent actors. The following entry, written early in her first month of teaching, showed the young teacher becoming a force to be reckoned with in her classroom:

> The scholars missed some lessons and had to stand on the floor. I had to scold Cora M. and shake Freddie Young. Jocie B. wanted to drop [Swanton's] grammar because there were things in it that she did not know; and I would not let her. There was a fight after school between Alden Sibley and Harry Bright. I didn't know anything about it until I arrived at Segar's but will give them a fine lecture to-morrow. I have changed some seats to-day too. Resolved to have order in that school hereafter or "bust." Look out for breakers![32]

Learning to be a teacher involved becoming comfortable with maintaining discipline, inspiring students to want to master their lessons, and achieving confidence with herself and her abilities. Emery's comments from late in her first term indicate a growing ability to manage the intricacies of school management. "Have succeeded admirably to-day notwithstanding the fact that Tuesday is generally a bad day. . . . I was obliged to stand Harry on the floor for misbehavior and Cora for missed lessons. Cora cried. I was very sorry for her but did not relent. She took all her books home to-night and declared that she wouldn't miss any more lessons."[33] In the next week, the same confidence in her actions was apparent. "I rather like George Jenkins. I stood him on the floor for whispering to-day. I was really half afraid to tell him to go; but he went like a gentleman and did not open his mouth to whisper all the rest of the day."[34] Over the course of her first term, Emery made the transition from naive newcomer to an assured teacher, and there was little happening within her small domain about which she did not know and exercise a certain amount of control. As the years passed, these concerns about student misbehavior became less frequent as she learned to manage problems in pedagogy and discipline.

*In this picture, typical of many rural Minnesota schools, teacher Hermie Johnson
poses with her students outside a schoolhouse near Lake Elmo, Minnesota, June
1913. Notice the sheepish expressions on the big boys at the right of the picture.
Photo by John Runk. By permission of the Minnesota Historical Society.*

Another element of the education of a rural schoolteacher was accommodating oneself to life in someone else's home. Teachers often boarded
with their students' parents or with other families in the district. It was a
situation to which Rhoda Emery never quite resigned herself. Some boarding situations were quite comfortable, and the family made her feel at home.
Other families were less accommodating, and the homesickness she inevitably suffered took over. Boarding in someone else's home could even be
frightening. On November 20, 1889, Emery wrote, "How I wish I could go
home and stay there! I wonder if I will ever have a settled home. I sleep with
a knife under my pillow."[35] Unfortunately, she never explained what had
frightened or unnerved her. Had she revealed her fears to her parents, she
might have found herself at home again—and unemployed. One of her primary goals was not to worry her parents. She vowed not to tell them of her
homesickness, and she was careful to overeat in the days just before she
went home to visit, "so as to make a good appearance at home."[36] Arriving
at home looking thin and lonely would have concerned her parents, and
Emery was always the dutiful daughter, conscious of not overburdening
them.[37] Unfortunately, boarding never became easy. Emery was generally

far happier when she could teach in a school close to her parents' farm and work from home. Her loneliness was only too apparent in comments made on learning she had lost the opportunity to go home and teach in a neighborhood school.

> I was very much disappointed about the school. You see all my hope about getting home for a time are all knocked in the head and I must keep roaming. . . . Mame C. and Harvey Brockway were married Thursday. She is only fifteen. I pity her some but still I almost envy. Just think she can stay at home now as long as she lives and she will have in her husband at least one true friend. . . . My school was small to-day but I got along very well only I almost cried two or three times for homesickness. I suppose though "whatever is is right."[38]

Home, where she was known and comfortable, was infinitely preferable to the stresses and strains of boarding.

As Emery's experiences with boarding illustrate, there was a second story in Rhoda Emery's life. She was not only a schoolteacher, but also a dutiful daughter whose economic and social world continued to be defined by her relationship to the larger family unit. Her responsibility to her parents and their economically fragile farm required her to subsume her own wants and desires to their needs. As much as she might be the adult and authority figure in her school, Rhoda Emery continued to be her parents' child, and her labors contributed to the survival of their enterprise. And even though she worked through the day during the school year, her evenings, weekends, and holidays often belonged to her family. Her earnings belonged to them too. Clearly, the Emery family struggled economically. Their eighty-acre farm was probably too small to support a family of eight adequately, and Helen and Caleb Emery relied heavily on the earnings of their children. The pain and frustration this duty caused was apparent in Rhoda's anguish over her desire to purchase a small luxury for herself—a bicycle. Bicycles became fashionable in the late nineteenth century, and Rhoda dearly wished to spend some of her hard-earned money on one. In fact, Wellington Clay, a friend and suitor who lived in St. Paul, eagerly helped her locate one. Daughterly duty, however, intervened. Instead of buying the bicycle she wanted, she bought the carriage her parents believed they needed, going $65 into debt on their behalf. Her disappointment was achingly apparent:

> Well to-night I am $65 more in debt that I was last night. I went to R[ochester] with Pa to-day and bought a two-seated buggy at that price due Dec. 1. I don't care,

leastways mostly I don't for Pa and Ma will I guess take a good deal of comfort out of it, and I will probably manage to live some way though it means no more clothes even next fall, and I have had none for two years, and never any bicycle.[39]

Rhoda reconsidered her words the next day, swallowing her disappointment. "I guess I couldn't have bought anything we would all take more comfort in, and will have time enough to live for myself after it is paid for."[40] Rhoda's words are suggestive of the true meaning of being a "dutiful daughter." It meant living for one's parents and family instead of living for oneself, and unmarried daughters might have to wait well into their twenties, thirties, or beyond before achieving any degree of independence.[41] Becoming an adult was a difficult process, and parents did not relinquish their children easily. Because of their financial distress, Helen and Caleb Emery may have exerted more pressure on their children than the average.[42]

The complicated relationship between children and their parents often extended beyond questions of what one owed to one's parents; older siblings also had responsibilities to their younger brothers and sisters that could be quite onerous. This might account for the very poor reception that Rhoda's youngest brother, Robert, received upon his birth in 1890. The two eldest Emery children, Clara and James, were gravely displeased with his arrival and treated their mother badly, a situation that greatly distressed Rhoda. Perhaps Clara and James believed that given the family's straitened circumstances and the heavy responsibilities that Helen and Caleb Emery expected their older children to assume, having another child was entirely unwarranted and irresponsible. This would have been particularly important to them because the older Emery siblings, like many in the late nineteenth century, were not only asked to support their parents, but also their brothers and sisters.[43] Helen Emery believed that her oldest daughters, in particular, should be responsible for the expenses associated with educating their younger brother and sisters. Clara described this situation to Rhoda in 1892: "Ma says that the girls have started to school at Oronoco. It will be a long ways for them. She suggested that the girls & I stay in [Rochester] next winter while you amused yourself by teaching and paying our expenses. I don't fall in with that idea at all but perhaps I could get something to do there. . . . We must manage to get the girls to school next year."[44] Clara Emery had absorbed her mother's teachings and was willing to help to raise and educate her younger sisters, although perhaps not in quite the manner that her mother suggested. Under these circumstances, Clara might have perceived the addition of a new brother as an imposition; only gradually would she come to love and accept young Robert.

Economic stresses and the problems they caused were not the only points of tension in the Emery household. Perhaps because of her own background as the daughter of a local attorney and Civil War army officer, Helen Emery disapproved of the neighborhood youth and believed that her own children were superior to the locals with whom they came into contact. This selectivity, warranted or not, might account, at least partially, for the late age of two of the Emery daughters' marriages; when Clara and Nell married and left home, both were about thirty years old. There are also indications that Caleb Emery discouraged the young local men from courting his daughters; Rhoda's longtime suitor, Wellington Clay, was apparently unacceptable to her father, perhaps because of a cleft palate.[45] Neither Rhoda nor her younger sister, Mary, ever married, and Mary would spend a lifetime caring for her elderly parents.

The Emery daughters were not the only children facing difficulties. Oldest son James, who by the standards of the day should have been a source of support to his parents and his siblings, was instead a heartache and expense. When he left home in 1896, it was because he had accumulated debts he could not pay. There was also some suggestion in his mother's writings that he had been involved in illicit sexual activities with local girls that might have resulted in pregnancies. Even James knew that he had been a disappointment. As he wrote in a letter to Rhoda, "I always have been and probably always will be the great moral and financial drawback of the Emery family."[46] Rhoda Emery's home was no tranquil rural haven. The stress of financial difficulties and parent-child conflict were more than evident, and James's inability to live up to his parents' expectations and needs certainly increased the burdens on Rhoda as a wage-earning daughter.

Although Rhoda Emery's diary tells the story of one farming daughter, it was the story of many. Rhoda Emery was one of a long line of wage-earning American farm girls, a line that stretched backward toward Puritan families who bound out their daughters to work for other families and early nineteenth-century New England parents who sent their daughters to Lowell's mills. In this struggling but proud family, older children became teachers in order to supplement an agricultural income that was often inadequate to the family's needs and wants. For this family, like many others, the cash a daughter could generate was more important to the family than her continued, full-time presence and labor on the farm. The Emery family's economic strategy was a common one. Rhoda Emery's life also illustrates that even a hundred years ago the line between childhood and adulthood was problematic. Although many youngsters had working experiences both on and off the family farm that might have defined them as adults, their relationship to their parents, and their parents' farms, continued to define their daily lives as dependent and subordinate to their parents' wishes. Whereas the response of some young people, such as James Emery, was rebellion, the response of others, such as Rhoda and her sisters, was submission. Duty drove Clara and Rhoda to work as teachers and to support their parents and their younger siblings. It kept all four daughters close to the farm, working on their parents' behalf, well beyond their teenage years. Clara and Nell only left at thirty. Mary never left and labored a lifetime caring for her aging parents in their home. Rhoda purchased and maintained a neighboring farm; she more than likely spent most of her working years supplementing her parents' income from her farm receipts and her wages as a teacher. It was a heavy burden to undertake as a seventeen-year-old, and one she seemed to be aware of from a very early point in her life.

The weight of her family aside, however, in 1889, seventeen-year-old Rhoda Emery was still a teenager, like any other. Although the term *teenager* was not invented until the twentieth century, young people in the late nineteenth century were not so different from those in the early twenty-first. Rhoda Emery experienced all of the anxiety, passions, and exuberance of any girl her age. She worried about her looks and her personality. She wondered about the propriety of going to dances and parties escorted by the local boys. She was greatly excited by her opportunity to become a teacher, as well as a bit bewildered by her new authority. At seventeen, she was beginning a new chapter in her life. No longer a schoolgirl, she was now a schoolteacher and embarking on a road she would travel, sometimes with enthusiasm and sometimes with trepidation, for the remainder of her working days.

Rhoda Emery continued her teaching diaries through October 1894. Now in her early twenties, she was an experienced teacher, and very little she encountered in the classroom was either new or daunting. Her writing took on a plaintive tone as she wrote, "I am so glad tomorrow is Saturday. I am so tired, so awfully tired of school. I have not missed a single term since I was four years old."[47] A desire for further education seems to have been at the core of Emery's fatigue and dissatisfaction. Her activities as a young teacher made clear her love of learning and quest for something beyond rural teaching. Like Hermann Benke, she studied while her students worked, then into the night. She began correspondence study of Latin with one of the Sisters of St. Francis at Our Lady of Lourdes Convent in Rochester. She attended every teachers' institute possible. Books were a consuming passion, and Emery purchased many, one of her few personal indulgences. For example, in the winter of 1892, her book purchases included Nathaniel Hawthorne's *The Scarlet Letter,* Charles Dickens's *Barnaby Rudge,* Susan Bogert Warner's *Queechy,* Edward Bellamy's *Looking Backward,* and Lew Wallace's *The Fair God, or the Last of the 'Tzins: A Tale of the Conquest of Mexico.*[48] As early as 1890, at the end of her first academic year of teaching, she was chafing at her situation: "I want some change I guess, though I don't know what it is. Every thing is a disappointment & I am tired of drudging along teaching country-school. If I only had the means to go to St. Paul and go through the training-school, how I should welcome the change; and I would earn so much more too. I guess I am blue to-night so I will write no more."[49] She further articulated her desire to pursue higher education in an undated letter, written in the spring or summer of 1895. "They [friends] urge me to go with them next fall and go to school. There is nothing I should like so well but suppose my duty lies in another direction. Only if I just could go to school, a little more."[50] Education was the only possible way to improve her lot as a working woman.[51]

For a country teacher, improving one's prospects generally meant finding employment in a city school district where monthly salaries were higher and the school year was longer. In urban locations, teachers could live relatively independent lives. As a life's work, it was far more attractive than remaining in the country schools, earning a sporadic living and boarding with relatives and the families of students. As late as the spring of 1895, however, employment in Rochester, let alone St. Paul or Minneapolis, must have seemed quite impossible to Rhoda. The chief barrier to Rhoda Emery achieving a career in Minnesota's urban schools was her limited education. Rhoda had attended neither high school nor college. As early as March 1868, the Rochester school board had adopted the following resolution: "Resolved, that we employ none in the public schools of this city expect [*sic*] normal school graduates, or those having had long experience as teachers in graded schools."[52] The author of a local history asserted, "Though the school authorities have not always adhered to this rule, the city has had her full share of able teachers from our own normal schools, and from other institutions of learning near and far."[53] By the 1890s, the city would have had an adequate pool of well-trained, experienced teachers from which to choose.

Rhoda was experienced but lacked adequate formal training, a situation she felt keenly.

In the fall of 1895, although it is entirely unclear how it happened, Rhoda was able to pursue her dream and embark on a one-year teacher training course at "the Normal," in Winona, Minnesota. She enrolled in the Elementary Course, which provided a year's study of topics useful to teachers of the elementary grades, such as psychology, school management, and methods of teaching drawing, reading, geography, and grammar.[54] As long as Emery declared her "intention to teach in the public schools of the State for at least two years" and remained in communication with the school's president, her tuition would be free.[55] She began school with a real cross section of Minnesota's aspiring teachers. In 1895's entering class, the students ranged in age from thirteen to thirty-four, although most were in their late teens and early twenties. She attended school with the sons and daughters of farmers, bookkeepers, grocers, bankers, lawyers, blacksmiths, and teamsters.[56]

Rhoda Emery graduated on May 27, 1896, with her one-year teaching degree. Even in that year, however, family duty threatened to thwart her ambitions.[57] While Rhoda was away at school, her grandmother in Rochester became ill, and her younger sisters tried to take care of her while going to school. Rhoda, perhaps under pressure from her mother, began to contemplate leaving her studies to go to Rochester to help. Clara Emery protested vigorously, defending her sister's hopes for further education.

> I do so want Rhode to stay where she is till she gets through. . . . If she should be foolish enough to come home I hope you will send her right back again. It seems as though a good deal depends on her finishing up now she has begun. Excuse me for giving you so much advise [sic] but it seemed to be what you wrote to me for was to get my opinion about things.[58]

Clara had become defender of her sister's hopes, arguing forcefully in her favor. Rhoda remained in Winona and graduated with her class, and within a year, the Board of Education in Rochester, Minnesota, had appointed her to teach sixth grade for $40 a month. Appropriately, her class had chosen as its motto "Out of the harbor into the sea."[59] She was on her way.

Rhoda Emery taught sixth and seventh grade in the Rochester schools from the fall of 1897 until the spring of 1909. When she began, she earned $40 a month; by the time she left Rochester, the average female teacher earned more than $60 a month.[60] Given her years of service and normal school degree, as well as the regard with which the superintendent of schools held her, she must have earned at least that amount. Emery was evidently quite an impressive teacher because in 1905 the state hired her to be a "master teacher," to instruct other continuing and prospective teachers in a summer institute at Rochester, preparing them for Olmsted County's examinations. The superintendent of schools recommended that she teach U.S. history and geography. "I have a high opinion of your ability as an instructor," he wrote, "and I should expect you would use your best endeavors to make a profitable summer school and to get results for the teachers in the examination. I think I can secure your appointment, and will do all in my power to bring it about."[61] J. W. Olsen, the superintendent of the Minnesota Department of Public Instruction, made the appointment two days later. Emery would work for six weeks, at $32 a week, a very handsome sum for the early twentieth century.[62]

Perhaps it was these activities in summer schools that brought Emery to the attention of the superintendent of the Board of School Inspectors in St. Paul; perhaps she simply applied for a position, having achieved a substantial degree of experience in Rochester. In either case, in the fall of 1908, the superintendent wrote Emery, attempting to convince her to give up her contract at midterm and come to St. Paul. "If you could secure your release on thirty days notice now, I will hold a place for you. If not, may we not look forward to your coming by the middle of next year, and if not the[n], certainly by next year?"[63] Emery honored her contract and remained in Rochester throughout the school year, but in the fall of 1909, she was bound for St. Paul to teach eighth grade at Douglas School. Her starting salary would be $750 per year.[64] Emery had achieved a very high level of economic security for a single woman of her generation. The vast majority of women who worked outside the home did so in occupations with far less prestige, and for half the pay, or less.[65] Many young women living and working in the Twin Cities in the 1910s earned less than $10 a week.[66]

Rhoda Emery's career would continue to develop. She enrolled in further course work at the University of Minnesota, although with mixed success. Her transcripts from the College of Education and General Extension Division show that she generally earned As, Bs, and Cs in her courses, but failed a quarter of Old English, and was only "Fair" in "Short Story Writing." Because she took most of her course work in the midst of the school year, it may have proven difficult to be both teacher and student at the same time. Although she stopped short of earning a university degree, the registrar noted at the bottom of the transcript, "Miss Emery is entitled to honorable dismissal."[67]

If the goal of her continuing education was to prepare for further academic responsibilities, Rhoda Emery succeeded. By the mid-1920s, she was the principal at Bryan School, a St. Paul elementary school. She also became the author of textbooks, further developing her credentials in education. In 1916, she coauthored with Grace Emery, a cousin, a grammar school textbook on Minnesota history entitled *The Story of Minnesota.* It covered all of the usual subjects and attempted to impart to its readers (with the expected prejudices of the age) a sense of the wonders and importance of the state: "Sixty years has seen in Minnesota a marvelous transformation from a wilderness inhabited by roaming bands of savages to a prosperous commonwealth which in scenic beauty, natural resources, and commercial advantage is unrivaled. Fortunate is the boy or girl whose youth is spent in an environment where Nature has been so benevolent and where She has afforded such liberal opportunities for mental, physical and moral growth— Hail to Minnesota!"[68] In 1928, she coauthored with George F. Howard a further text, *Outline of Study of U.S. History for Use in Junior High Schools and Senior American History Classes.* Although the book was, exactly as it said, an outline of United States history from the arrival of the Norsemen during the eleventh and twelfth centuries (very important in Minnesota, of course) through the presidency of Calvin Coolidge, the project did allow Emery to demonstrate her sense of humor and perspective on the teaching of history. On the subject of the Coolidge administration, she wrote:

> President Coolidge was elected President in 1924 by an overwhelming majority. The keynote of his administration is economy in government affairs, reduction in taxation, and a rapid liquidation of the National debt. While there have been many questions up for discussion in recent years, yet very little has been done that will make permanent history. "Happy is the country that does not make history," says one writer, and if that be true, the United States has been a happy nation during the years since the close of the great war.[69]

Subtle jabs at the current administration aside, Emery demonstrated her historical perspective in other ways. In addition to addressing all of the standard subjects, such as political and diplomatic history, the text included an outline of the "Development of Home Life," for its day a somewhat unusual foray into social history in a junior high and high school textbook.[70] In her outline, she included such topics as the development of education and the advent of certain agricultural and domestic tools and technology important to the home, such as the telephone and electricity.[71] Clearly, it was imagination, in addition to education and determination, that propelled Rhoda Emery onward.

Like most late nineteenth- and early twentieth-century female career teachers, Rhoda Emery remained single. Perhaps it was her thwarted romance with Wellington Clay that resulted in a decision to remain unmarried. The two corresponded off and on through 1896, but the relationship developed no further. On the other hand, it may have been a love of teaching, rather than a failure of romance, that kept Rhoda Emery independent, because it was virtually impossible in the late nineteenth and early twentieth centuries for women to pursue careers in teaching and be married simultaneously. In 1893, her correspondence with her brother seemed to foreshadow this outcome, when she wrote to him that "I really can't conclude whether we . . . are all getting to be old maids and baches or whether our contemperaries [*sic*] are all getting married too young."[72] A career, rather than domesticity, was to be her future.

Given her continuing importance to her family, a husband and children would have been heavy additional responsibilities, both emotionally and financially. Because of the size of her parents' farm and the strained circumstances they experienced in the latter years of the nineteenth century, it is unlikely that Rhoda ever relinquished responsibility for their support or that of sister Mary, who remained at home and cared for their parents into old age. Brother James never learned to manage his own affairs, and Rhoda continued to provide financial support to him until 1928, when he committed suicide as a result of poor health. Until her younger brother, Robert, established a career, she aided him financially as well as being a supportive big sister to him, and he admired her greatly. Their strong relationship began when he was an infant and extended into adulthood. It may very well have been solidified during Robert's teen years, when his mother wanted to protect and keep her last child, now well into his teens, a baby while he struggled for independence. Against her mother's wishes, Rhoda spent $13 to buy Robert his first gun and apparently urged him to think and act for himself. In this case, the stresses and strains of adolescence worked against mother-child bonds, but in favor of those with older siblings.

Robert Emery regarded his big sister as a combination of guidance counselor and guardian angel and referred to her at least one rural youngster headed for the big city. In 1913, he enlisted Rhoda's aid for a thirteen-year-old farm girl whose family sent her from rural North Dakota to Minneapolis. The youngster was planning to work for room and board while completing her education. Robert asked Rhoda to befriend and aid the girl. "There dont any of the bunch know anything about the troubles that a little country kid will have in a big city school and I wish you could find time to look the girl up and give her some of the advice you used to give me. . . . Wish you would look her up."[73] Robert Emery trusted his sister to be a port in the storm for country children making their way to the city, much as she had been for him years before.

Rhoda Emery seems to have made quite an impression on any number of people. Her grandnephew, James Wood (Clara's grandson), remembered his great-aunt as an indomitable, unflappable woman. In an essay he titled, "Yes, Virginia, There Was an Aunt Rhody," he described the woman who was a legend within her own family. Her driving, in particular, impressed the family with its daring awfulness. Once while attempting to revive her stalled 1925 Dodge in a busy downtown St. Paul intersection, she accidentally sent the car careening backward toward two impatient men in the crosswalk. "The two men seemed to fly as they leaped for their lives. Another man was standing on the corner reading his paper while all this was going on. Lowering the paper, he remarked, 'well, lady, you very nearly got two men that time.' 'Don't be ridiculous,' she replied, 'I've been trying all my life to get one.'"[74] Then in her fifties, Emery was quick-witted, funny, and a real presence within her family.

Although Rhoda Emery's life may not have evolved exactly as her seventeen-year-old self might have wanted, it was a life filled with achievement. When she died in July of 1953, she left behind a significant legacy. As both a classroom teacher and principal, she spent fifty years in schools, seeing several generations of children through Minnesota's educational system. In addition, she developed materials that would be used to teach students outside of her own schools. She served as a mentor for youngsters wanting to make their way from the farm to the city. For her struggling family, she was an essential source of support. It was a life that was defined by duty and service, but also by independence. Although she despaired for her future at age twenty-three, there would be more to her life than the limited existence she saw stretching out in front of her. By achieving an education, Rhoda Emery was able to provide the financial support that her family needed and yet live a life outside of the narrow bounds prescribed in her generation for women teachers in rural Minnesota. She had made it further, and with greater success, than the tired young woman writing the last resigned pages in her diary might have believed possible.

❖ ❖ ❖

HERMANN AND RHODA

The time that youngsters such as Hermann Benke and Rhoda Emery spent as teachers was time taken away from duties on their families' farms. As such, it represented a calculation on the part of their parents that such time would be better rewarded, either in the long or short run, than their efforts at plowing, weeding, milking, or any of the dozens of tasks that consumed farm children's time. We do not know why Hermann Benke's parents valued his intellectual efforts over his physical ones, but that seems to have been the case. Fortunately for Benke, this served his purposes as well, and he delighted in his role as teacher and quasi-adult, at least as he recorded it in his journal. His parents must have been pleased, too, with the wages his teaching brought into the family coffers.

Rhoda Emery's case is somewhat more clear, and somewhat different. Her parents depended on their children's wages, and Helen Emery's reservations about her daughters hiring out as household laborers more or less guaranteed that Rhoda would become a teacher. Rhoda Emery, ever the dutiful daughter, swallowed her own desires and supported her parents through her wages and continuing labor on her parents' farm. Her escape came in the form of higher education and an opportunity to teach in Rochester and St. Paul, which allowed her more secure employment, better wages, and a greater degree of privacy and independence than she enjoyed as a teacher in Olmsted County's rural schools. She continued in her duty to her family, but at a greater distance and with more abundant resources. Unfortunately, Rhoda Emery never left any indications of whether or not teaching was her ultimate goal or desire in life, but she did make clear that teaching in an urban context was preferable to teaching in a rural one. By earning a one-year normal school degree, she was able to leave rural schools behind. As the cases of Hermann Benke and Rhoda Emery illustrate, the experience of teaching, like other forms of farm children's labors, could have multiple meanings in the context of the family and the context of the young people's wants and needs. Young teachers educated generations of rural children and helped to support their families and themselves. In the process, many furthered their own dreams and plans for their adult lives.

Photographic Essay:
Growing Up in Dodge County, Wisconsin

Jennie and Edgar Krueger

Born on March 31, 1899, twins Jennie and Edgar Krueger grew up on their family's Dodge County, Wisconsin, farm. Their parents, Alex and Flora Krueger, were successful German American dairy farmers. Alex Krueger's grandfather, Wilhelm, had immigrated to the United States from Pomerania in 1851.[1] At the time of Jennie and Edgar's birth, four generations of the Krueger family lived on the Dodge County farm, in two households, one in a German *fachwerk* house, the other in a modern clapboard house.[2] Jennie and Edgar were surrounded by family and experienced a degree of comfort that many other midwestern farm children lacked. They were well loved by their family, both immediate and extended. As one of Edgar's daughters commented, "I sometimes think my dad and Aunt Jennie were kind of spoiled children. I think they were quite a novelty, the twins."[3]

They grew up with a father whose primary hobby was photography. Even before the twins were born, Alex Krueger was an avid and accomplished photographer. Throughout their childhood, Jennie and Edgar would be photographed at play and at work, with all of the trappings of childhood. This small sampling of the Krueger family collection, housed in the archives of the Wisconsin Historical Society in Madison, provides an intimate glimpse of children at work and play. It also provides a visual record of the material culture of relatively privileged turn-of-the-century farm childhood.

One of the earliest photographs of the Krueger twins, taken when they were toddlers, shows them in the yard, posed with a family dog and a chair hewn from a log. The photograph captures the similarity of clothing com-

Jennie and Edgar Krueger as toddlers. Krueger Family Papers. By permission of the Wisconsin Historical Society.

mon to small boys and girls. Both wore dresses, although Edgar's dress was made more "masculine" with the addition of a sailor collar and belt. As small children, their lives would have been very similar and marked by less gender division than would occur in later life. Even so, a gender division was visible in the twins' early toys. A picture of the family Christmas tree, taken in December 1901, captures the presents Jennie and Edgar received as two-year-olds. Under the tree were, among other items, a miniature broom and dustpan for Jennie, as well as dolls, and a train set and marbles for Edgar. Of course, just because parents bought gender-specific toys for children did not mean that the twins would follow these proscriptions. Also visible in the photograph is the apparent economic success of the Krueger family: the children's toys were expensive and store-bought, the wall behind

The family Christmas tree, December 1901. Krueger Family Papers. By permission of the Wisconsin Historical Society.

the tree is papered, and a sewing machine stands to the right of the tree, just out of view.

In another photograph, taken outside, the viewer receives a less rarified view of the Krueger children and their amusements. Here, they play in the farmyard with a cousin, Effy Goetsch Carr. Although the photograph is un-dated, the twins were probably two or three years old when it was taken. They both still wear dresses, the uniform of toddlers. Their outdoor play area includes a wide variety of homemade toys—rag dolls, spools on a string, and a number of small wagons, some made from recycled materials such as produce crates. The children also incorporated discarded items from the kitchen, such as spoons and cans, into their play. This collection of toys had much more in common with the average farm child's toys than those items pictured under the Christmas tree.

Jennie and Edgar Krueger with Effy Goetsch Carr playing in the farmyard.
Krueger Family Papers. By permission of the Wisconsin Historical Society.

From an early age, Jennie and Edgar Krueger also worked beside other
family members. One photograph shows the young twins participating in
cornhusking with their grandparents, August and Mary Krueger. Their
aunts, Tina and Saraphina (also known as Sarah), appear in the background.
Cornhusking was a laborious and time-consuming chore that generally required the efforts of all available hands. Gathering eggs, by contrast, was a
task that the children could do on their own. Although the photograph is
obviously staged, it captures Jennie and Edgar, age five, participating in a
chore common to farm children. One strong indication that this photograph
was staged lies in Edgar's costume. His mother, mindful of the laundry, was
unlikely to send him to the barn to do what could be a very messy chore
wearing a white ruffled shirt. Jennie's dark dress is much more sensible.

Photographs of the children at play are much more common to the collection than photos of work. Here, their father found the six-year-old twins
in the farmyard weighing a litter of kittens. At another time, he found them

The extended family, husking corn. Krueger Family Papers. By permission of the Wisconsin Historical Society.

Gathering eggs, September 1904. Krueger Family Papers. By permission of the Wisconsin Historical Society.

Weighing kittens, July 1905. Krueger Family Papers. By permission of the Wisconsin Historical Society.

The Bigalk and Krueger children playing with their wagons. Krueger Family Papers. By permission of the Wisconsin Historical Society.

Playing in the cattails, August 1906. Krueger Family Papers. By permission of the Wisconsin Historical Society.

playing with their cousins, Esther and Josie Bigalk. This photograph, again, shows a wide variety of homemade toys in use outdoors. The wagons were homemade, probably from discarded wheels and lumber. Esther pushed a child-sized wheelbarrow. The dolls in the wagon derived from an adult's imagination and skill: they were made by their Aunt Sarah, rather than being purchased from a store or mail-order catalog.[4] The dolls appear to be dressed in discarded children's clothing. When his children were seven, Alex Krueger photographed them in a nearby marsh, examining the cattails.

Having more than one pair of twins on the property presented Alex Krueger with special photographic opportunities. In one photograph taken in 1904, Jennie and Edgar are pictured feeding twin calves at the family's barn. The second photograph, taken two years later, shows Edgar with an-

Jennie and Edgar, feeding calves, April 1904. Krueger Family
Papers. By permission of the Wisconsin Historical Society.

other pair of twin calves, training them to walk in a yoke. This being a particularly boyish exercise, Jennie only appears in the background. Alex
Krueger captioned the picture "Training While Young." The implication
seemed to be that both boy and calves had a lot to learn.[5]

A 1905 Christmas photograph of Edgar and Jennie shows how their toys
changed as they grew. A set of alphabet blocks suggests the importance of
both construction games and reading. Both children appear to have received
stuffed toys. These were probably a combination of store bought and homemade; mothers could purchase cloth printed with various images and then
cut out, sew, and stuff them. A china-headed doll sits underneath the tree
with a tiny tea set. Their parents tied various types of reading material to
the branches of the tree. Although Jennie and Edgar had graduated to gender-

Edgar with twin calves, April 1906. Krueger Family Papers. By permission of the Wisconsin Historical Society.

The family Christmas tree, January 1905. Krueger Family Papers. By permission of the Wisconsin Historical Society.

Edgar Krueger, husking corn with Anson and Frank Goetsch, and Tramp the cat.
Krueger Family Papers. By permission of the Wisconsin Historical Society.

specific day wear, nightshirts or dresses were common to both boys and
girls, as well as men and women, in the early part of the twentieth century.

As they grew older, the twins continued to work and play with their extended network of cousins. One photograph shows Edgar husking corn
with his cousins Anson and Frank Goetsch. Frank Goetsch was pictured
holding Tramp, the long-suffering, patient Krueger family cat. Tramp, wearing baby clothes, also appears in a 1905 picture of Jennie. As with other farm
children, pets appear to have been an important part of the Kruegers' lives,
providing companionship and entertainment. At various times, the children's pets included guinea pigs, rabbits, gophers, and baby raccoons, as
well as the more usual cats and dogs.[6]

By 1910, the twins were eleven years old. Bicycles were a popular form of
entertainment, although many families did not have the resources to purchase
them. Here, Jennie and Edgar pose with their new wheels. Notice that these
are safety bicycles, rather than the earlier, taller, and more precarious versions.

As the twins grew older, they participated more and more in gender-
specific activities and forms of entertainment. A 1913 photograph, taken

Jennie and the ever-patient cat, Tramp. Krueger Family Papers.
By permission of the Wisconsin Historical Society.

when Edgar was fourteen, shows him with a mink he had trapped. Boys more than girls participated in hunting. Hunting was an activity with many purposes. It allowed youngsters to spend time in the woods and fields, away from more mundane chores. Many looked on it as a form of entertainment. If ducks, squirrels, or rabbits were the object, hunting might provide dinner. It also could be remunerative. Many farm boys earned pocket money, or more, from activities such as hunting and trapping. The children's grandfather even paid a penny bounty for mice and sparrows, animals classified as pests.[7]

Ultimately, Jennie and Edgar's paths would diverge in adulthood. Edgar, as the only son, became a farmer. At the age of thirty, he married Elna Som-

The twins with their bicycles, September 1910. Krueger Family Papers. By permission of the Wisconsin Historical Society.

merfield, who had also grown up on a Wisconsin farm. He would work in cooperation with his parents until their deaths. Edgar's son, Robert, farmed with his father for a while, but eventually he decided that other occupations were preferable. In 1987, he and his wife sold the farm and much of the family property.[8] At the time, six generations of Kruegers had farmed the land. Jennie Krueger pursued a different course, in 1920 marrying Ernst C. Breutzman, an accountant. The young couple moved first to Watertown and then to Milwaukee. This was not an enormous leap because her uncle, Henry Krueger, and a number of cousins already lived in Milwaukee.[9] Although she lived at a distance from the family farm, she maintained an interest in the property and influenced family decision making until her parents' deaths. In fact, her concerns may have reinforced her parents' reluctance to retire and hand over the farm to Edgar in a timely manner. She did not believe that she would feel at home on the farm if it belonged to her brother rather than her parents. Edgar would only purchase the farm from his mother in 1957, when he was nearly sixty years old. Jenny had a strong

Edgar with a mink, 1913. Krueger Family Papers. By permission of the Wisconsin Historical Society.

sentimental attachment to the farm, even if she chose to pursue her life in an urban location.[10] Like many other siblings, Jennie and Edgar Krueger chose different paths, one of which led away from the farm.

The Krueger twins enjoyed a not entirely typical farm childhood. Their family was relatively well-to-do, and their father was a progressive farmer. He took several agricultural short courses at the University of Wisconsin and embraced the idea of scientific farming. On the basis of lessons learned in the dairy short course, he improved his animals' feed, bought better stock, and acquired the newest machinery: a tractor, binder, seed drill, and hay loader. These purchases reduced the physical load on his family and improved its material well-being. But more cautiously, Alex Krueger avoided going into debt to make these improvements, helping to ensure financial well-being.[11] Jennie and Edgar had no siblings, limiting the amount of competition over resources. And because they had a wide network of grandparents, aunts, uncles, and cousins, they were insulated from the possible problem of a lack of labor in a too-small family. Because of the family's relative affluence, the children were able to participate in the consumer revolution of the late nineteenth and early twentieth centuries. They owned a number of store-bought toys, including blocks, dolls, books, and bicycles, although their parents, grandparents, aunts, and uncles continued to make them toys as well.[12] Theirs, too, was an unusually well-documented childhood, the result of Alex Krueger's hobby. Had he not been a photographer, their story would likely have been lost to all but their families. As it is, these photographs and the others preserved at the Wisconsin Historical Society provide as complete a visual record of life for one turn-of-the-century farm family as is available anywhere in the midwest.

5

"It Surely Pays to Go to a Circus"

Farm Children and Youth at Play

❖ ❖ ❖ ❖ ❖ ❖ ❖ ❖ ❖ ❖ ❖ ❖ ❖ ❖

A circus came to Nebraska City a year ago last September and we decided to go. . . .
We ate our dinner and then watched the parade. It was fine and consisted of a
colored band, a horseback band, elephants, and wagons containing wild animals.
We went to the performance, which I thought was good. I saw every wild animal
and bird of which I had ever heard, excepting a camel and a giraffe. It surely
pays to go to a circus.
—*Herman Bretthorst, age fourteen, Burr, Nebraska, 1916*

If any activity exemplifies childhood, it is play. Although farm parents generally valued work and education over play, children found the time and
energy to devote to their pursuit of recreation. As much as any children, they
enjoyed opportunities to partake of organized activities, such as the circus,
but such events were special treats, few and far between. Time for play had
to be wrested from hours spent plowing, weeding, and milking. Although
their playtime may have been limited, children inevitably found ways to entertain themselves. As children in urban areas increasingly played in adult-
scripted ways, with store-bought toys and on purpose-built playgrounds,
farm children continued to innovate, often making their own toys, creating
their own amusements, and playing wherever the spirit moved them. They
even challenged the tyranny of work by making their labors into amusement. The farms and fields were their playground.[1]

As with work and school, the nature of children's play and its meaning shifted according to the particular circumstances of the youngster involved. To play is to engage in recreational activities, or to amuse or divert oneself, but the content of that play, amusement, or diversion can be endless. Because of their parents' busy lives, the content and setting of children's play was far more likely to be determined by the children themselves than by their parents, a characteristic that increasingly distinguished rural from urban childhood in this period.[2] Obviously, factors such as a farm's stage of development influenced a child's ability to play. The newer the farm, the more work there was to be done, and potentially less opportunity a child had to play. But as Elliott West has found in his study of children in far western communities, newly established farms, in novel locations, could also generate innovative recreation, such as collecting Indian artifacts, snakeskins, and new varieties of insects.[3] Likewise, a family's financial condition affected a child's leisure activities. The more impoverished a family was, the less likely it was to be able to allow its children much time for play, or to have much money for toys. Conversely, relatively well-to-do families may have expected little work and allowed much time for education and play. A family's economic priorities would also influence a child's access to toys, books, and games. Parental attitudes toward play also shaped a child's options. Very traditional parents without a concept of play as needed or desirable may have provided very little time for recreation and put little or no family resources into their children's leisure activities. Toys would have been few and far between. Other parents, sensing the importance of play to youngsters, would have arranged schedules, at least at slack times, to allow them more freedom. But in either situation, children themselves would have created opportunities for play. Barbara Hanawalt's research on childhood in medieval London shows that even in times and places where adults allowed children very limited special treatment, they found the ways and means to play. These differences and qualifications aside, healthy and able farm children were united in their pursuit of amusement and diversion. Child's play and child life, despite parental strictures, seem to be inseparable.[4]

Toys and games formed an important part of young children's entertainment. Although in 1870 few store-bought toys were available, by 1900 manufacturers had vastly increased the range and number of available toys. Given the idiosyncratic contents of the average country store, it is perhaps easier to examine what toys were available to children by way of one of the most common forms of reading material in farm homes, the Sears catalog.

THE

NEBRASKA FARMER

Nebraska's Real Farm Paper

ESTABLISHED 1859   JUNE 2, 1915   VOL. 57. NO. 22

AND THE FISHING IS FINE

Nebraska Farmer Company, Lincoln, Nebraska

This 1915 frontispiece from the Nebraska Farmer *recognized the tension between work and play with the caption "and the fishing is fine." From the Collections of the Nebraska State Historical Society, by permission of the* Nebraska Farmer.

❖   128   ❖

In the 1902 catalog, for example, children might find a wide variety of mass-produced toys and games, most at relatively modest prices. For little girls, Sears, Roebuck and Company offered a selection of dolls, ranging from the "Majestic Doll," which at $4.25 boasted moving parts, a wig of human hair, and "indestructible composition flesh," to less elaborate kid, bisque, and rubber dolls, priced at fifty cents or less. Dolls' heads were also available for as little as ten cents, and mothers or the children themselves could sew and attach cloth bodies to complete them and then sew their wardrobes. Creating and clothing the doll might be a part of the child's play. Toy tea sets could be purchased for as little as fifteen cents, or as much as $1.40. Cast iron and tin toy stoves came in several models, priced under a dollar. Sears also sold a fully functional miniature sewing machine, "suitable for the little miss, for the nursery maid, for all kinds of plain family sewing, and is adapted largely for kindergarten use." Interested boys might find miniature steam engines, priced from ninety-five cents to $3.50, mechanical ships and automobiles costing less than a quarter, wagons ranging in price from $1.20 to $5.00, and the least expensive of store-bought toys: four-cent slingshots. Sears also sold a number of items suitable for either sex, such as banks, blackboards, kites, and board games. Checkerboards, backgammon sets, and dominoes could all be purchased for twenty cents or less.[5] Not surprisingly, many of the available toys reflected the adult roles children would one day assume, with homemaking featured in girls' toys and mechanical pursuits demonstrated in those for boys.[6] Children, however, might subvert this carefully constructed gender division of play and playthings. Little boys, as well as little girls, played with dolls, and little girls might prefer vigorous pursuits, such as skating or bicycle riding, to quiet play with gender-specific toys. Girls, too, might play with their dolls, but in ways that might shock and dismay their parents. Late nineteenth- and early twentieth-century children regularly conducted doll surgery and dentistry, funerals, and even executions. Girls could be remarkably rough on their dolls, a fact that led to increased manufacture of soft, less easily broken models.[7] This apparently common type of doll abuse, however, did not appear in the diaries or memoirs of any of the farm children studied for this book. Perhaps the sheer scarcity and expense of purchased toys limited the cruel treatment to which children subjected them, fortified with the knowledge of sure parental retribution for wasting precious resources.

The items in the Sears catalog, whether dolls, steam engines, or checkerboards, represented possibilities that were often beyond the range of the av-

Small children's toys often mimicked adults' tools. Eddie Wendorf pushes his wheelbarrow, October 20, 1901. Photograph by Alex Krueger. By permission of the Wisconsin Historical Society.

erage farm family.[8] Although adults might purchase a variety of mail order items for their homes and farms, children's toys were far down the list of ways to spend precious dollars. As Maurice Minor, who grew up in central Illinois, noted, "Many toys commercially made were available, but to us they were only pictures in the mail-order catalog and far beyond our wildest hopes ever to possess. Christmas was a time when you thrilled over receiving a large orange or a colored popcorn ball but very seldom a toy."[9] Necessities and work-related items came first, with luxuries such as toys a distant second. It was the unusual farm youngster who might own an assortment of items such as toy stoves, iron wagons, and jumping jacks.[10] Although children's diaries rarely mention toys, memoirs of farm childhood are more explicit on the subject. Some women remembered owning a store-bought doll, but rarely more than one. Those dolls might be china-, bisque-, or wax-headed, with a homemade cloth body. Predictably, such fragile playthings often met with disastrous fates. Girls often dropped and broke their

In this 1905 scene, Wilma and Hazel Warren enjoyed both extremes of children's toys, the "homemade" corncobs and the store-bought doll. Warren Collection. By permission of the State Historical Society of Iowa.

china dolls, unless their mothers carefully supervised their play. Wax dolls were also subject to accident. Addie Thompson Sinclair, who grew up in rural Kansas, noted that she and her sister, in an attempt to keep their wax babies warm in winter, melted them by putting them too close to the heating stove in the living room.[11] More commonly, mothers or the youngsters themselves made dolls from paper, cloth scraps, rags, and corncobs. Even a bootjack, with its two "legs," might be dressed and put into service, sometimes wearing "trousers and a jacket" or "wearing didies and long dress and a bonnet." Iowan Louisa Boylan recalled that she and her sister picked ears of corn with particularly long silks and "played they were our babies." Her parents put a stop to that game when they discovered their daughters had been picking and wasting green corn.[12]

Fathers often made toys for children, including sleds, wagons, swings, and even merry-go-rounds.[13] But part of the joy of toys could be making them oneself. Such toys ranged from the simple to the elaborate. Hoops could be salvaged from broken-down farm equipment. Popguns, slingshots, bows and arrows, and darts were relatively simple to make. Children made paper windmills or pinwheels to turn in the breeze. Children also enjoyed noisemakers, carving whistles from willow and spools and constructing cornstalk fiddles. For Maude Keene Gill, a long list of found objects filled her toy box. Corncobs became blocks, while acorns became animals, and corn, sticks, matches, and tablespoons became other farm animals, implements, and structures. She and her brother created entire imaginary neighborhoods.[14] One youngster devised a particularly clever toy, a hand-cranked tractor, made "from a discarded apple peeler clamped to a short piece of board with skate wheels nailed to its ends." Even though the boy had to use his imagination to see a tractor's form within his machine, he was enormously proud of this creation: "My! how it clawed at the dirt to gain tractive power as I turned the crank at the top."[15] Although some children devised their own playthings, a generous brother or sister might also build a toy for a younger sibling. When Agnes Mary Kolshorn longingly described a doll bed she had seen at a store, "no doubt realizing that money was not going to be spent on such things," her older brother offered to make one for her from an orange crate. "I watched him carefully separating the boards on the crate, making a smooth, sturdy bed and painting it blue gray; a bed that far surpassed the smaller, fragile one I had seen in the store. I was delighted! It was mine! Made for me! I treasured it for years."[16] Making toys represented two different types of entertainment: the entertainment inherent in inventing and building, as well as the enjoyment of playing with the toy. Children exercised their imaginations and ingenuity, and they often felt an enormous sense of satisfaction in their creations.

Families also indulged in games, some of which might include purchased components: checkers, dominoes, jacks, and tiddlywinks (also called tiddle-de-winks). Checkers and dominoes, in particular, were important to evening entertainment.[17] Children and parents might play card games such as Authors together, while other parents forbade the playing of card games of any type, on religious principles.[18] In the 1870s, a minor croquet craze swept the midwest. The Stilsons of Linn County, Iowa, purchased a croquet set, and daughter Sadie regularly brought friends home to play, or went to their homes to play too. In 1879, in Trempealeau County, Wisconsin, various neighbors owned croquet sets, and the older sons of the Wood family made a croquet ground out of a pasture, putting clay on it "to make it hard and smooth."[19] In the early 1890s, the game was still popular, and Ralph, the Wood family's youngest son, still played with family, friends, and neighbors.[20]

Beyond toys and games, literary diversions also occupied youngsters. If a father subscribed to a farm publication such as the *Nebraska Farmer*, the children's page within that publication was available to his family. These pages published stories and puzzles of interest to children, but more importantly, they published letters written by children. A young reader could entertain him- or herself by reading the adventures of other children living in very similar circumstances, and by writing to the editor of the children's page with tales of work, play, and school. Finding one's name and stories in the pages of the newspaper had to be a particular thrill. Families with a few dollars to spare might allow their children to subscribe to papers and magazines published specifically for them. From the mid-1870s until 1882, the publishers of the *Kansas Farmer* also produced an agriculturally oriented children's newspaper, *American Young Folks*, intended for the "amusement and instruction" of the young. As might be expected of a children's publication (and especially one published in Kansas), it was a highly moralistic newspaper, pro-temperance and anti-tobacco. Its articles and poetry promoted industriousness and cheerfulness in all circumstances. An 1876 article was entitled "How Girls Can Learn to be Housekeepers." Another in 1878 praised an eleven-year-old Iowa girl, a "plucky little miss," for writing to Uncle Sam, requesting her own homestead. Boys could read articles directed toward them as well. A piece entitled "Chore Boys" commiserated with hard-working lads while encouraging them to become accomplished in their tasks. The youngster who did not, the author warned, would be "only a chore boy all his life."[21] It is difficult to judge how entertaining children found this type of material. The moral and educational messages could be heavy indeed. For example, building on farm children's undoubted experiences with the devastation wrought by grasshoppers, the editors published a poem entitled "'Tis Only a Grasshopper." The writer noted that a single grasshopper posed little threat to anyone: "Don't mind him, come, now, he shall not spoil our fun." Grasshoppers in profusion, however, were another matter:

> The 'hoppers are coming, they're now in the west,
> They soon will be here; O, the terrible pest!
> Just look at their coming, like a cloud in the sky,
> Just look at their dropping, like snowflakes they fly.
> See, millions on millions now cover the ground;
> And millions on millions are flying around!

Just look at our corn fields, the stalks eaten bare,
Just look at our fruit trees,—no apple, no pear,
Just look at our vineyards,—no grape to be seen,
Just look at our gardens—they're all eaten clean
Just look at our pasture, field, meadow and tree
They've eaten them all, *desolation I see!*

There was a lesson to be learned from this dramatic comparison:

My friends, I've no doubt, the moral you've guessed,
A bad habit or two, you pass with a jest;
But evils like 'hoppers, when grown to a pest,
Will ruin the richest, the wisest, the best.[22]

Admonitions such as these were common to literature for children and may have limited its appeal and entertainment value. Many children, however, were happy to read just about anything. As May Crowder reminisced, "Reading was scarce and we read everything we could get our hands on."[23]

Even if moralistic stories and poems in *American Young Folks* had limited appeal, the letters young subscribers wrote to "Uncle Frank," and later "Aunt Mary," the fictitious adults who edited the children's writings, had to have been particularly interesting. Young readers might learn about new and different parts of the country, where wolves roamed and Indians camped. They might compare their workloads with those of others who also plowed, harrowed, hoed, and chored. The letters also offered the opportunity to commiserate with other children who also had seen their families' crops destroyed by grasshoppers, who had lost siblings to accidents and disease, or who were lonesome because the school year was over and the nearest neighbors were some distance away.[24] *American Young Folks'* readers must have been disappointed when, in 1882, the editors ceased publication. Moralistic or not, the paper provided diversion from the ordinary and an opportunity to learn more about the lives of other farm children across the midwest and the nation.

Some parents made a practice of reading to their children. One particularly well-read Norwegian immigrant family took numerous papers and magazines, but the *Youth's Companion*, the longest-lived and most successful young people's religious paper, was a favorite.[25] The mother not only read to her four children, but made the reading into a test of memory. As a daughter reminisced, "We were required to remember 'out loud' just what had taken place the week before. This was good mental practice, our parents thought."[26] Young Ralph Wood, of west-central Wisconsin, enjoyed both listening and reading. Sometimes his mother read to him, and sometimes he read to himself. In either case, nonfiction was his preference. As a ten-year-old, he commented, "Ma red to me about Rodents and how celluloid is made," as well as "a story about pioneer life in Dakota." She also read to him from the Bible. For himself, he too read the Bible, and read about "boys hunting bears," and "a story of a boy make-ing maple suerip."[27] Although he did not indicate the source of the stories he read, they probably came from a children's paper. Some parents recognized the potential for reading to lighten the family's evening work. Frances Olsen Day's mother and father "took turns reading aloud while the others sewed carpet rags or shelled seed corn or some other tedious job. As soon as we children could read we took our turn at it and many an interesting tale was impressed on our childish memories in that very pleasant fashion."[28] Parents might perceive reading as education, entertainment, or an inducement to cheerful compliance with an evening's labor.

Numerous books published specifically for children were available in the late nineteenth and early twentieth centuries, although it is difficult to gauge what books were available to an individual child. Among the most popular forms of children's literature were adventure stories, historical novels, and morality tales. By the latter half of the nineteenth century, the morality tales had taken on a more subtle form in novels than that found in children's newspapers, with some of the best loved being Louisa May Alcott's books, such as *Little Men* and *Little Women*.[29] Some families purchased books for children, but the precarious farm economy made such purchases, in most cases, few and far between. Again, Sears offered an assortment of books, ranging from atlases to encyclopedias, advice books, and novels, some available for fifty cents or less.[30] Other children borrowed books from libraries and friends. For example, eighteen-year-old Minnie Mae Moon, of rural Towanda, Illinois, was able to make use of the library at Illinois State Normal University, in neighboring Normal, Illinois, even though she was not enrolled as a student. There she borrowed books such as Louisa May Alcott's popular novel, *Rose in Bloom*.[31] Truly voracious readers, if in possession of funds, might even invest that money in the creation of small family libraries. Rhoda Emery, an Olmsted County, Minnesota, teenager, spent a substantial amount of her earnings as a teacher on books. A reader of the *Youth's Companion*, she took advantage of offers in the paper to buy discounted volumes. In 1889, in her first term teaching, she planned to pool funds with her older sister, Clara, in order to buy a set of Charles Dickens's works and a bookcase, purchases totaling $5.50. That Christmas, she bought her sisters two books, *The Pilot* and *The Last of the Mohicans*.[32] Buying books from the Montgomery Ward catalog and the *Youth's Companion* continued to be a special treat. In the winter of 1892, she purchased and read *The Scarlet Letter, Barnaby Rudge, Queechy, Looking Backward,* and *The Fair God,* a combination of fiction, historical fiction, utopian, and self-improving works.[33] Reading offered an escape from the ordinary, as well as the busy world of a farm daughter and rural schoolteacher.

How-to books were dual-purpose children's literature, providing the entertainment of reading as well as information on how to devise other types of fun. If any child should be unsure about what to do with his or her time, there were numerous tomes providing descriptions of games and diversions galore. One such publication, *The American Boy's Book of Sports and Games,* introduced youngsters to any number of games and forms of recreation. Its nearly six hundred pages described everything from playground games, such as hopscotch, to basic figure skating. Children might learn how to raise animals from pigeons to rabbits to dogs. For the truly ambitious, there were various magic tricks to be mastered. Tolerant parents might allow "chemical amusements," such as the creation of a small Mount Vesuvius in a flask. Although the writers justified their book of games as training boys to be wholesome and courageous men, its appeal must have been in the careful, step-by-step instructions it provided for games (and even mayhem) of all sorts. It was a place to begin, if a child's imagination ever left off.[34]

Store-bought toys and books were precious to farm children, but they represented only a portion of children's play. In addition to the possibilities inherent in these items, farms themselves offered children other opportunities to create their own diversions. The rural environment itself provided a certain level of entertainment. A Nebraska girl claimed that farm children "always have a good time," citing her opportunities for skating in winter and gathering flowers in summer. A Kansas girl enjoyed the wildness of her surroundings, writing, "I often take long walks in the woods, which are very beautiful now, and gather bouquets of leaves and grasses." A boy noted his love of hunting, his enjoyment in the birds and flowers, and his opportunities to "go galloping over the hills." Even watching men at work could provide amusement. As ten-year-old Olive Everts, of Discord, Iowa, noted, "Sometimes we go down to the hay field and watch the men put up hay,

Children found many ways to entertain themselves in the barnyard. Emma Ray and her cousin, Ada, on a farm in Randall, Minnesota, circa 1905. By permission of the Minnesota Historical Society.

which we think is nice fun."[35] Imagination, and a certain amount of freedom to meander the surrounding countryside, could be all that was needed to provide a morning's or afternoon's entertainment.

The built environment, as well as the natural environment, was a playground. Barns were a favorite place for play, and rope swings allowed children to fly "across the barn from one ledge to the other above the horses and cows." More daring sorts would simply jump from the haymow onto the hay below. On an earthier note, Milo Pitcher of Story County, Iowa, spent a good deal of time concocting the perfect ball of cow manure for throwing. It needed to be of the correct consistency to stick to the side of the barn, something that he mastered, but his city cousins never did. Pitcher was not the only child who entertained himself by throwing cow manure. Thirteen-year-old Curtis Norton, engaging in the sport, missed his brother and hit his sister. "I hit Mary in the eye with a cowturd It was a dry one At first she said she could not see I was throwing at Charley but hit Mary She houled like a nailer."[36]

Pets, too, were an important form of diversion. Farm children accumulated an amazing assortment of animals, because space, noise, and odors were less of a problem than they would have been in an urban environment. Most commonly, children owned dogs. Dogs often were dual-purpose pets, playmates to children but also useful for various tasks, such as hauling, herding, and controlling rodents. Horses of various varieties plowed fields and carried children to school, but they could also provide endless fun in the form of horseback riding. As one girl wrote, "Some other girls and I go out riding nearly every day and have lots of fun." Although most youngsters owned the usual cats, dogs, rabbits, and birds, others boasted more exotic pets as well. Frankie Woita owned a goat, noting that he could "ride it and drive it whenever I like." The goat, apparently with good reason, had a short temper, "and he tries to hook us but we run up the tree so he can't hook us." A thirteen-year-old boy made a pet of Pete, the rooster, and trained him to ride on a sled in the winter. "When I turned a little quick he'd fall off and stay there until I came back and put him on my sled." Children and animals were a natural combination, and one of the great joys of farm living.[37]

Loving an animal, however, could be one of the sorrows of farm childhood as well. Animals, like any other living being, were mortal, and that mortality could cause grief and disappointment. An eight-year-old girl mourned the passing of a pair of burros: "Our two burros, Jane and Polly, died recently. We think it was cornstalk disease that killed them. We are so sorry, for we were planning so much fun with them this summer. They were thirty years old." Given the vigor of children's games, the quite elderly Jane and Polly might well have been relieved to pass on and avoid a long, hot summer of riding, racing, and exploring. Children's animals met less natural ends as well. Pets that misbehaved, and particularly those that threatened a family's livelihood, would generally be killed. A cat that caught and ate chickens could not be tolerated, as a nine-year-old Nebraska girl discovered. "Mamma had some little chickens and Bessie began to catch and eat them, so as I hated to have her killed, they carried her away and I never saw her again. I was very sorry." Farm animals adopted as newborns also grew into adults, with all of its implications. Bottle-fed lambs, as adults, had to be turned out to pasture with the other sheep. Hand-raised pigs had to be slaughtered or sold. A boy whose pig grew too large to be a pet sold it to his father for $20, and soon after it was slaughtered. As his brother wrote, "At first after it was dead John used to go down to the garden every morning to feed it, but it wasn't there. He felt pretty sorry, but he didn't cry."

A horse could be a child's best friend. Here, George Collier, of Agenda, Kansas, is pictured with his horse, circa 1910. By permission of Mary Thompson Riney.

Some youngsters anticipated this transition with a bit more detachment. An eleven-year-old, knowing that the day was soon coming when his pet calf and "playmate" Blink would be sold, commented, "When he gets big I am going to sell him and buy a bicycle."[38] Whether the joys of owning a bicycle would actually assuage the grief of Blink's departure was yet to be discovered. Pet ownership was one area where the joy of farm living collided with its realities. None of the children encountered in this study, however, commented that the realities kept them from wanting to raise pets.

Beyond simple enjoyment of nature and time spent with animals, the farm and its environs became a playground for these children. There were enormous opportunities for a wide variety of child-initiated and child-scripted activities. Water, in all its forms, was full of possibilities. In winter, ice and snow offered obvious diversions. Children employed both sleds and skates to the great enjoyment of all. As one young girl wrote, "There has been a snow here and the children are having lots of fun . . . skating and breaking their heads on the ice." Skating, as children defined it, did not necessarily require special equipment, because they could slide quite successfully in just their shoes. Ice-skating, in particular, was a well-loved diversion, but it of-

A homemade goat cart provided entertainment for two Iowa boys. Alden Family Collection. By permission of Special Collections, Parks Library, Iowa State University, Ames, Iowa.

fered numerous opportunities for misadventure, with youngsters falling through weak ice, soaking themselves or worse. Sledding was also a favorite activity. Children pressed any and all hills into service, but a cooperative parent might apply the power used to grind corn to drag boys across relatively flat pastures and farm yards. Choosing an inopportune place to sled could be as dangerous as skating on thin ice. For one youngster, fastening his sled to a hay rack and then traveling through a pasture filled with hungry horses led to a kick in the head, unconsciousness, and two stitches. "Since the accident," he wrote, "I have never tied my sled to the rack when we are going through a pasture." Skating and sledding were not the only water-based diversions farm children indulged in; water in any form was a temptation. In the spring, a flooded schoolyard and a stock tank might provide the opportunity for an afternoon of "boating." In the summer, swimming or wading in stock tanks was common, although, given the possibility of drowning and accidents, parents often disapproved.[39]

At any time of year, speedy movement across the landscape was a thrill. In months without snow cover, children harnessed animal power, as well as

Children often made farm animals into pets. Pictured here is Ralph Munson with his pet pig, circa 1912. By permission of the Minnesota Historical Society.

gravity. A variety of animals, not necessarily just horses, found themselves drafted for duty. Unhappy calves hauled carts around farmyards, sometimes running away "through three fences and [breaking] the cart all to pieces." Rolling buggies and wagons down hills also achieved children's desire for speed. Two brothers and a sister dragged an old buggy to the top of the hill and rode down, taking two cats and their dog along for the ride. After success in the first run, they found a steeper hill. Although the buggy "broke down" after this treatment, none of the children was injured. "At last we pulled the buggy home and repaired it and that ended our fun for the day." Old wagons left around the yard might be pushed up hills and ridden down again. Of course, not having an effective steering mechanism might cause some problems. Two Nebraska girls crashed their wagon into the barn. "Sister was in the seat guiding the wagon, and when we hit the barn she was thrown over the dashboard on her head. I was in the back seat and was not thrown out. It was the last time we took a ride like that."[40]

Even learning to fly might become an obsession. After observing the effortless flight of buzzards, eight-year-old Illinois farm boy Walker Wyman joined forces with his cousin, Jim, to devise a method of flying. They whittled shingle extensions and attached them to Walker's arms. After some

Children's imagination often made good use of no-longer-functioning vehicles.
Alden Family Collection. By permission of Special Collections, Parks Library,
Iowa State University, Ames, Iowa.

practice flapping his "wings," he climbed to the top of the hen house "and made ready for one of the greatest experiments of my life. Could I fly away just as the buzzards seemed to do so easily?" On the count of ten, he leapt from the roof, "but instead of soaring away I went straight down to the ground with a thud." Fortunately, Wyman was uninjured, and neither he nor his cousin wished to repeat the stunt.[41] The high incidence of risk-taking and mishap involved in farm children's play may help twenty-first-century readers understand why so many modern parents prefer to script and control their children's play, instead of leaving them to their own devices.[42] Left on their own, farm children pursued any number of entertaining, but highly dangerous, diversions. Although often battered and bruised, most lived to tell the tale.

In some children's descriptions of their activities, it can be difficult to distinguish those undertaken as work and those undertaken as play. The line between the two could be thin at times, with children making their work as entertaining as possible. Children might find chores involving the use of animals particularly enjoyable. Riding a pony after the cows could be fun.

The cows themselves could add to the entertainment, although they probably did not appreciate their role in children's capers. When nine-year-old Georgia Finnigan went with her two brothers to get the cows, she decided to ride one of them. The cow, predictably, bucked her off. Other children rode cows, hoping for a wild ride. These activities provided the same dangerous thrills as sledding, skating, or riding discarded farm equipment. Fishing, hunting, and trapping, largely boys' activities, also fell somewhere between work and leisure. Each of these activities produced either food or income, but it also allowed youngsters relatively unsupervised time in and around the fields, woods, or water. They also often involved cooperation and camaraderie with other children or adults. A parallel indoor activity might be cooking. When done in volume, on a hot day, under pressure from many hungry people, cooking was definitely work. Done because a child, usually a girl, wanted to do so, cooking could provide entertainment while also serving the purpose of educating the child in the art of feeding a family. Little girls experimented with their first layer cakes and pies, and as might be expected, they also wanted to make candy. Left at home with their father, eight-year-old Clifford Woodbridge and his brother decided to make "a surprise for mamma. So we got the recipe book and found a candy recipe. . . . We were about one hour making it. After it was cooked and cooled my brother wrapped it up and I did my chores." The rest of the family was impressed with the results, "but mamma had to wash the chairs and other things which got covered with candy." Evidently the fun of making candy had not included the decidedly less enjoyable task of cleaning up afterward.[43]

Transforming work into play, farm animals into pets, and the built and natural landscape into a playground were some of the most important forms of recreation for farm children. Unlike store-bought toys, or many of the community and family activities described later in this chapter, such types of entertainment did not require a parental commitment or investment. What was required was a child's imagination and willingness to steal a few moments from a busy day in pursuit of entertainment. As such, this entirely unscripted and child-driven play represented the most universal and easily accessible form of entertainment for youngsters on farms.

In addition to these unscripted occasions for entertainment, family traditions might also create special spaces for children's activities. Many families designated holidays as important occasions for feasting, play, and diversion. The Story family, of Buffalo County, Nebraska, struggled economically, beset by injuries, illness, and an inability to make a sufficient living on their acres. Even given the family's straitened circumstances, parents Charles and Melvina made a special effort to make holidays special for their children. The first family Christmas in Nebraska, celebrated in 1879, required innovation. "As we have no trees within five miles of us, we could afford no Christmas tree for the children so we had a Nebraska tree, made as follows. I pinned my brown dressing gown up under the mantle piece, & decorated it with the ornaments from last Christmas, & filled the cornicopia [sic] with candy. The affect was quite pretty & when the children got up this morning they were delighted." The Christmas feast included roast chicken, mashed potatoes, bread, butter, pickles, preserved plums, and two kinds of cake. November of 1880 saw the family celebrating Thanksgiving with "a quite nice dinner for this miserable State. A brace of roast chickens, roast potatoes, mashed potatoes, pepper cabbage, bread & tea." Later that evening, the family feasted on doughnuts and popcorn. Although the parents were feeling "dreary" because there were "no presents for the little ones," a month later the Storys celebrated Christmas with stockings filled with "doughnuts, pop-corn kisses, and mixed candies." The parents took a wild plum tree and transformed it into a Christmas tree with "little cupids, fairies, angels with red wings and other candy and attractive ornaments."[44]

Other farm children, whose families were in better financial condition, received presents for Christmas. Like the Storys, Sarah Gillespie's Iowa family also had a plum tree for a Christmas tree, but hung on it presents such as cards printed with mottoes, ribbons, handkerchiefs, journals, slippers, and small pieces of jewelry.[45] The Armentrout family of Wilton, Iowa, gathered together for the Christmas holiday and shared modest gifts such as letter paper, envelopes, and cologne.[46] In addition to these family observances of Christmas, communities sometimes sponsored holiday gatherings, usually at the school. These evening events might include refreshments, plays or spoken pieces, and a communal Christmas tree. Parents generally contributed so that every child would receive some sort of present, even if it was just a bag of candy or a popcorn ball.[47] The celebration of Christmas with feasting and presents was not, however, universal. In 1889, Mary Van Zante, who grew up in the Dutch area surrounding Pella, Iowa, noted the lack of a Christmas holiday in her community. "Christmas today. But none of us got anything today. Lizzie and Evert went to school but there were only 12 scholars. I stayed at home to sew on our dresses. We got them a nice little ways."[48] Given the presence of twelve youngsters in school on Christmas, this disinclination to celebrate the holiday indicates a community practice, rather than an idiosyncrasy of the Van Zante family. Mary's diary also shows that on December 6 the family did not celebrate St. Nicholas Day, perhaps the most important part of the Dutch celebration of the Christmas season. As members of the Dutch Reformed Church, they shunned any holiday observances that might be considered worldly. Only in the twentieth century would the community begin to celebrate Christmas in ways that were similar to the dominant society.[49] Religious and ethnic traditions shaped holiday observances in other communities as well. Swedish immigrants in some Minnesota communities, for example, celebrated the summer solstice and St. Lucia Day, among other holidays.[50]

Independence Day was also the occasion of community celebrations, often attended by whole families. The standard midwestern elements of the holiday were picnics and fireworks, either in a neighborhood gathering place or in town. Mamie Griswold, of Greene County, Illinois, noted her family's attendance at a picnic and fireworks to celebrate Independence Day. In Wisconsin, the Woods and their neighbors gathered "on the hills" for dinner, firecrackers, and blueberry picking. Likewise, in Iowa, the younger Stilsons went to a local grove for an evening's entertainment while their father remained home to mow hay and attend to chores.[51] Much more elaborate events took place in the region's larger towns. For July 4, 1877, Rosa Armentrout was able to travel to Davenport for a day's festivities. In fact, a large number of the young folks from rural Wilton, Iowa, made the journey by train. The day's events included a steamboat ride and croquet. She also feasted on special holiday treats. "We had so much ice cream, lemonade, soda water, candy, peanuts, oranges, apples & & we were most sick." She enjoyed herself so thoroughly that she missed the train home on the fourth and remained until the fifth. She reflected on the day's entertainment: "I have never spent a better day that is I never had a nicer time than yesterday."[52]

Although considerably less common than Christmas and Fourth of July celebrations, some parents allowed their children to attend parties on New Year's Eve. In 1892, Minnie Mae Moon traveled from her parents' home in Towanda, Illinois, to nearby Lexington for an evening of food and dancing: "Went to Lexington this afternoon. to night went to a party given by the business men. . . . about Midnight we all went over to Goddards for supper and then returned to the Opera House where we continued dancing until 12 o'clock when we went home."[53] In most homes, and in most communities, however, New Year's Day was little celebrated, perhaps marked by a special dinner, such as turkey and oysters at the Wood family home in north-central Wisconsin. When youngsters noted the passing of the old year and the beginning of the new, it usually rated a simple notation, such as "Today is the last day of the old year," rather than a description of dancing and parties.[54]

In the latter years of the nineteenth century and the beginning of the twentieth, Halloween was both similar to and different from its current incarnation. For young children, afternoon parties at school seem to have been fairly common. These might include special food, candy, and games. The children might also host events for the whole community. At one country school, the children decorated the classroom with jack-o'-lanterns, served oyster soup, and sold popcorn and candy. Their carnival included fortune-telling and guessing games. The object of the evening's entertainment was to raise money for the school, and the students earned $21.65.[55] Such school-sponsored events usually encompassed the small child's experience of Halloween and are not terribly different than school-sponsored parties and carnivals today. Trick-or-treating had yet to become an American institution, and hardly would have been practical, given the state of transportation and the long distance between homes in most rural communities.[56] Among older youths, particularly boys, Halloween was the occasion for pranks and misbehavior, such as tipping over privies and moving buggies onto roofs.[57] Adults probably wished they could exercise as much control over the activities of older children as they did over the younger.

Aside from holidays, circuses were a particular delight and treat. When the circus came to town on a weekday, teachers might find their classrooms completely empty, as did Minnesotan Rhoda Emery on one June day in 1894: "The Ringling Bros. gave a circus in R[ochester] yesterday so though I came up here to the schoolhouse I had no pupils and no school. Bessie and I went down to see the parade. . . . There was a great crowd in town."[58] As the chapter's opening quotation from Herman Bretthorst indicated, the parades and shows fascinated youngsters. Bands entertained the crowd, and children saw firsthand many animals they had only previously read about. They might also have their first view of people of another race. Stunt riders and trapeze artists thrilled the children, and clowns made them laugh. Some circuses included novel acts, such as aerialists ascending into the skies with the aid of balloons, a stunt that to one youngster appeared to be "very Scary." Youngsters might even be treated to lemonade, popcorn, and candy. As Herman commented, "It surely pays to go to a circus."[59]

A trip to the circus might also provide the script for future games. One boy was so impressed by the spotted pony at the circus that he painted spots on one of the family horses and tried to teach it to run in circles, "he being the ring-master." The youngster, upon his father's discovery, received a spanking. This might partly explain why other children played circus only when their parents were away. Many of the imitative activities of children were physically dangerous or potentially damaging to the family's property. The Gelhorn children, growing up on a farm along the Iowa River, enlisted their dogs and cats as "wild animals," and they used all the quilts in the house to make a big top. They walked a tightrope, turned somersaults, and attempted to imitate as much as possible the performers they had seen at the circus. For them, it was not so much the daring performances that caused problems with their parents, but dragging their mother's quilts into the yard. The children in another Iowa family would hitch up four horses and imitate the circus wagons that thundered around the ring. "They would go to a 5-acre patch of land south of our house, and drive around and around as fast as the horses could go. It was a very dizzying and noisy game. A neighbor once saw it and reported it to our folks, and that ended the circus." Unfortunately, ending one dangerous game did not prevent the children from finding another. Forbidden to play circus, the children would drive down to the creek "and see how far into the quicksand they could go, and out again. The neighbors couldn't see us there, and that lasted for some time."[60] Circuses appealed to children on many levels, allowing them to experience pageantry, excitement, and danger vicariously. Many then attempted to adapt that experience to their own environment.

Although circuses were occasional and very special activities, other activities, such as church, were an important part of the weekly ritual of families, for recreation as well as worship. Attendance at Sunday services was a welcome break from a week's labor. Mary Eleanor Armstrong, an Iowa farm girl, viewed Sunday services as an opportunity to mitigate her loneliness. "I haven't been to church for a long time. I am awful lonesome and cross."[61] John Stilson, also an Iowan, regularly attended church activities and clearly enjoyed this opportunity to get away from the farm and meet with other people. In his diary he lamented, "O dear how lone some[.] there is neither Sunday School nor Church." His younger sister, Sadie, however, could be a little more critical in her comments, writing on a Sunday, "We listened to another of Mr See's long sermons[.] he was here to dinner."[62] Sunday services, however, were not the only religious activities. Churches also sponsored numerous events throughout the week, such as prayer meetings and fund-raising dinners. These events drew people of all ages, but those in their teens and twenties in particular used them as opportunities for gathering and for meeting the opposite sex.[63] Minnie Mae Moon regularly went to church, acted as secretary of the Sunday School, and attended events and sociables at the Christian, Methodist Episcopal, and Congregational Churches in neighboring Normal, Illinois. She also belonged to Christian Endeavor, a young people's social group affiliated with the Methodist Church. Sometimes she attended services and meetings at several different churches on a single Sunday. In her case, the opportunity to attend a variety of local gatherings seems to have been more important than denominational loyalty.[64]

Churches also brought together people in their late teens and early adult years for their own meetings and programs. The Baptist Young People's Union of Hudson, Illinois, for example, held regular prayer meetings on a variety of topics. In the winter and spring of 1891, members met on a weekly basis, discussing such topics as "Helping Our Brethren," "Is My Heart Right with God?," and "Hearing and Heeding God's Message." In 1896 and 1897, the group discussed missionary work in Cuba, China, and Japan, as well as temperance, self-denial, and baptism by immersion.[65] There is abundant evidence that churches filled a similarly important role in the social lives of youngsters in immigrant communities. Among Norwegian Americans, for example, the Young People's Luther Leagues were an extremely important place for socializing and worship.[66] For many young people, the opportunity to meet and mingle and to assess the latest styles may have been just as or more important than the religious content of the evening's program. On a Saturday evening, sixteen-year-old Mary Eleanor Armstrong joined with a group of friends entertaining themselves by attending a youth program at a local church: "Gene, Lucy, Jen & I went to the Dutch church in the evening. Ha! Ha! We learned a new song. Lucy and I wore our hair curled." Armstrong seems to have made this trip to what was probably a local Dutch Reformed church for purposes other than the religious, because her hairstyle received more comment than any teaching there imparted.[67] From the perspective of young people, church-sponsored gatherings had the great advantage over other forms of entertainment of being classified as safe and respectable, characteristics that made even conservative and cautious parents more willing to allow their children to attend.

Also deemed respectable were the many educational events available in the evening, sometimes attended by families and sometimes by older youngsters on their own. In any one community, there might be a number of singing schools, debating societies, and literary clubs. As a fifteen-year-old, Oliver Perry Myers, of Washington County, Iowa, joined the geography school that met during the evening. The students pooled their resources and hired a teacher, paying him $35 for twelve weeks of instruction. As Myers commented, "It is very Interesting and Instructive." Additionally, Myers joined and was elected secretary of the local literary society, which met on Tuesday evenings.[68] Parents in developing communities sometimes lamented the lack of such wholesome entertainment for their children. Wrote farm mother Mary Norton of social conditions in thinly settled central Kansas, "I wish our children had singing school to attend or some pleasant way of spending an evening occasionally with improvement to themselves. Lottie would feel better for a little recreation occasionally."[69] Not long after she made this observation, social activities for youngsters and their families began to develop in the Nortons' community. In January of 1880, most of the family attended an evening spelling school: "Ma spelled down the whole school the first time and Johnnie was second best." Mary Norton approved of the educational effects of this activity. "The spelling school has waked the children up about spelling."[70] A local lyceum, or literary club, also developed, but met irregularly. Hermann Benke, also of central Kansas, commonly attended evening literary meetings that included debates that ranged from the philosophical to the practical. On March 2, 1886, the proposition was "Deceit is never justifiable."[71]

Mamie Griswold, growing up in Greene County, Illinois, in the 1870s and 1880s, experienced a whole range of entertainment activities organized by various groups in her community. Apparent within her accounts of local activities was a seasonal round of family-oriented entertainment open to people of all ages. Many of the activities were concentrated in the winter because there were fewer pressing farm chores at that time.[72] Temperance societies were active in Greene County, and throughout the year they sponsored lectures and meetings in the local schools and churches. In the winter, Griswold often attended lyceums, or literary meetings, and magic lantern shows. On the lighter side, winter was also the season for dances. In the spring, outdoor activities commenced. In May 1878, her church sponsored a "strawberry & Ice cream festival." Summer brought picnics. In 1878, the local temperance society sponsored one such event, and as Griswold commented, "Had a very good time The members all had on blue cambric sashes." In the fall, bees of various sorts took place on local farms. Griswold, in particular, mentioned an apple cutting bee, a step in the preparation of dried apples or apple butter. Area families attended local agricultural fairs but also traveled as far as St. Louis to the fairgrounds there. In 1884, Griswold had the opportunity to visit New York City, a great adventure that also spoiled the local fairs for her. Upon her return, she commented, "Went to Carrollton to Greene Co Fair[.] Did not enjoy it very much. . . . it is because I have seen so much that is far ahead of it."[73] Griswold attended a wide variety of events, but never anything quite as exotic as the phrenological lecture Sadie Stilson attended at the Universalist hall in Linn County, Iowa.[74] Even so, accounts such as Griswold's illustrate that in established rural midwestern communities there were numerous opportunities for entertainment involving the whole family.

In some communities, there was a regular whirl of activities oriented specifically toward older teenagers and young adults. These events appear to have been largely age-segregated, in that younger teens and older married adults generally did not take part. Mary Eleanor Armstrong, of Jones County, Iowa, attended many dances and parties from the age of sixteen onward. Just before her sixteenth birthday, she wrote, "I do hope there will be a dance soon. I am just aching to go." More than likely, her parents had forbidden her to attend such gatherings until she turned sixteen, and she was eagerly anticipating the day's arrival. Her first dance came on December 4, 1891, just after her birthday: "Went to the dance, Katie, Lizzie & George R. Went with us. Had a splendid time. I danced 12 sets, every set but 5. I made two new acquaintances. . . . We got home Sat. morning 20 minutes after 4." After just a few hours' sleep, she was surprised to discover that she "didn't feel very bad after all. Helped do the housework." The next Friday night, she was dancing again. About a hundred young people attended, and Mary made her way home at nearly 3:30 in the morning. As she began her Saturday's work, however, she noted, "I don't feel very well." Evidently, Mary's dances were causing some problems with her parents. On December 29, she excitedly announced that "Ves Miller came to the schoolhouse and asked me to go to the dance with him. Of course I said I would go. I didn't know that Pa didn't want me to go with him. Oh! My! What a time! Oh! Oh! Whe-e-ew." In spite of her father's objections, she attended the dance, but "didn't enjoy myself a bit." Her father's concerns either eased or were ignored, and in January she went to dinner again with Ves Miller and attended another two dances. Her parents allowed her brothers to organize a dance at the family home in February.

In the winter of 1891 and 1892, Mary Armstrong's accounting of her activities gives the impression of a community of young people proceeding from house to house, and dance to dance, often staying out until the wee hours of the morning. In March, when there was a lull in the action, Mary complained, "I wish the young folks would have a sociable or something."[75] If Armstrong's experience is at all representative, parents allowed their older children a certain degree of leeway in pursuing their own social interests. Winter was the slack season on the farm, and as long as the day's work and school lessons were done and the next day's were not neglected, a Friday night dance might be allowable. What is surprising about these events is their sheer number and that parents allowed their children to remain out dancing until three and four in the morning. If most of these dances, like the one in the Armstrong household, occurred in family homes, parents must have assumed that other adults were chaperoning, or at least keeping an eye or ear on the proceedings. Given the size of most farm homes, parents could hardly have avoided the sights and sounds of the event. Not all girls, however, were allowed as much freedom as Mary Armstrong. In some families, parents allowed boys to go to dances, but not girls, fearing for their reputations and virtue.[76]

Dances were not the only social events for young adults organized in Armstrong's rural community. In 1896, a depression year, she attended a "poverty party":

> We thought we were dressed awfully, but the rest of the crowd looked more poverty stricken than we, rags & patches predominated. There was a large crowd & nearly everyone was dressed according to the times, & everybody had bushels of fun. Each one was asked in turn to recite a verse from memory. Every verse seemed quite appropriate. Some were composed for the occasion. George McPherson rec. the booby prize for being the best dressed. & Lillie rec. a box of bonbons for wearing the shabbiest. Arrived home cold & weary *yet perfectly happy* about 2 A.M.[77]

In addition to singular events, such as this poverty party, the teens and young adults within other communities might form their own social organizations. The "country young people" from Shelby, Iowa, formed a club, as a "diversion from the monotony." Although the content of those club meetings is unknown, they probably were much like other gatherings of young people, including singing, spelling bees, debates, dances, candy making, and other common forms of entertainment.[78] Even without the formal structure of a club, young people might gather in each other's homes for parties. The Norton children, in Pawnee County, Kansas, noted their attendance at parties where the boys played cards while the girls played dominoes. Refreshments included popcorn. Will, who was twenty, noted, "Twould have been more pleasant had there been more girls."[79]

The coming of the twentieth century brought a whole new list of possible diversions, some of them depending on a youngster's access to transportation. Seth Adolphson, born just before the turn of the century, grew up on a Rock County, Wisconsin, tobacco farm. Adolphson maintained and drove the family automobile, which allowed him to attend a wide variety of events in neighboring towns such as Edgerton and Janesville. Going to the movies was a notable occasion, and in 1917, he was able to see *Intolerance.* Other new technology aided his pursuit of leisure and a social and romantic life. The family owned a Victrola, which allowed him to listen to music. He also had access to the telephone, which made it easier for him to remain in contact with his many loves. The ability to go to town and partake of the amusements available there no doubt led Adolphson into activities of which his parents would not have approved. A memorandum in his diary listed his New Year's Resolutions for 1918, among them to quit smoking and "not to play pool for at least two months."[80] Changes in transportation and communication technology made it increasingly possible for young people to pursue separate social lives from their families, and to create a separate and distinct youth culture.

The existence of a range of social events within a community did not, however, guarantee that any one youngster would be able to attend. Work came first, and only after it was completed did parents generally allow their children to take part in social activities. Divisions within communities might also exclude some young people from the activities of the group. One particular familial example illustrates the forces that worked against inclusion for some young people. Both economic circumstances and concerns about the character of young people within the community limited the range of possible social activities for the Emery children, living in Olmsted County, Minnesota. In the 1890s and early 1900s, this family consisted of six children and their parents. The family was in debt and depended on its older children for economic support. Additionally, the mother, Helen George Emery, was the daughter of a prominent local attorney. The place of the George family in Olmsted County may have accounted for Helen Emery's distaste for many of her neighbors, most of whom she believed to be unfit companions for her children. The combination of economic distress and perceived social divisions made it difficult for the Emery children to participate in the social activities that so many youngsters, such as Mary Armstrong or Mamie Griswold, took for granted. When the circus came in June of 1904, work and a lack of funds kept the youngest Emerys at home. "Circus day & Nell wanted to go & so did Robt but they are hoeing beans instead. poor children. guess we can manage for them to go next time."[81] More often, however, it was Helen Emery's concerns about the state of the neighborhood that kept her children at home. At various times in the late nineteenth and early twentieth centuries, Emery referred to her neighbors, directly or indirectly, as improper, impious, uncivilized, and vile.[82]

The Emery daughters faced serious restrictions on their social lives. If the parents did not believe that the venue or the company was respectable, the daughters would not be allowed to attend an event. This was not an uncommon parental position, but the senior Emerys seem to have been far more strict than most parents. When attempting to socialize with others her own age, Rhoda Emery regularly encountered her parents' objections, as well as those of her proper older sister, Clara. Although she was quasi-independent, living away from home and teaching, Rhoda felt compelled to live at all times by her parents' rules. At Christmas in 1889, she went home to celebrate with her family and received invitations to join in neighborhood events. She wrote, "There was an oyster supper at Ed Nelson's Tuesday night & the boys came for us to go and we could not. Pa objected and Clara thought the crowd not respectable. Frank was very angry because we did not go and poor little Lewis was very much embarrased."[83] Even though she would have been escorted by Frank and Lewis Moulton, the sons of old family friends, she was not free to attend an event that might be frequented by a less-than-respectable crowd. Her parents also restricted her right to accept invitations from young men, as they had decided opinions about the suitability of young men as potential beaux. Thoughtless acceptance of an invitation caused Rhoda great consternation. "Oh dear! dear, dear, what shall I do. Bird Sheldon stopped this morning & asked me if I would go to the dance at Hartz's to night & I said I would & I don't know him well at all and Pa will be mad & I hadn't ought to go. Oh darn it, dash it, confound it, oh, oh, oh! I wish it would rain pitchforks, bombshells and rotten eggs so I would have to stay home. It is sprinkling some now, maybe it will rain. Why couldn't I have said no. It will ruin my reputation to go to such a place, and if I go once, how can I help going again?"[84] Much to her relief, the weather did intervene on her behalf. She wrote, "I didn't go. It did rain all night, not pitchforks or pot-hooks but just a quiet steady rain all night and all day to-day."[85] On the other hand, some activities, such as socializing with the children of old family friends, were acceptable, particularly if carried out within the bounds of the family home. "Frank and Lewis were over Saturday night and we had an old-time sing & good time but they staid so late and I was so tired."[86]

By the time Rhoda's younger sisters, Mary and Nell, were old enough to begin courting and attending parties, Helen Emery had come to the conclusion that making her home the primary site for occasions was the only way to improve her daughters' social lives: "I am going to try to keep open house for all the respectable young people who will come here & see if the girls will not enjoy themselves better than heretofore. they have always been in a great measure restricted to the select few whom my people considered proper."[87] Whether she was successful or not, she did not note. Helen Emery never seems to have been willing to challenge the idea that "her people's" concerns should dictate the social lives of her children. The elder Emerys' selectivity and conservative approach to their daughters' social lives, warranted or not, might help to account for the marital histories of the Emery daughters. Family legend contends that Caleb Emery discouraged young local men from courting his daughters on general principles. Neither Rhoda nor her younger sister, Mary, ever married, and Mary would spend a lifetime caring for her elderly parents. Clara and Nell eventually married, but at approximately thirty years of age.

Although some parents restricted their daughters' activities but allowed their sons greater leeway, the Emerys were quite careful with their younger son as well. When Robert Emery's lack of funds kept him home from a sociable, his mother commented, "Poor little Robt has worked hard hauling up wood & is feeling abused because he has no money to go to the Neighbors social this week—would get him money for anything respectable but do so hate to have my clean bright boy get in the notion of associating with Idle & the refuge crowd who attend all the Neighbors doings in Oronoco. If only I can keep him as good & honest as he is now till he is older & better able to judge people."[88] In other words, had his mother approved of the neighbors' company, she would have made it possible for him to attend the sociable. Because the neighbors were, in her opinion, disreputable, she did not. When Robert was fourteen, she cringed at the thought of him attending as seemingly innocuous an event as a school picnic: "The children are all getting ready for the school picnic to be held at Oronoco Friday. I dread it. am always afraid Robt will get hurt at such places."[89] Even when he was a sixteen-year-old, she restricted his participation in local activities. "Rob does not look well or eat much & the children going by to the party make him feel badly—wish he could live in a civilized community."[90] Emery seems to have realized, however, that the days of her control over Robert's social life were numbered. "Robt seems possessed to run & play ball & make himself sick—that slink of a Wading boy was here to invite Robt to a Sunday afternoon party. I cannot say he *must not* do things much longer—but so long as I have any influence over the dear little boy he will not go mery [sic] making on Sunday with such people as the Wadings—He feels abused but has sense enough to know that such things are wrong."[91] Helen Emery's protectiveness may very well have reflected her failures with her older son as much as her concerns for the younger. Her oldest son, James, the black sheep of the family, was a grave disappointment, continually in trouble over debts and misadventures with local girls. Having lost control of the older boy, she may have been particularly concerned to maintain the innocence and respectability of the younger. The outcome, however, was a severely restricted social life for her youngest child, much as the lives of his older sisters had been.

Issues of respectability limited the social lives of the Emery children. For others, differences in race, social class, and ethnicity surely played a similar role, restricting their access to the activities in their localities. For example, given the prejudices of native-born farming families about the work of young women of Scandinavian and German descent, it is possible that native-born parents, or perhaps even their children, may have found such young women unacceptable social contacts, perceiving them as coarse and unfeminine.[92] Ethnic considerations could cut the other way as well, with members of immigrant communities remaining within the group as much as possible for their marriage choices. In the late nineteenth century, for example, many Swedish immigrant youth practiced high levels of endogamy. Such strictures, however, might loosen over time. In the early 1880s in Trempealeau County, Wisconsin, marriages outside of one's own ethnic group were very rare, generally less than 15 percent. By 1905, one-third of all marriages of native-born, old-stock Americans were to Norwegians. In 1930, the proportion reached 50 percent.[93] Changing marriage patterns would have meant changing patterns of socialization between the young of different ethnic groups. For others, particularly African Americans,

Asians, and Native Americans, such interaction and intermarriage would have been highly unlikely. Impoverishment, either relative or absolute, would also have limited the number of homes and events open to young people. Especially in the case of male-female interaction, one's playmates were potential lifelong associates and partners, and the suitability of these associations in racial, ethnic, and class terms, among others, was serious business.

Children's accounts of their own activities, and the memories of play remaining in the minds of farm-raised adults, make it clear that recreation in all of its forms was extremely important to youngsters. This was time that was their own, and it provided an essential escape from a world that was too often (in their opinion) dominated by agricultural and household labor. A lack of entertainment and diversions could be a painful situation indeed. Effie Elsie Converse, of Eau Claire County, Wisconsin, felt a deep need for companionship, excitement, and drama. School, because it was dominated by a group of boys she found to be unpleasant, did not fulfill her social desires. The nearest Sunday School was eight miles away, and she lamented, "I wish we had a nice meeting and Sunday school and good scholars so that we could go on Sunday and not have such a long day." She longed to attend school in a town, such as Eau Claire, or a neighboring community, such as Mondovi. Above all, she wished for some excitement. In one of her more expressive moments, she wrote, "I would like to be by the side of a large herd of wild buffaloes that were frightened." Buffalo being in short supply in rural Wisconsin, she had to content herself with a new school year and the arrival of a new teacher who kept better order and organized events, such as spelling bees, for the whole community.[94]

In February of 1912, Freda Mae Rockefeller, living in Midvale, Nebraska, practically on the hundredth meridian, voiced this sentiment. "We are twenty-six miles from a railroad station. . . . I am the only child and get very lonesome; no amusements; no school and no church to go to, nor any books to read. I am very fond of reading. A neighbor's little girl loaned me her Sunday School papers which I have read over and over." She, like Effie Converse, keenly felt her lack of social contacts and entertainment. Time, and a little help from fellow readers of the *Nebraska Farmer*'s children's page, helped to remedy the situation. Months later, Freda Mae wrote, "We are now surrounded by neighbors, which seems very nice. We have a new school house three-quarters of a mile from our home and we had nearly four months of school. We have also had church here, and wish we could do so oftener. I have received many letters, papers, and books which were sent me by friends who read my last letter. I appreciate them so much and wish to thank one and all for their kindness. I still get lonesome, but will make the best of it."[95] Fortunately, this sheer absence of schools, churches, books, and other youngsters was a situation relatively few suffered. The presence of social, educational, and religious institutions, as well as other children, created the opportunity to devise games and activities, a prospect that children seem to have considered their right.

If all we knew about farm children was the content of their working lives, it would be easy to conclude that those young people were not children at all. From a very young age, they participated in their families' work, and work generally was the most important component of their day. There was little to indicate in their working lives that a childhood, as defined by modern notions of play and leisure, existed. Examination of the accounts of farm children, however, tells us something very different. Vigorous pursuit of play was an important part of farm childhood, even if it had to be squeezed into the odd moments between work and school. Children received and made toys. Many of them enjoyed reading. In most families, children expected, and indeed received, some sort of holiday celebration. Even discouraged, desperate parents, such as the Storys, attempted to create a spirit of celebration in a dismal location. Even more importantly, children created their own diversions, making use of the landscape and the resources offered them by the farm. Their imaginations allowed them to create playgrounds where others might only have seen a working environment. As they grew older, they carried their desire for diversion into the community, taking advantage of the resources offered there and developing their own organizations and pastimes. Although not all youngsters had equal access, as the case of the Emerys well illustrates, it was a rich world of play and leisure, and in many ways, it was a world that children themselves created.

6

"This Case Is a Peculiarly Hard One"

Farm Child Welfare and the State

❖ ❖ ❖ ❖ ❖ ❖ ❖ ❖ ❖ ❖ ❖ ❖ ❖ ❖ ❖

The mother and stepfather reside in Richford and are farmers. They have in part abandoned the children. That is they have failed to suitably support and care for them. . . . They are exceedingly ignorant and indigent and are cruel & inhumane in their treatment of the children. . . . Their father is dead.
—Description of the circumstances of Schret (age thirteen), David (eleven), Joseph (nine), and Harry (six), Waushara County, Wisconsin, 1895

One of the most difficult tasks a historian faces is telling the story of those who have left no written records of their own. To this point, the story of midwestern farm children has largely been told through the words of youngsters who recorded for posterity—or for their own purposes—the stories of their days. If the history of farm children, however, was derived entirely from the records of those who wrote letters and diaries, numerous children's stories would never be told. In particular, the stories of the poor, neglected, abused, and unprotected would rarely become a matter for historical scrutiny. Children such as Schret, David, Joseph, and Harry would disappear entirely from view. Without examining their lives, it is difficult, and perhaps even impossible, to measure the quality of child life on midwestern farms. Measuring a child's quality of life is also a difficult task. It is particularly difficult to measure a group's material conditions and to make a determination that fits the entire body. This chapter, by making use of public records from the state of Wisconsin, rather than children's letters and diaries, attempts to create a fuller, more complete picture of the contours of children's lives and provides a window into the well-being of farm children, especially those who lacked the capacity to speak for themselves.[1]

One measure of the well-being of children is the degree to which the children of certain classes of individuals became the wards of the state. Presumably, parents who fed, clothed, and sheltered their children adequately, and who provided them with a stable family situation, would rarely, if ever, relinquish their children to the state, or would not be forced by local officials to do so. On the other hand, children who were poorly fed, clothed, and sheltered and whose parents could not adequately care for them might become the charges of private charitable institutions or local or state governments. The best-known late nineteenth-century mechanism for dealing with indigent and dependent children was the Children's Aid Society's orphan trains, which transported youngsters from New York City to locations throughout the country, largely placing children with farming families in need of labor. Over time, the Children's Aid Society's methods lost favor, largely because of the wholesale distribution of children to homes of unknown quality and the lack of supervision of these placements.[2] In response to these concerns, state legislatures developed "importation and exportation laws" governing the interstate movement of dependent children. States made it increasingly difficult for organizations to transport children across state lines for foster care, although individuals continued to be able to do so legally in order to adopt youngsters.[3]

Less well known than the Children's Aid Society were the many other structures that existed for the care of needy children in rural communities. Throughout the midwest, impoverished farm families that had reached the end of their resources might apply to their local governments for "outdoor relief," or aid administered outside of the poorhouse. The general procedure once a family had appealed to the public coffers for aid was for the poor commissioner to make an investigation. The commissioner or other county official would visit the family home and gather information from neighbors. A family classified as among the "worthy poor" might receive some sort of aid from the county (groceries, food, clothing, fuel), whereas the unworthy poor might be sent to the poor farm or called into court.[4] In Polk County, Wisconsin, for example, several different types of families qualified as the worthy poor. Family tragedies classified as acts of God tended to qualify otherwise respectable families as members of the worthy poor. If an unexpected death occurred, for example, the poor commissioner was likely to take pity on the suffering family. When Hans Madsen died in 1883, his widow petitioned for aid and received provisions, clothing, and incidentals including "a yoke of steers, to be Co[unty] property." Over the course of two years, the family accepted more than $100 in material aid. The poor commissioner classified others as "temporary paupers," needing aid to survive unexpected (and unfortunately undefined) setbacks. To several families experiencing such setbacks, the poor commissioner awarded food and clothing, as well as seed wheat. Another farmer, facing setbacks three years running, received aid including "team hire." When in December 1883 Fritz March broke his leg while chopping wood, his neighbors, as well as the county, came to his aid. As the poor commissioner recorded, "He is a hard working, sober & honest man, has 5 small children, no means, german by birth. The people of Oseola [township] wishing to aid him, started a subscription list & I signed for the county & paid by order." The taxpayers of Polk County contributed $10 to the aid of the March family, in addition to the private contributions of friends and neighbors. The March family, as well as any other, exhibited the characteristics of the worthy poor, being sober, honest, and hard working.[5] In cases where the family was large and their problems were likely to be transitory, limited and carefully circumscribed outdoor relief was the accepted way to cope with poverty.

Not everyone's problems, however, could be solved with the careful application of $10 here, or $20 and some seed wheat there. Counties were ill-equipped to cope with the chronically poor and had little patience with those they considered to be the unworthy poor. The itinerant rural poor, without permanent abodes and with reputations for trouble, found themselves quite literally driven from community to community as counties attempted to control demands on their poor funds. One family of at least ten members, which in 1913 came to rest in Eau Claire County, Wisconsin, quickly learned that it was not wanted and would not be tolerated by local authorities. County officials knew the father and oldest sons to be "great Boose Fighters" and that the oldest daughter was an unmarried mother. Evicted previously by the sheriff of Chippewa County from a farm near Cadott, they were then driven from land they had squatted on in Eau Claire County. After leaving Eau Claire County, they moved on to neighboring Dunn County. In each location, they owned no property and quickly exhausted the patience of those on whose land they camped. As rural poor people without permanent address, they had no right to the largesse of Eau Claire County, or any other.[6] In the 1920s, a Children's Bureau report noted that when poor commissioners and other officials in rural counties dealt with impoverished and troublesome residents, they generally used expressions such as "cleaned up the nest," "wiped out that hole," and "broke up that outfit," indicating in strong metaphorical terms what local officials and communities generally believed about the poor in their midst.[7]

The most indigent of the resident poor might become the wards of the county in which they lived and move into the county poorhouse or poor farm. Poor farms generally provided room and board for destitute widows and their small children, unmarried mothers, the indigent elderly, and the mentally and physically disabled. Children, however, posed a special problem because of the seeming impropriety of housing them alongside the mentally, or morally, unfit, as the poor were often judged. An examination of poor farm records shows why, by the late nineteenth century, localities were beginning to try to find alternative locations to house dependent and neglected children. Between 1885 and 1887, the poor farm in rural Polk County, Wisconsin, sheltered more than twenty inmates. Some came because they were ill and had nowhere else to turn. When they recovered, they left the poor farm. The poor commissioner recorded the majority, however, as either insane or "imbeciles," some of whom he or a judge considered dangerous when at large. Only one minor male, of unspecified age, described as a rowdy, suffering from syphilis, lived at the poor farm.[8] The poor farm was not, perhaps, the best choice of accommodation for youngsters.

By the late nineteenth century, midwestern states were beginning to formulate other solutions to the problem of indigent children. Michigan was one of the first states to address this issue, its legislature in 1871 passing a law designed to create a state institution specifically for the education and care of poor children. The state intended to remove children from county poorhouses and to avoid state subsidies to private institutions for the care of such children. Michigan's school opened in 1874.[9] The Wisconsin state legislature, following Michigan's lead, created the Wisconsin State Public School, a home for dependent and neglected children. The State School, in Sparta, is an excellent vehicle for studying midwestern child welfare because of its pioneering nature, the long duration of its existence, and the completeness of its records. Before the creation of the school, there were few options, beyond the poorhouse, for the care of dependent children. The Wisconsin Industrial School for Girls and the Wisconsin Industrial School for Boys accepted incorrigible children, but those whose only crime was familial poverty or dissolution might be committed there too. Criminal records for Polk County, Wisconsin, demonstrate the circumstances under which local judges might commit minors to the industrial schools. In 1882 and 1883, Polk County sent four children from one family to the Industrial School for Girls in Milwaukee. The county court committed the oldest child, age fourteen, for "leading a depraved and abandoned life" and frequenting "the company of lewd, wanton and lacivious [sic] persons." Her father was convicted and imprisoned in December 1882 for "having been found guilty of the crime of rape upon the person of his own daughter." Three other children, two boys and one girl, all aged eight or younger, also went to the Industrial School for Girls, their mother testifying that they were in danger of "falling into habits of vice without a careful education." Their mother also attested to her poverty and her inability to support her children. The judge ordered that the boys be transferred to the Industrial School for Boys once they turned ten.[10] Had their cases come before the court just four years later, the oldest would still most likely have gone to the State Industrial School for Girls, but the younger children would have been committed to the State Public School.

The legislature created the State Public School to remedy many different familial situations, including the one above. The home opened in 1886, was renamed the Wisconsin Child Center in 1947, and finally closed in 1976. Between 1886 and 1912, the years for which the records of the school are both open and most complete, school officials considered 3,887 children for placement.[11] The school received children from all parts of the state and from nearly every ethnic and racial group then present. Records indicate that many were the children of the native born, but many were also Irish, French, Norwegian, German, Polish, African American, English, Belgian, Canadian, Welsh, Scottish, Dutch, Danish, Bohemian, Swedish, Swiss, and Italian. Although county officials suggested some Native American children for placement, the State Public School generally redirected them to the Indian School at Wittenberg, Wisconsin.

Most of the children were not orphans in the sense that both of their parents were dead. Instead, many were "half orphans," with one living parent who was generally unable to care for them and to some degree dependent on the public coffers. Some of the youngsters were residents of county poorhouses or had been abandoned. Others were the children of alcoholic parents (called intemperate in the nineteenth century) or parents who were incarcerated in one of the state's institutions, such as the prison at Waupon or the mental hospital at Mendota. Many had living family members, but they were either unwilling or unable to care for them.[12] An early twentieth-century study of the school found that more than 50 percent of the children the school indentured and that more than 25 percent of the children the school placed for adoption had "two living parents who had evaded their responsibility for the care and support of the children, or from whom it had been necessary to remove the children because of neglect or bad home conditions."[13]

The circumstances from which children came are an excellent corrective to the idea of a mythic past in which children were better treated and more carefully raised. Many, like young Charlotte, whose case is described here, came from appalling situations. Investigators described her mother as "devoid of moral sense" in her illicit relations with men, her drinking, her stealing, and her "almost inhuman" treatment of her own children. Her son had been crippled by a fall from the porch that occurred while she was drunk; a daughter's ear bore a scar from an injury she inflicted. Charlotte's mother attempted to persuade her to become a prostitute to help support the family. Dismayed by his wife's behavior, Charlotte's father abandoned his family.[14] Unfortunately, Charlotte and her siblings were not alone in their woe. Among the most common reasons children came to the State School were parental immorality, desertion, neglect, intemperance, poverty, and lack of financial support.[15]

In the years between 1887 and 1901, the children committed to the State Public School from Eau Claire County showed essentially the same characteristics as the larger body of children, except in the limited range of their ethnic origins. Most of those from Eau Claire County were native born, although youngsters of Norwegian, German, and French Canadian heritage also appear in the record. In fourteen years, county officials sent sixty-two children from thirty-five families to the school. Only five of those children, from two families, were farm children. Just over half the group, or thirty-four children, were half orphans, with either their mother or father dead. Only two children were completely orphaned. Thirty-one had been abandoned by one or both parents, and several by both their birth and adoptive parents. It was not uncommon for these children to have a parent in the poorhouse or judged insane. Several had parents who were awaiting trial or in jail for crimes including prostitution, assault and battery on a child, and larceny. One youngster's father was serving a life sentence in Waupon for having poisoned his mother with strychnine. The woeful circumstances affecting the larger body of children in the school were mirrored by the sad stories of the youngsters in Eau Claire County.[16]

For families from throughout the state, the school functioned in several different ways. First, it did indeed care for and educate children from families that could not or would not care for their children. The goal was not, however, for children to remain permanently in residence at the school. Before the turn of the century, the school's administrators did not admit children under the age of three because it did not intend to act as an adoption agency or to provide custodial care for small children on site. The legislation creating the school specified that it would be only a "temporary home," pending the placement of children with "good families." The state expected that within sixty days of admission, most children would be placed in suitable households.[17] As a result, the school indentured a large number of children with families throughout the state, in precursors to modern foster homes. The indenturing families requested children from the state and signed contracts promising to send the children to school, teach them a useful occupation, provide them "kind and proper treatment as a member of the family," and pay them a set sum of money upon release from their indentures.[18] In the period between 1913 and 1917, less than half, or 43 percent, would spend their time in a single indenturing home. Many would live in two, three, or more homes over a course of years.[19] School officials placed children in successive indentures until they reached the age of sixteen, were returned to their families, were adopted by an indenturing family, or ran away. Families would legally adopt approximately one-sixth of children sent to the school.[20] Some children were indentured to their own families, an arrangement that allowed them to remain with their parents but receive supervision from school investigators. School officials also allowed some boys to strike out on their own before the age of sixteen, if they were physically and mentally mature and capable of self-support.

The school rejected some children as unfit or inappropriate for the purposes of the school. The school returned a large number of physically handicapped children to their home counties, presumably because the school was unequipped to deal with their problems and the children were believed to be unable to complete indentures. Even so, some children with handicaps did arrive in Sparta. Uncertain that local governments would adequately care for them, school officials allowed a number of them to remain. Only in 1921, however, did school policy specify that it would accept youngsters with serious physical limitations, and then subject to the proviso that those physical conditions were "amenable to cure or amelioration by surgical or other means." Children who proved incorrigible went to either the Industrial School for Girls in Milwaukee or the State Industrial School for Boys in Waukesha. Children with developmental disabilities were redirected to the State School for the Feeble Minded, while the courts committed insane children to the state hospital at Mendota. A selection of records of children rejected by the school indicates that school administrators judged them to be "Diseased and Deformed" and "Feeble Minded." Others "could not talk," "had spells when . . . insane," or were "partially paralyzed."[21] The State School was prepared only to serve the physically and mentally fit and the tractable.

When parents relinquished their children or the courts removed them from their homes, those children were potentially gone for good. When a child went to the State Public School, the state took custody of that child and could then arrange for the child's care as it pleased. Although state law did not specifically allow it, judges could arrange for temporary commitments for families suffering what was presumed to be temporary stress. The vast majority of parents, however, retained no right to regain custody at a future date, although they could petition to do so. Parents were sometimes surprised to discover that the school had the right to transfer their children to other institutions without appealing to the courts and to put them up for adoption without the consent of the parents, because the school was empowered to act on the child's behalf. Although local officials were supposed to make this situation clear to parents when their children were committed to the school, they did not always do so. Only after 1920 did the Wisconsin Supreme Court rule that the school had to obtain parents' permission before children could be placed in adoptive homes.[22]

Farms and farming families maintained a complex relationship with the State Public School. The way in which the agricultural community was most tightly tied to the school was through its placing out system. Families requested that children be indentured to them. From the beginning, the school's administrators preferred to place youngsters in farm homes because of a philosophical preference for farm homes and rural communities common to the era: "The absence of doubtful associations in the communities of which they are a part, give the great number of chances in favor of a safe growth in the formative period."[23] Additionally, school officials may have been concerned about the impact of institutionalization on children's health, preferring that they live in the countryside rather than in a crowded boarding school environment, where children often died in large numbers.[24] The children themselves had no choice about their ultimate destination or the type of work they would engage in.[25] Among children indentured between 1913 and 1917, 81 percent went to farm homes, 3 percent to villages, and 16 percent to cities. A Children's Bureau investigator explained this phenomenon: "Most of the homes secured are on farms, because the families there are in constant need of the kind of help that can be given by a boy or girl."[26]

In the years between 1889 and 1906 (again, the years for which records are available), the majority of applicants requested children between the ages of ten and fourteen, children of prime working age. Requesters asked for boys and girls in roughly equal numbers, reflecting the need for both field and domestic labor. School officials investigated each individual and family applying for a child, and the officials' comments indicate a sensitivity to the quality of the homes in which children might be placed. The school's officials had no objections, on general terms, to placing children with farming families. When the Fitzpatrick family requested a fourteen-year-old boy in May 1889, the investigating officer approved the application, because "party is good honest industrious farmer." The Richardson family, applying in March of 1891, also received approval: "Mr. R. is a retired farmer of considerable means, and will give the child a good home."[27]

The State School's investigators, however, also rejected many farming families because of the treatment that indentured children might receive in their homes. Although it was acceptable and expected that families would employ their indentured children, it was not acceptable for those families to work children too hard. Notes on a rejected application for a ten-year-old girl read: "The woman is very cross, and peevish. She wants a girl for work only." Another application, made the next day, received essentially the same comments: "Would work children very hard and would hardly ever give them enough to eat." A Mr. McHugh requested a boy, age fourteen or fifteen, and was also rejected: "Drinking man. Expects a boy to do a man's work & he sits around." Another rejection read: "This man wants a hired man. Have no boys at the school able to do the work required." The school expected indenturing individuals and families to desire a child first, and a worker second. Families' prior treatment of their own children also figured into the equation: "Has worked his own sons (12 or 13 yrs) till they ran away from home."[28]

Appropriate levels of work were not the school's only concern. The agency demanded that indentured children be allowed to attend school to age sixteen. Several applicants were rejected because they would not pledge to send older children to school: "Mrs. R. would not agree to send children to school after fourteen." Others, regardless of what they said about sending a child to school, lived too far from the schoolhouse, in the investigators' estimation. Families living more than two miles from schools (the limit beyond which a family was no longer required by state law to send a child to school) might also receive rejections.[29] Appropriate gender roles also concerned investigating officers. Families wanting boys to do girls' work, such as tending infants, received rejections, as did families in which women did field work. The school rejected a family requesting a seven- or eight-year-old girl because the "girl would be expected to work out doors if necessary, and I think it would be necessary." The Stemmers, who requested a twelve- to fourteen-year-old girl, were rejected on the same grounds. "Mrs. S. is today working in the field. Home not neat & clean. As there are no girls at school who can be both hired man and hired girl, I have rejected the house." The Schultz rejection was more terse: "Home dirty. Woman does man's work."[30] These comments reflected urban, middle-class assumptions about the nature of work, failing to recognize the necessity of women's field work for many families, as well as failing to understand ethnic differences in the gender appropriateness of work that operated in many German American and Scandinavian American homes.

Beyond requiring an approved balance of work and school, the moral climate of indenturing families was extremely important. Many applicants failed in their quest for a child because of a history of drunkenness, or even because they were related to the local saloon keeper. Investigators rejected others because they had unspecified poor morals, or had raised unruly, badly trained children. Concerns about maintaining girls' chastity lurked behind other comments, such as "there are three worthless boys in the house" and "he is a widower, and I do not think it best to place a girl there."[31] The experience of one youngster, indentured to a New Richmond farmer, underscored the necessity of careful investigation of foster families. Her case worker wrote, "Emma had a disagreeable experience with Mr. Christopherson and was in the Woman's Christian Home at St. Paul for one year. Christopherson was arrested and sentenced to Waupon for the term of fifteen years."[32] Although the information in the school records is not complete, the description in the register, coupled with county records, paints a clearer picture. According to Polk County court documents, Christopherson was convicted of "carnal intercourse with a female under the age of 14 years."[33] Given the length of Emma's stay in the Women's Christian home, a home for unwed mothers, she probably gave birth to a child and put it up for adoption before returning to the school and again being indentured. This was certainly not the type of moral climate and indenture experience that the school's officials wanted for its charges.

Although the agency's investigators rejected many applicants for State School children, they also accepted many, and large numbers of children coming through the school spent some time, if not years, either in one or a series of indentures. They would have fulfilled their indentures by attending to the normal duties of farm children and, if the foster family followed the terms laid down by the agency, attending school. Sometimes the placements worked well, and children remained with their foster families for years, treated as a "member of the family."[34] Families might go beyond what was expected by the school and adopt the children placed in their homes. This was most common for youngsters who were indentured as very small children, age five or younger. Other placements were less satisfactory. A Grant County farmer returned one eleven-year-old after the youngster "set fire to hay stack and was very mischiveous [sic] and unruly." He was sent on to other, presumably equally unsuccessful, indentures, and two years later ran away, never to appear in the school's records again.[35] Other children had fatally unsuccessful indentures, dying in farm accidents, such as being kicked by a horse or run over by a wagon.[36] Other youngsters survived the experience in good form, and the school emancipated them, convinced of their ability to fend for themselves. After serving a series of indentures, the school superintendent emancipated a young Frank Jenks. "This boy on account of his age and his knowledge of farm work, his size, strength, etc., was permitted to go away and work for himself." The superintendent gave him $6 to pay his way to Spring Valley, Minnesota, to begin agricultural work. "There is no doubt but the young man can support himself and lay up some money."[37]

Although some children's cases were well documented, other children simply slipped from view upon their indenture. In some cases, this was the result of deliberate acts on the part of foster families. As was noted in one girl's case, who was admitted as a three-year-old and immediately indentured out, "Mrs. Huganir [the indenturing party] was very much attached to the child and wished to adopt her and the agent recommended adoption and blanks were sent but nothing farther was done in regard to the adoption. It is possible that Mrs. Huganir wished the school to lose trace of the child, as sometimes our guardians fear the parents will claim them and take pains to leave no trace of their residence." The record concluded, "Sometimes people become very much attached to our wards, especially if they have them when they are very small and fear they will be taken from them."[38] For most children, there was not even this degree of explanation of their experiences, but instead a list, short or long, of indentures, permanent placements, returns to their home communities, marriages, and sometimes deaths. What is clear, however, is that most of the children spent time on farms, and that in the late nineteenth and early twentieth centuries, the State Public School served as one of the largest employment agencies in the state of Wisconsin, placing thousands of workers on farms, albeit very young ones.

It is not surprising, given the attitudes of the age, that relatively few families indenturing children actually adopted their charges. Most indenturing adults seem to have had work in mind when they brought a child into their homes. Maintaining a child as a worker in the home did not require or even suggest adoption. Additionally, fears about a child's heredity would have prevented many from legally adopting State School children and making them a permanent part of the family. Americans generally assumed that parental traits such as shiftlessness, poverty, and promiscuity were inheritable. The environment into which a child was born was presumably inescapable, making children with questionable backgrounds unappealing choices for adoption.[39] That the majority of children at the school still had one or two living parents also would have been a barrier to adoption, as potential adoptive parents often feared that a living relative, at some future date, would try to reclaim the child.[40] Other families, in spite of developing a strong tie of affection with a child, might reject official adoption in favor of a lifelong, unofficial association. Legal adoption was expensive, time-consuming, and complicated, and many families "simply did not place a great deal of importance on a legal piece of paper." As historian Julie Berebitsky has commented, other families rejected the idea that a court's decree "contributed to the legitimacy of their family."[41] The officials of the State Public School did not pursue the issue, seemingly content with finding foster families, preferably on farms, for its wards.

The other relationship that farm families maintained with the State Public School was as contributors of charges. This, however, was a minor role, compared to that of employer of wards of the state. Although between 1886 and 1913, the case histories of 3,887 youngsters appear in the school's records, only 208, or slightly more than 5 percent, were identified as the children of farmers or farm laborers. Although the investigating official did not always list an occupation for the parents of the child, he or she attempted to do so if that information was at all available. That only about 5 percent of these children were the children of farming families is a somewhat surprising statistic, because in 1900 agriculture employed 36.8 percent of all adult workers in Wisconsin.[42] Farm children were vastly underrepresented within the population of youngsters at the State Public School. In fact, in those cases where a parental occupation could be determined, the great majority of those youngsters who ended up wards of the State School were the children of common laborers, unskilled workers who survived by taking whatever form of work was available. In Eau Claire County, for example, among those youngsters whose parents' occupations were identified, five were the children of farmers, nine were the children of skilled laborers, and twenty-two were the children of common or unskilled laborers.[43] Among the farm children who came to the State School, parental illness or disability, death of one or both parents, and the advanced age of the father were most often the culprit, sending ninety-three children to the school. Parental desertion sent another thirty-eight children to the school, while thirty-one arrived due to parental cruelty or neglect. The others came to Sparta for a variety of reasons: a parent's institutionalization or alcoholism, a child's incorrigibility, or general familial poverty. After 1901, the school increasingly served as an adoption agency, as it began to accept infants and place them in permanent homes within weeks or months of their admission. Between 1901 and 1912, eleven infants, either the children of unmarried farm daughters or farmers, found new homes through the State School.[44]

In theory, the State Public School served as a safety net for farm families lacking support from friends, neighbors, and extended family. If an obliging judge provided an order of temporary care, parents might be able to retrieve their children; otherwise, they might very well lose custody permanently.[45] Unfortunately, the type of commitment was rarely recorded in the school's intake records. Instead, we find cases such as that of the Hovede family, which in 1895 sent four of its children to the school. The mother had been committed to the State Hospital for the Insane, and with five other children at home, the eldest being physically disabled, the father could no longer care for his family. Three children fulfilled indentures, while the fourth went to the Wisconsin Home for the Feeble Minded.[46] The Morrison children, a nine-year-old and two-year-old twins, came to the school because their mother had died and their father was ill, waiting on an operation for appendicitis. Unable to care for his children himself, he also could not afford to hire anyone to care for them. All three children were indentured.[47] Seven-year-old Stephen Warpechowski's case was a particularly sad, and well-documented, one. He ended up at the State School as a result of his mother's death and his father's poverty and inability to care properly for him, in the judgment of the investigating officer. Although his father was "greatly attached to him and desirous of retaining the custody thereof," Stephen lived more than four miles from the nearest school, with the roads being "nearly impassable." The father, trying to develop a forty-acre homestead with only two acres cleared, spent a great deal of time working away from home. Because his father was unable to afford any sort of hired help, seven-year-old Stephen spent much of his time alone in the family's windowless cabin, with the nearest neighbor more than three miles away. The investigating officer noted that "this case is a peculiarly hard one." The state took Stephen from his resisting father, "with the hope that within a year or so, this child may be returned to his father upon proper showing that his circumstances and surroundings are such as will make it proper for such return." There was no indication, however, that Stephen ever returned to his father's homestead.[48]

A particularly interesting question, and one that cannot be answered completely, is why farm children came to the Wisconsin State Public School in such small numbers, relative to the proportion of farmers in the general population. As previously mentioned, the vast majority of youngsters whose parents' occupations could be determined were the children of common laborers. After 1901, most of the infants surrendered to the school had been born to domestic servants, their fathers unknown. Any number of interpretations of these facts are possible. On the negative side, this may have been the product of the public nature of poverty and neglect in urban areas. Impoverished, dependent children in an urban environment would have been far more visible than children in isolated, rural neighborhoods. This relative invisibility may have led to fewer farm children being sent to the State School by public authorities. Another possible interpretation is that, relative to common laborers, farm families had more resources with which to care for their children. Common laborers, without property and finding themselves unemployed, would have been hard pressed to feed their families and care for their children. Domestic servants, generally single and living and working in someone else's home, would have had even fewer resources. Farmers, on the other hand, except in the most dire circumstances, would have had land upon which to grow gardens and to raise chickens, pigs, and cows, and thus would have had the bare essentials with which to feed their families. By the 1870s, although just over 30 percent of Americans lived in cities, two-thirds of convicted vagrants came from urban centers.[49] The land provided a safety net of sorts that unskilled laborers did not have.

Farm families may have also had access to informal networks of child support that other working families did not. Children had high value within the farming community as laborers and would have been attractive to extended family, friends, and neighbors as potential workers. As was demonstrated in Chapter 2, some families hired their children out simply for room and board and did not ask for wages. If a family was in trouble and needed to send children away temporarily, there was a strong possibility that an aunt, uncle, or grandparent, or even a neighbor, would be willing to take that child into their home, at least as a stopgap measure. Perhaps the best evidence for this interpretation was that there were thousands of families throughout Wisconsin that were willing to apply to the State School, have their circumstances investigated by the school's agents, and bring a completely unknown child into their homes, in order to have another set of hands to do either field or domestic work. Instead of sending large numbers of children to the State School, farm homes served as the means of providing what state officials hoped would be a better atmosphere and a more hopeful future to the state's dependent and neglected children.

The history of the indenture program of the State Public School also provides an additional means of evaluating the well-being of children on Wisconsin's farms. In the early 1920s, Emma O. Lundberg, an investigator for the Children's Bureau, wrote a draft report about the conditions under which children indentured by the Wisconsin State Public School lived. The Children's Bureau never published the report, which was in many ways quite critical of Wisconsin's efforts. Instead, in 1926, the Children's Bureau published a report on fostering that criticized placing out and indenture systems in general.[50] Nevertheless, the unpublished report contains a treasure trove of information about childhood indenture on Wisconsin's farms. The Children's Bureau studied all children indentured between 1913 and 1917, gathering demographic data and interviewing children and, when possible, their biological and foster parents. During those years, 452 children participated in the indenture program; of that group, 298 found adoptive homes. Lundberg eliminated from the study those children who had been adopted (most of whom were very young and who had very short indentures), as well as seventy-seven who were, by the time of the study, geographically inaccessible. She focused on the case histories of the remaining seventy-seven individuals who had fulfilled indentures in the four years before World War I.

The stories of these seventy-seven provide telling insights into child life on Wisconsin's early twentieth-century farms. Certainly, their lives and experiences cannot be classified as typical. Many lived in appalling conditions before being sent to the State Public School. At best, they came from families that were loving but terribly poor. At worst, they had been abandoned, abused, and forced to witness all varieties of parental misbehavior and depravity. Their experiences provide several lenses through which to view midwestern child life at the century's turn. First, these children's histories can tell us about some of the worst conditions under which impoverished and neglected farm children lived. Second, they can tell us under what conditions farm families employed child laborers. And finally, these stories can tell us about the range of children's experiences on turn-of-the-century midwestern farms, because some families treated indentured children exceptionally well, while others neglected and abused them badly. These seventy-seven young people, who spent at least part of their early years on farms, attest to the many problems and possibilities facing youngsters in rural communities.

The testimony Emma Lundgren collected is an excellent corrective to the idea that farm homes provided, in all cases, the best place to raise children. Parents who made serious miscalculations about their ability to support their families on the land might have little to offer their children but drudgery and poverty. In 1916, Alma and Alfred (their surnames were not revealed, for reasons of privacy) became wards of the state when their immigrant father was no longer able to support them. After his wife's death, their father was left with four children whom he attempted to support on "an 80-acre stretch of sandy, valueless land." The old schoolhouse the family planned to move to the farm as their home lost its internal plaster and external clapboards during transport, leaving only "an old, one-roomed log house." With a $600 mortgage and no one to help him, the children's father believed he had no choice but to appeal to the township, and then the county, for aid. Because of the impoverished condition of the family, county officials encouraged the father to send his two middle children to the State Public School.[51]

Although Alma and Alfred's family was poor and motherless, there was no evidence of abuse or serious neglect. For four-year-old Marian and her three siblings, the situation was much worse. Their father, unwilling to do his share of work on the family's "unfertile acres," left the running of the farm to his wife and small children, while he "frequently lounged around saloons and pool halls." The mother soon tired of contributing her earnings from gardening and care of the family's livestock to her husband's gambling and drinking and began to spend her time in the pool halls as well, becoming a prostitute. "Four little children, cold and hungry, were often left alone at the little farmhouse all night." The poor commissioner investigated the home and attempted to help with food and cash for rent. An aunt who wanted to adopt them was not allowed to do so because she had six children herself and lived in a home that was "dirty and much overcrowded." When officials found the children alone once too often, they committed Marian and her two sisters to the State Public School, while their infant brother remained with their mother.[52] These stories, unfortunately, were all too typical.

After the state took (or parents surrendered) children from poor, but loving, or poor, abusive, and neglectful homes, it sent them into a range of foster families almost as broad as the range of families from which they had come. Lundberg and the Children's Bureau classified virtually all of the homes of origin of the State School's wards as unsatisfactory and detrimental to their physical or emotional health, stating that these homes were the source of "degenerating influences." Under the best of circumstances, the farm homes to which the school sent youngsters "may in many cases have meant better opportunities for the children to build up bodies and character." Unfortunately, investigation revealed that many of the foster homes were not of the best quality. In spite of the efforts the State Public School's officials put into finding suitable homes for children, those efforts fell short of their goal. This was, perhaps, a foregone conclusion, given the limited number of investigators who carried out their work over a large state, many parts of which were poorly served by roads. Following the Children's Bureau's study of 540 homes indenturing children, Lundberg concluded that nearly half of those homes, or 262, provided conditions that were detrimental to foster children. A number of factors went into a classification of detrimental, such as foster parents neglecting a child, depriving the child of school, or making the child work too hard. A "morally bad," "ignorant," or "disorderly" home also fit into the same category. Another 236 homes were satisfactory. She judged only forty-two of the investigated homes to be "high grade," providing the best possible conditions for a child's healthy growth and development.[53] Some of Lundberg's objections reflected an antirural bias, as well as a lack of understanding of the workings of, and familial constraints operating within, rural communities. Other objections reflected fundamental problems with a foster care system that relied on indenturing children to individuals who had no long-term interest in the health and well-being of the youngsters in their care, something that should unfortunately be unsurprising even to observers in the twenty-first century.

Given the Children's Bureau's emphasis on the importance of education, Lundberg's primary concern with the experience of indentured children in farm homes was the neglect of their education. "The home in which this fundamental of child welfare is neglected," she wrote, "can not be considered a satisfactory one, no matter what its other attributes may be."[54] The State Public School required that indenturing families send children to school 120 days of the year, significantly less than the 160-day school year she believed to be appropriate. Although 60 percent of the children in indenture homes attended more than the minimum schooling, a full 40 percent of the children whose records she and her investigators examined had not even attended 120 days.[55] The histories of these children often showed a marked lack of attention to education: "Boy, three-year period from 13–15 years of age: School attendance 109, 83, and 69 days out of 160-day school year. Grades 4–6. Kept out for work. Boy did not like school and would not study." "Boy, 14 years: Grade 3. Attended 47 out of 180 days. Four weeks late entering fall, and other absences due to work." "Girl, 13–16 years: Irregular attendance. Teacher reported that the girl was always tired, and that she did poor work. She believed the girl worked so hard that she did not have time to prepare her lessons."[56] The ultimate result of poor attendance was often a child who could not keep up with his or her peers in the classroom.

> As a result he would fall below grade, gradually become older than most of the children in his grade, grow to dislike school, and be glad of any excuse to remain out. Then the parents would say that the child did not like school, did not want to attend, made no progress in school, and preferred to stay home and work. These excuses were used as pretexts for withdrawing the child from school.[57]

Children who labored under serious disadvantages often failed to receive the benefits that even a grammar school education would have afforded them.

The Children's Bureau, however, wanted even more for these youngsters. Lundberg noted that only the smallest number of them lived with families that sent them on to high school or additional training. Most high schools were more than five miles away from foster homes. In such cases, to attend high school would have required access to transportation or boarding in town, expenses not easily borne by foster parents. Additionally, sending a child to school out of the immediate neighborhood deprived the indenturing family of the youngster's labor, the reason for which most families had accepted a child. Because the indenture contract required children to go to school until age sixteen, and youngsters might finish the eighth grade by age thirteen or fourteen, they ended up repeating eighth grade several times, if they attended school at all. "Naturally the child hated school, became a behavior problem, was absent frequently, and gained no advantage from attendance." In many ways, by setting high school and further vocational training as the standard, the Children's Bureau was suggesting that the dependent wards of the state be given more in terms of education and training than many foster families, especially farm families, could afford for their own children.[58] In 1920, in most rural communities, a high school education remained the exception rather than the rule.

For indentured children, as with most farm children, it was work that interfered with attendance and achievement in school. Christina, indentured on a farm with her twin brother at the age of eleven, lived more than two miles from the school. The two attended roughly sixty days of school each year. The balance of her time was spent in doing a great deal of housework for a foster mother who was in poor health and helping with the milking. The neighbors agreed that "the foster parents expected an endless amount of work from the two children."[59] Nine-year-old Elbert worked on a rented farm for his foster parents, "hoeing corn and potatoes all day, even on Sundays. Besides this he did chores, pulled weeds, gathered eggs, and carried wood. Much of the work was beyond the boy's strength." Although 135 school days passed while he lived in this home, he attended 100 and was only in the first grade.[60] Seventeen-year-old Sophie, brought into her foster home to be a maid, cared for the family's children and did "practically all the housework." Another youngster who had once lived in the same home commented, "They always treat you rough in that place and expect you to work." Because of years of repeated absences, by the time Sophie was sixteen, she had only achieved the academic skills of a child in the third or fourth grade.[61] Unfortunately, the Children's Bureau investigators did not include the kind of information that would make it possible to compare the absences and hours of work of indentured children with those of children born to these families. In some cases, it is likely that all children in the household would have been deprived of schooling and would have labored under equally difficult workloads. Neighbors considered the farmer who indentured Christina to be quite "mean": "he refused to have extra help, insisting that the members of the family should work the farm themselves."[62] In other cases, families indentured youngsters to spare themselves and their own sons and daughters from work.[63]

The lack of "advantages" present in farming communities also concerned investigators. As Lundberg wrote, "No attention appears to have been paid by the State school to any kind of cultural development in the homes in behalf of the children placed there." In particular, she worried about the lack of organized recreation for children, such as Boy and Girl Scouts, Camp Fire Girls, and similar youth-oriented social activities, although she did note the beginning of activities similar to those found in 4-H clubs. She also lamented the lack, in some communities, of Sunday schools or other church-related activities for young people. At home, children had little access to musical instruments or reading material. They might not even be taught about "the beautiful natural surroundings in which they lived." As a result of the lack of amenities, she believed that the older children were being drawn into dubious pursuits. "Young people would think nothing of driving 35 miles or more to dance halls, which were generally survivals of the days when beer and stronger drinks were served in them. In these entertainments the older of the indentured children frequently took part."[64]

Whether there was such a complete lack of social activity in rural communities, or whether investigators simply chose not to look too deeply, is unclear. As discussed in Chapter 5, other young people, born and raised in the country, commented on a fairly healthy variety of formal and informal social events available in rural communities. Whether State School children, or others who were economically, ethnically, or racially outside of the mainstream, would have been included in the round of community events for the young is another matter altogether. There is evidence that because of their origins as dependent children and wards of the state, indentured youngsters experienced prejudice in both foster homes and their communities. The prevailing view of children born to less-than-perfect homes being permanently tainted by their parentage would have made adults wary of the character and suitability of State School children as playmates.[65] Investigators claimed that adults exaggerated the faults of the children, and other youngsters absorbed those prejudices. "In several instances the State school children refused to go to school because the boys were rough to them and they were made to feel uncomfortable because other children would not play with them and only picked on them and called them names."[66] As stressed previously, not everyone was made to feel a part of the larger rural community, and in many cases indentured children remained needed but still unwelcome visitors.

Worst of all were cases where children went from abuse in their homes of origin to abuse at the hands of foster parents. Herman, deserted by his mother, who was later declared insane, went to work at age eleven for a family whose home "showed every evidence of shiftlessness and poverty." He was kept out of school, worked hard, and beaten "unmercifully." As an adult, his back still showed the scars from the beatings he endured. When he moved to a second indenture, his new foster mother "found the little fellow's back all raw, and his filthy underwear blood-stained where the lashes had cut through his skin."[67] Elbert, whose story is told above, also experienced abuse that went beyond overly taxing work expectations. After being whipped severely, he ran away. His foster parents' neighbors joined in the search for him, not to return him to his abuser, but to protect him. When they found him in an apple tree, he would only come down when promised he would not be going back to the same home. The neighbors discovered that his body was "black and blue and cut from the lashes he had received. Seven of the neighbors went to the home and accused the farmer of cruelty and abuse, and he acknowledged having whipped the boy."[68] Fortunately, the State School subsequently placed both Herman and Elbert with caring families. Elbert's new foster mother, in fact, "treated the boy as one of her own children, and . . . he seemed to be quite happy there."[69]

As the above would suggest, there was a significant range of indenture experiences, just as there was a significant range of farm children's experiences in their own homes. Although many of the indenture experiences were quite unpleasant, others provided youngsters with a happy home and a strong foundation for future life. Eleven-year-old David went from poverty in a home with immoral and drunken parents to a comfortable home on a large farm. Although his foster parents lived modestly, their home had "the necessary comforts," and they treated David "as an own son." The family provided him music lessons, books, and magazines, took him to Sunday school, and encouraged him to maintain contact with his mother. The foster family gave him more than six years of love and support.[70] David was not alone in his good fortune. The state indentured Felix for four years with a farm family that provided him reading and recreation. When he fell in with a "wild gang" of local youths, rather than returning him to Sparta, his foster family forgave him and helped him mend his ways.

His farm experience prepared him for work after his release, and at the time of the investigation he was earning $35 a month as a laborer and maintenance man.[71] Myrta found a home with a family that provided her "not at all a home of culture, but one where there was plenty for comfortable living, and there was much kindness." Upon her release from the State School, she continued to live there, earning $5 a week doing domestic work. "She said she loves the home—she was not nagged at nor were any heavy demands made on her. . . . She expressed a hope that it would always be her home."[72] Agnes found a similar situation. Although she worked hard, her foster parents provided her with music lessons and a job when she was released from the school. "She seemed satisfied and consented to stay for $4 a week wages."[73] In each of these cases, foster parents provided a supportive environment to the children they indentured and tried to make them feel as if their placement really was a home, not just a way-station in a series of indentures.

What even these positive stories illustrate was one of the most lasting problems the Children's Bureau saw with the indenture program: children indentured on farms were rarely, if ever, trained for a life beyond agriculture and housework. With a grammar school education and most of their vocational experience on farms, they had no specific training for adult occupations. As a result, the largest number of boys for whom information was available went to work as farm laborers on their release from the State School's jurisdiction. Although the occupations of many young men were unknown, more than 50 percent of those whose occupations were known were working on farms, many on or near farms where they had lived while indentured. Others were factory workers, in the armed forces, or working at other types of unskilled and semiskilled labor. Perhaps not surprisingly, among those women whose occupation was known, most were either married and housewives or did domestic work. This accounted for more than 60 percent of the young women. Others held positions such as clerks in stores, factory workers, and telephone operators. There were many youngsters that could not be accounted for, and the Children's Bureau believed that their situations were grim. They had come from villages and cities and had returned there upon their release from the school. "Having had no contact with life in the cities or experience with the employments to be secured there, they drifted from job to job, their former work having meant nothing to them in the way of vocational preparation."[74]

In spite of the problems children experienced in foster homes, the Children's Bureau did not advocate as a solution returning them to their parents. When the Children's Bureau studied the 17 percent of indentured children who were returned to their parents between 1913 and 1917, investigators concluded that many of them had been returned to homes that were detrimental to them. Investigators were able to track thirty-six youngsters, and they found that twenty-one of their homes, or 58 percent, were unsuitable. The reasons for this unsuitability included the child being neglected, abused, or worked too hard. The state had returned children to parents who were alcoholic, feeble-minded, insane, criminal, or "morally bad."[75] Rather than encourage returning children to bad home environments, the Children's Bureau suggested more and better institutional care, tighter supervision of placements, and ongoing social work with problem families.

The experience of Wisconsin's children who came to the attention of the state tells us many things about farm childhood in the late nineteenth and early twentieth centuries. It tells us that farm children, like other children, experienced poverty, family dissolution, abuse, and stress. If a "respectable" family experienced transitory misfortune, it might be able to appeal successfully to the local government for aid. If a family's distress was ongoing, or if its members were not considered to be members of the worthy poor, it would have fewer options, many of them decidedly unpleasant, such as commitment to the poor farm. Farm children, in some ways, were more fortunate than the children of laborers. Because of their importance to the family economy, they had a significant value to their extended families and neighbors. When times became too tight, they might be able to find shelter within their communities, rather than being uprooted and sent into the care of strangers and institutions such as the Wisconsin State Public School.

The experience of youngsters who were indentured by the State School can be used, in a sense, as a proxy for understanding the experience of very poor, abused, and neglected farming children, those who received little protection from their kin or their communities. They would have received far less education than even that which was commonly available in rural districts. Their workloads would have been extremely heavy. Parents, overburdened with the care of their farms, often would have been unable to provide secondary or vocational education for their maturing children. They might find that their opportunities for social interaction with other children within their communities were limited by their very differentness—by the fact that no one wanted to be associated with their troubles. If they were fortunate, they might find shelter with caring neighbors. Many, however, did not. In the end, as we will see, the reactions of the State School children to farm life were rather similar to those of hard-working and disadvantaged youngsters born there: "Many remembered with no enthusiasm their experiences on the farms where they were indentured, and had been eager to get away from the drudgery."[76]

7

"I Wouldn't Live in the City Always for Anything"

Growing Up and Making Decisions

❖ ❖ ❖ ❖ ❖ ❖ ❖ ❖ ❖ ❖ ❖ ❖ ❖ ❖ ❖

*I wouldn't live in the City always for anything. Get an Education there and a
good start in life and then let me have a farm. If I had to live in the City always
the very thought would kill me.*
—*Frisby Leonard Rasp, age sixteen, May 9, 1888*

Defining what is meant by the term *grown up* is a difficult task. In any society, there are a number of markers of maturity, including achieving a certain age and physical development, taking on work responsibility, completing school, participating independently in leisure activities, and leaving
home. Attempting to measure a farm child's degree of "grown up-ness" in
relation to these markers is problematic. Achieving a certain age and degree
of physical maturity did not automatically make children grown up but did
make them more valuable to their parents as workers. In terms of responsibility and their importance to the family, youngsters became more than a
little grown up at an early age, although this did not signify independence
from parents. Boys, not yet teenagers, herded their families' cattle, sometimes through the night, without adult supervision. Very young girls took
responsibility for their siblings while mothers did the laundry or went into
the fields to work. Both boys and girls contributed their labor to their families in important ways. And yet being grown up meant more than being a

significant contributor to the family fortunes. The term implied a degree of autonomy as well. When Martha Foote Crowe, writer and proponent of the Country Life movement, attempted to define the term *American country girl* for a 1915 publication of the same name, she was at a bit of a loss. Her "girls," meaning young women living and working on the parents' farms, still dependents, ranged in age from fifteen to twenty-nine. She reasoned, "Some farmers' daughters become responsible for a considerable amount of labor value well before the age of fifteen; and on the other hand the energy of these young rural women is abundantly extended beyond the gateway of womanhood, far indeed into the period that used to be called old-maidism, but which is so designated no more."[1] In the world of the farm, "girls" and "boys," too, might be fifteen years old, but they might be twenty-nine, as well. Being an integral part of the family's economic structure might also mean having an awareness of one's family's economic fragility at an early age. Farm-raised youngsters did not have to be adults to understand the weight of their parents' troubles, and a childhood free of economic worries was probably a luxury.[2] Even leaving school did not necessarily mean that a youngster was grown up but perhaps only that the child's parents needed him or her at home. In this world, growing up did not just mean making a significant, or even adult, contribution to the family enterprise, but gaining autonomy and eventually leaving the family home.

For most youngsters, an important part of being grown up is believing that one is, in fact, an adult. Although it is somewhat difficult to uncover the dawning of this important self-perception in individuals who lived decades ago, the diaries of some youngsters revealed that they faced young adulthood with many of the same emotions as young people today. When eighteen-year-old Iowan Oliver Perry Myers left school, it was a day for reflection and embracing what he perceived as his newly adult self. He wrote, "Perhaps I am to Sentimental but I can not help but think of the young Scholars that are growing up to take my place as I have done others places. I think if they had my experience they could do a great deal better. . . . I enjoyed my self very much in the Innocent youthful plays of my childhood. I can now see my errors & mistakes—and I will now have to battle with the Real hardships of the world."[3] For Myers, entry into the world would mean admission to the University of Iowa. At roughly the same age, Mamie Griswold, of Greene County, Illinois, also made a transition out of school, but into the world of full-time farm work rather than a university education. She expressed her new maturity in disdain for the social activities of neighborhood youngsters. Although she often violated her own resolutions, she planned to quit dancing, seeing the fortune teller, and attending lyceums. These activities were "foolishness," and she professed herself to be "too old." Part of her new maturity included a spiritual decision to confess "the name of Jesus" and her resolve "to live a Christian life."[4] Maturity meant setting new priorities and living like an adult rather than a child.

Like many young women today, Mary J. Aberle, a Kansas farm daughter in her teens, demonstrated her growing awareness of her age and maturity in worries about her looks. "I have been indulging in a fit of the blues and wondering why such an ugly girl as I am was ever created—it looks as it were not fair for me to be so plain." Her lamentations about plainness segued into fears about her marriageability. On her birthday she wrote, "This is my birthday and I suppose wrinkles and crowfeet will begin to make their appearance after a while and they will commence calling me old Maid too."[5] As a fifteen-year-old, Lucy Van Voorhis, growing up in rural Iowa, also lamented the shape of her physical being. In an autobiography, written for school, she wrote, "My height is five feet five inches. I have black hair and eyes, and a dark complection. My weight is about one hundred and twenty five pounds. . . . I am much larger than most girls of my age. I consider it a misfortune." Perhaps that is why she mused, at the essay's end, "I am going to be an old maid, and teach school in a little yellow school house in the backwoods of Dakota, if it is proper to speak so of a prairie state."[6] As they left school, assumed new work responsibilities, and interacted socially with other young people, sons and daughters were made aware of their changing status within the family and the community. They were growing up, but growing up could be a difficult and uncertain process.

One of those difficult and uncertain areas about which historians know very little is the experience of puberty and sexual maturation. The modesty of young diary writers precluded much of a discussion of this topic, so integral to the process of growing up. Historians Linda Peavy and Ursula Smith, compiling their work *Frontier Children,* found a great deal of evidence on the puberty ceremonies of western tribes such as the Cheyenne and Navajo but relatively little firsthand information about puberty among white settlers, who did not mark the occasion with ceremonies.[7] The traditional, adult-formulated ritual was accessible to historians, whereas the youngster's lived experience was not. Youngsters' reticence, even in their own personal writings, becomes easier to understand when one examines the influences shaping their attitudes about sexuality. Youngsters received little in the way of sexual education, and much of what they received simply encouraged them to not think about the topic. The Women's Christian Temperance Union, in addition to being active in temperance and prohibition, also promoted social, or sexual, purity. The "White Shield Pledge for Girls," distributed at temperance events and in schools, required girls to pledge to "repress all thoughts, words and deeds which I should be ashamed to have my parents know" and to "avoid all conversation, reading, pictures and amusements, which may put wrong thoughts into my mind."[8] Adults encouraged youngsters to suppress their thoughts and shield their eyes, before they even had the opportunity to reflect on or write about what they were experiencing. The intense physical changes of the teenage years, for the most part, remain hidden from prying historians' eyes.

Instead, it is easier to see maturation taking place within the context of youngsters' daily activities. For rural youngsters, work was an area in which they could exercise a certain amount of independence but rarely any autonomy. Their farm work often required that they act and think independently of their parents, but ultimately parents controlled the shape and content of that work and its rewards. The needs of the family enterprise guided youngsters' actions, as they planted, weeded, harvested, shucked, milked, and herded. Parents taught their children the proper ways to accomplish these tasks, and then expected them to carry them out competently and without additional instruction, either alone, or in concert with them or with other children. Any number of tasks made up the repertoire of farm children, from gathering eggs and firewood, to planting gardens, to husking corn. Herding was one of the most independent jobs children assumed. The Norton boys, ranging in age from twenty to fourteen, herded the family's cattle day in and day out, with little or no supervision from their father. As a fifteen-year-old, Curtis, or Curtie, Norton's responsibilities included watching the cattle overnight, without any company from brothers or adults. Wrote his mother in the family journal, "Curtie has gone to camp to stay alone tonight. He was willing. His dog is company."[9] This was not an unusual occasion, and less than a week later Curtie was again "at the camp alone. I hope he will rest well tonight. If it keeps cold Will must go over tomorrow night and stay all night."[10] In later years, other younger brothers and then sisters would continue the tradition. The Norton family's livestock operation could not have existed without the unsupervised labor of their children, but the decisions regarding the herd, the disposal of the cattle, and the assets accruing from their sale belonged to their parents. As the Norton boys matured, and as the family fortunes faltered, they contributed their labor to the family in other ways as well. In the summer of 1880 and winter of 1881, William, John, and Curtis, aged twenty-one, seventeen, and fifteen, traveled long distances from home to do whatever form of work they could find, in order to help support the family. They remained away for months, largely out of touch with their parents.[11] The farm essentially became home base for the older boys, and they alternated between time spent working for their parents and time spent away, working for others, sending their wages to their parents. At home or away, until they surpassed the age of twenty-one, family considerations, needs, and desires guided the Norton children's working lives.

Graduating from the eighth grade, passing a teacher's exam, and taking up a position in a local school might seem to qualify a youngster for a type of adulthood, but even then parents often remained the masters of their children's fate. Although they might be adults in the classroom, young teachers often remained their parents' children. Rhoda Emery, whose teaching career is described in Chapter 4, did not loosen her ties to her family when she taught in the rural schools of Olmsted County, Minnesota. She came home on weekends and between sessions to help her parents run their eighty-acre farm. The elder Emerys continued to control her social life, deciding where she could go and with whom. The knowledge of their strict standards kept her on the straight and narrow, even when boarding away from home. Her parents laid claim to her earnings as well. Although she did use some money for her own purposes, she also helped her parents pay their taxes and meet other expenses, putting aside her own wants and desires. She sacrificed her dream of owning a bicycle to her parents' need for a buggy. It was perhaps a small act of revenge when, as a young woman, she helped her younger brother, Robert, to assert his individuality against his parents, and his mother in particular. When Robert was fifteen, Rhoda bought him a gun, something his mother greatly disapproved of. In her diary, Helen Emery protested, "Robt came bringing in a hateful little gun that Rhode had squandered 13$ on for him. . . . will keep me very uncomfortable watching Robt & that infernal gun until I make out to get rid of it."[12] This evidently was not the only occasion on which Rhoda, or one of her sisters, defied their mother's wishes. Helen Emery lamented that Robert "would be so good to me & we could take so much comfort together if the girls did not all set him up to think his mother an idiotic old tyrant. I wish they would leave me my one dear little boy—if they are tired of me themselves."[13] It appears that the Emery daughters, weary of their mother's domination of their lives, encouraged their brother to be more independent. Farm parents had a very strong understanding of the relationship of the child to the farm, and the child's first responsibility was to contribute to the family's fortunes, rather than his or her own. As Rhoda Emery's diaries indicate, conforming her life to her parents' needs was an ongoing struggle.

These struggles between parental claims and youngsters' desires were not isolated to rural communities. Among working-class youngsters in urban locations, striving to achieve autonomy took the form of an increasingly vibrant youth culture. Like farm youth, urban youngsters often faced difficulties in achieving the autonomy they craved. In some sense, they had more independence than farm youngsters, but they faced the same familial restrictions on their activities. They, too, lived in a world where their wages were central to the support of the family. Their wages were essential to the family achieving a livable income, and their efforts were an extremely important component of the family's safety net, in the event of a parent's disability, unemployment, or death. Instead of working for their parents, however, many worked for wages outside of the home. Another essential difference was that these wages came in the form of money, and employers generally placed pay packets directly into their hands. Parents then expected that their children would hand those pay packets over to them, unopened, at the end of the week. Increasingly, youngsters began arguing for some sort of control over their wages, and over their free time. After putting in long hours laboring in factories and shops, the young believed they should have the right during their leisure hours to turn their energies, and some of their hard-earned funds, to the serious business of socializing and entertainment. With varying degrees of success, young people challenged their responsibility to contribute their all to the family coffers and began to use some of their wages for fashionable clothing and entertainment. Although a familial world of walks, talks, and gatherings over food and cards continued to exist and fill young people's leisure hours, an exciting new world of amusements beckoned from outside.[14] Young people joined clubs in order to meet and mingle with the opposite sex and to pursue social activities in a more congenial environment.[15] Increasingly popular were less structured and considerably less respectable pursuits that included dance halls, amusement parks, and movie theaters. Fearful of the results of this new independence, urban-based reformers such as Jane Addams argued for greater adult control of youngsters and their activities; at Addams's Hull House, this took the form of supervised social clubs and night classes for young workers.[16]

In rural communities, the developing youth culture might take somewhat different forms. As discussed in Chapter 5, a whole range of activities within the community included children and young adults, and often their parents as well. An important part of growing up was the moment at which parents surrendered a degree of control and allowed their children to attend evening events meant largely for young adults, with other family members playing a very minor role. Within what parents presumed to be a chaperoned setting, young men and women played games, danced, and visited, often staying out until the small hours of the morning. Parents may have assumed more supervision existed than there actually was; after all, how much could a person see in a dark house, barnyard, or barn, in the days before electric illumination? They may also have underestimated, or simply have chosen to ignore, the amount of unsupervised contact that could occur on dark walks or rides between entertainment venues and home. Even so, the assumption was that youngsters would entertain themselves in a familiar world, a neighbor's home, with familiar companions, their neighbors' children, under familiar social rules. Within this context, parents hoped that little would go wrong. The arrival of the automobile, which made the sights, sounds, and experiences of urban areas easily accessible, increased parental worries. Youngsters gained access to unfamiliar worlds and unfamiliar companions, and their parents worried that the accepted social rules would disintegrate under their influence. In the early years of the twentieth century, however, rural youth had more hurdles to jump than urban youth in gaining access to new cultural activities. Like urban youngsters, rural youngsters needed their own pocket money, but they faced greater problems with transportation. Boys were more likely to have their own funds and know how to drive a car, and they faced less parental opposition to their activities than their sisters.[17]

There was also an informal youth culture existing below the surface of the rural community, in which the young, and particularly young men, defied the rules of their parents and other authority figures. Older boys attending school in order to harass the teacher was a part of this larger phenomenon. Accounts of students and teachers would suggest that this particular challenge to authority periodically occurred in nearly every community, and professional educators' journals treated this "boy problem" as a given. School, however, was not the only forum for defiance of adult authority. In the Ise family's community in north-central Kansas, the young men often gathered at the home of an older bachelor "to smoke and chew tobacco, tell smutty stories, play cards, and even drink beer occasionally." Even though these activities distressed and angered parents, they seemed to be powerless to prevent them entirely. These same young men engaged in other disruptive activities, including a charivari, or a rowdy postwedding celebration, that led to the near destruction of the newlyweds' house. Their misbehavior went as far as disruption of church services, almost to the point of their arrest on charges of disturbing the peace.[18] Curbing these activities took relatively mild forms. After the charivari, parents insisted that the young men pay the cost of repairing the house they had damaged in order to avoid a lawsuit against them. After the troubles at church, Rosie Ise objected to the minister's intention to swear out a warrant against the young men, and she and her husband restrained their son from attending church after the minister declared his intentions. Beyond this, however, parents seemed to be unwilling to act, perhaps on the assumption that this was a phase in growing up and that someday the young men would become responsible adult members of the community. And that is exactly what happened: "The young hoodlums soon grew into staid and dignified manhood."[19] In some ways, this community attitude seems very much like that adopted by the Amish in relation to their young. Before committing themselves to the church and the community for life, Amish youngsters are allowed a period of experimentation and lax supervision known as *rumspringa,* or "running around." Adults assume that when they are ready, the young will come back to the fold as responsible members of the community.[20] As long as youthful activities did not go completely beyond the pale into serious criminal activity, adults seem to have taken those activities in stride and assumed that the day would come when the exuberant young would take their place as mature adults.

These descriptions of raucous adolescent and young adult behavior included only young men. If young women participated, they escaped notice, or they failed to note their participation in their diaries and reminiscences. What is more likely is that parents maintained relatively greater control over daughters. Studies done in farm communities in the 1920s and 1930s showed that although many young men pursued the bulk of their recreational activities away from the farm, young women were more "home centered" in their leisure.[21] Much more was at stake with a girl's indiscriminate behavior than a boy's. A badly behaved young man might be said to be sowing wild oats. He could be redeemed by a sober and industrious adulthood. Girls who too visibly deviated from responsibility, chastity, or sobriety might very well have ruined their possibility for marriage and respectability permanently, especially if a premarital pregnancy resulted. A girl's reputation was much more fragile than a boy's.

When aberrant activities included only young men, families could be accepting of those activities. Changing rules governing the relations between young men and women, however, complicated this situation. An important part of this social revolution was the evolution of the concept of dating. In the years before 1900, calling predominated as the way in which young people respectably courted. A young man presented himself at a young woman's home, and she and her parents decided whether or not to admit him. Visiting occurred in the family home or on the front porch, under the watchful eyes and ears of family members. This, at least, was the theory under which courtship operated. Youngsters, however, had a talent for subverting the system and claiming more privacy and intimacy than their parents believed was proper. This is very much evident in the remarkable diary of a young Nebraskan. In the mid- to late 1870s, young Rolf Johnson lived in the central part of the state. He and his parents had emigrated from Illinois with a group of Swedes. Rolf carried on a number of romances, including one with a young farm daughter, Clara Mathilda, or Thilda, Danielson. Thilda's parents objected to their daughter seeing Rolf Johnson, and her parents "upbraided her for her intimacy" with him. Thilda's parents, however, were unable to force their daughter to give up her relationship with Rolf. Thilda's response to parental admonitions was to send Rolf a note, inviting him "to call this afternoon as she would be alone." Johnson wrote that he "called and found her all alone, her folks having gone visiting. Spent the afternoon very pleasantly and staid until about ten o'clock this evening, and we played 'love in the dark' as we lighted no lamp not wishing to be watched from without through the windows." It is unclear exactly what Johnson meant by playing "love in the dark," except that Thilda's parents would certainly have objected to their activities. Thilda's parents caught Johnson leaving the house, and she had a "stormy interview with her father last night after I was gone. He was very severe, called her a prostitute, and accused her of being my mistress."[22] Although Thilda would have been happy to regularize their relationship through marriage, Johnson commented that he was "not quite prepared to leave a state of single blessedness for that of double misery."[23] Despite parental objections, Johnson continued to see Thilda Danielson off and on until his 1879 departure for adventures in the west. By the time he returned, she had married, perhaps to someone more acceptable to her parents.[24]

In theory, the system of calling was supposed to prevent intimacies such as those that occurred between Rolf Johnson and Thilda Danielson by locating courtship firmly within the home, under the supervision of parents. Youngsters, however, seem to have preferred to manage their relationships themselves and to have wanted greater privacy and intimacy than calling allowed. The system of dating, as it developed in the late nineteenth and early twentieth centuries, met these desires. Under the dating system, young men and women took their courtship out of the family home and into the public, spending time on their own, generally beyond the direct supervision of their parents. Instead of staying home, young people went "out," attending events and enjoying amusements beyond the family home. In rural communities, the number of places a couple could go might be limited, although the advent of the automobile greatly increased the number of destinations as they ventured further afield into towns and cities. Before easy access to the automobile, going to parties or to local church- and school-sponsored functions, such as singing schools and debates, might be the only organized recreation available. There were dance halls in some rural locales, but young people frequented them much more commonly in the 1920s, 1930s, and beyond, when autos became more available.[25] For urban working-class youth, who lacked parlors or front porches but who had access to a myriad of venues outside of the home, going on dates was far more practical and attractive.[26] From the point of view of the young, although generally not their parents, this had the added advantage of increasing the privacy of courting couples.

Assertions of independence that took the form of premarital sexual activity were the ones that most concerned late nineteenth- and early twentieth-century reformers and parents. By the early years of the twentieth century, a sexual revolution was under way in the United States. Although the incidence of premarital sex among young men remained relatively steady, premarital sexual intercourse was increasingly common among young women. Although young women had many reasons for pursuing intimacy (not the least of which may have been the desire for closeness with someone they loved), rebellion was certainly a possible motivation. In many ways, engaging in premarital sex was as great a statement of independence as a young female could make, asserting that her body was her own, to do with what she pleased. She was asserting that she did not belong to her parents.[27] As the years passed, assertions of this sort were increasingly common. Studies done in the early twentieth century with upper-middle-class, college-educated young women indicated that among those born before 1890, 90 percent were virgins upon marriage. Among those born between 1890 and 1899, 74 percent were. Of those born between 1900 and 1909, only 51 percent were.[28] Although the proportion of sexually active young women was likely to have been lower in conservative rural communities, late nineteenth- and early twentieth-century observers spoke in general terms of a rising "girl problem." Although young men were certainly part of the problem, judges and juvenile officials rarely punished them for their partnership in sexual experimentation. In urban areas, officials dealt with the "girl problem" by enforcing age of consent laws against young women and by prosecuting and incarcerating those who had transgressed the boundaries of propriety by engaging in premarital sexual activity. This, reformers argued, was for the good of the girl and the good of society.[29]

In both rural and urban America, sexual experience ranged widely among the young. In 1883, eighteen-year-old Mamie Griswold was socially quite active but clearly not sexually experienced. In her diary, she expressed great delight at an evening's flirting. "Will Carter & his three cousins came & spent the evening *'Made a mash!'* "[30] Describing her interaction with the young men as "mashing" implied a bit of flirting, or even perhaps a bit of kissing, but no more serious contact. Even in the years immediately preceding World War I, it was possible to be "dumb and green and shy" and to approach courtship with almost no sexual experience of any kind. Edith Bradley, growing up in a conservative southern Illinois family in which children did not even kiss their parents, fell in love with Bill Rendleman, her husband-to-be, because of his gentlemanly ways. She reminisced, "I had been raised so strict it would have scared me to death if one [a young man] had made a pass at me. It was months after we started going together before Bill kissed me good-night."[31] Edith Bradley and Bill Rendleman's experience was at one end of the spectrum. Other young men and women were far less conservative in their behavior; increased levels of premarital sexual activity were not simply an urban-based phenomenon.

Although the numbers do not differentiate between urban and rural women, and rural women rarely, if ever, wrote about sexual matters in their diaries and letters, there is certainly evidence that some rural daughters were sexually active. The stories of unmarried farm daughters, unable to support their children, may be found in the records of the Wisconsin State Public School for Dependent and Neglected Children. Around 1900, unmarried mothers began to leave infants and toddlers whose fathers had failed to support them at the school, in preparation for indenture and adoption. Some of their mothers resided in the poorhouse, rejected by their parents, while others remained at home. Such was the case of an infant, Elizabeth, whose father was unknown and whose mother was a farm daughter who attended school and helped her parents on the family farm. Eventually, Elizabeth's grandparents were no longer either willing or able to provide for her support, and her mother surrendered her to the State School. Like most infants and toddlers left at the school, she soon found an adoptive home.[32] Far more common to surrendered infants were mothers who were domestic servants rather than farm girls. This was a somewhat ambiguous designation, however, because many of those young domestics may very well have been farm daughters, making their way from rural areas to towns and cities. Urban communities were a place where parents could send wayward and headstrong daughters, hoping to conceal illicit sexual behavior and premarital pregnancies from the neighbors.[33] Research done on the activities of young single women who lived in Fargo, North Dakota, during the Great Depression suggests that many young rural women migrated to the city, became domestic servants, and found many new ways to express their freedom, including premarital sexual activity.[34] Given the evidence from the records of the Wisconsin State Public School, there is little to suggest that young women's activities were much different than those a decade or two earlier.

The pursuit of pleasure and intimacy was not without risk. Although sexuality was an important part of coming of age, it was also fraught with danger in the late nineteenth and early twentieth century. Young people often had limited knowledge of human reproduction, and even less of contraception, so any forays into premarital sexual intercourse carried the risk of pregnancy. If a pregnancy resulted and the couple married, the problem was, in the eyes of the community, solved.[35] If, however, a marriage was not in the offing, the young woman faced shame and ostracism. A 1915 case of suspected infanticide in rural Dane County, Wisconsin, illustrates the worst-case scenario that many parents must have imagined as their daughters left the confines of the family home in order to interact with the opposite sex. It also graphically demonstrates the dangers premarital sex posed for young women, the fears young women struggled with, and the apparent inability of a rural community to adequately deal with a young woman in need of social support.

At 9:30 on the morning of December 2, 1915, at a schoolhouse near De-Forest, Wisconsin, the teacher, seventeen-year-old Alma Christiansen, dismissed class after only half an hour. The students, concerned for their teacher, called their parents to the schoolhouse. Someone also summoned the local doctor, and he arrived fifteen minutes later. The assembled adults found the teacher "almost in a condition of collapse from loss of blood." The teacher's podium and desk at the front of the room showed evidence of the teacher's distress. "The platform on which she sat was covered with blood; everything was covered with blood; her clothing was soaked with blood."[36] The teacher claimed that "she had a sudden flow and all she needed was a warm bed and a few days rest," but the students' mothers, who had arrived to help, were suspicious. Other evidence discovered on the school grounds indicated that the problem was far more grave than a surprisingly heavy and unexpected menstrual period.[37] On December 3, after searching the grounds, two students' mothers discovered the body of a small and poorly developed newborn infant at the bottom of the pit in the outhouse. The teacher had given birth in the classroom, left the infant in her clothing until she could hide it in her desk, and then had attempted to hide the body in the outhouse. Alma Christiansen remained in a state of collapse for several weeks and was only well enough to participate in a coroner's inquest in late December.[38]

Testimony by Alma Christiansen, members of the school board, students, and others revealed the sad story behind the birth and death of her child. According to her mother's evidence, Alma and Ray Anderson, a young Green County farmer of twenty or twenty-one years, had gone to town together several times the previous spring, but he had stopped visiting Alma not long thereafter.[39] She became pregnant sometime that spring and was expecting to give birth in mid-January. In spite of this attenuated courtship, Alma was also expecting, or at least hoping, to marry Ray Anderson. Alma was to be disappointed in her hopes. When she told Anderson of her pregnancy, he denied paternity and refused to marry her. When the coroner asked Alma what Anderson had said to her when she told him of the pregnancy, she answered, "He first accused me of something and he didn't think he was guilty." He had even been to the schoolhouse to demand that she tell no one that she was pregnant with his child.[40] Nevertheless, when the coroner asked Alma what she planned "with respect to the child, what did you intend to do?" She replied, "I intended to go home and get married."[41]

Perhaps not surprisingly, Alma told no adults other than Anderson about the pregnancy. Her parents only found out about the pregnancy and birth when the doctor called them after her collapse and asked them to come and retrieve her.[42] She had been spending most of her time since the end of the summer boarding away from home, and they may not have had much opportunity to see the physical evidence of their daughter's condition. Those in closer proximity to Alma also feigned ignorance. Neither the school board members nor the parents of students at the school had confirmed knowledge of the pregnancy, although some of them apparently were suspicious. Oscar Heisig, a school board member who lived near the school, received a report four to six weeks before the birth that the teacher might be pregnant. He believed that Ferd Rademacher, the clerk of the school board, had spoken with Alma. Mr. Rademacher, even though he was suspicious about the teacher and had told Oscar Heisig of his concerns, had not taken any action whatsoever. Mrs. Josephine Rademacher, with whom the teacher had boarded until September, claimed to have had "some" suspicions but had not discussed them with Alma.[43] No responsible adult who might have been able to change the course of events and prevent this tragedy had found the courage to broach the subject to a vulnerable, scared youngster. In fact, the whole community seems to have been embarrassed by the happenings of that December day. Although reports of an unknown infant's death and the successive postponements of the inquest received notice in the local paper, the *DeForest Times,* no information about the substance of the inquest or its verdict ever appeared. Another local paper, the *Brooklyn Teller,* completely ignored December's scandalous events.[44] Local papers existed to boost the community, and no one would benefit from publicizing such a shameful incident.

Because the infant was apparently premature and no real evidence of wrongdoing existed, the coroner's jury found "no one was criminally liable for the death of said infant."[45] Although Ray Anderson had been to the Christiansens' house, promised to talk to Alma when she was well, and "acted quite friendly" with her father, a marriage was not forthcoming. When the census enumerator visited the Christiansen farm in 1920, the now-twenty-two-year old Alma still lived with her parents, working on their farm.[46] Her presence there, in a single state, was unsurprising. She had transgressed the bounds of decency in several ways, being involved in premarital sexual activity, becoming pregnant, and failing to marry the baby's father. She had also failed in one of the more important tasks of the schoolteacher, which was to be a model of propriety for the area's children. Escaping the stigma of her past could not have been easy and most likely would have involved moving to the relative anonymity of an urban area, such as Madison or Milwaukee, to start again. In Alma Christiansen's case, premarital sexual activity had come with a very high price of pain, anxiety, and public humiliation, not to mention the death of her child, whose life might have been spared had a responsible adult known of Alma's pregnancy and aided her in the last months of her pregnancy, as well as the delivery.

Alma Christiansen's experience served an educational function, in several ways, for other young women in her community. Although there was, according to the children's testimony, surprisingly little to see or hear that December morning, eight or nine children, three boys and five or six girls, were in the room during the birth. Four of those girls, ranging in age from eleven to sixteen, testified at the coroner's inquest. If they had not previously known that babies came from women's bodies, they would certainly have known it after that morning's events and the subsequent investigation. Perhaps unsurprisingly, the coroner called none of the boys to testify, presumably because of the delicacy of the matter. Given the informal channels of communication operating in most rural communities, however, all of the children would have emerged from the situation knowing something more about the shame, pain, and mortification involved with becoming an unmarried mother in that time and place. Given Ray Anderson's refusal to marry her, Alma Christiansen faced her dilemma with few options. An abortion would have been illegal and potentially life-threatening. She could, as she did, attempt to conceal the pregnancy and birth, hoping that nothing would go wrong and that no one would notice. In that attempt, however, she failed. She could have told her parents; perhaps they would have sent her away to relatives or to family friends to have her child in another community and encouraged her to put the baby up for adoption. Other farm daughters in similar situations gave their children to the Wisconsin State Public School in Sparta, or other state or private charitable agencies. Only a few charities, such as the Florence Crittendon Homes, encouraged unmarried mothers to keep their babies while helping them to find work to support them. It was also highly unlikely that she would have remained an unmarried mother, raising her child on her parents' farm. Hers was a situation unlikely to have a happy ending.[47] Alma Christiansen's story, told in whispers, likely served as a cautionary tale for a generation or more of young women in rural DeForest. It reinforced every admonition parents had given their children, and especially their daughters, about the dangers of premarital sexual relations. By the early decades of the twentieth century, organizations such as the Young Women's Christian Association (YWCA) were pushing for systematic instruction in sex education for country girls, in the hopes of curtailing the incidence of premarital sex and pregnancy.[48]

The more common script followed by most young people included marriage. Courtship, as indicated above, could be carried out in several different ways. Generally, young people met and became acquainted with each other, judging each other's suitability as lifelong partners. School and church were common venues for such introductions. Seth Adolphson and his intended, Ella Stanke, carried out a fairly typical early twentieth-century courtship. Adolphson, of Rock County, Wisconsin, was the son of Swedish immigrant tobacco farmers. He attended grammar school, stayed at home and helped his parents for several years, and then attended two years of high school at Albion Academy. He was the third oldest child in his family and his parents' only son. He greatly enjoyed his time at Albion Academy, and part of its appeal was social. Leaving school made him "terrible lonesome."[49] After meeting Ella Stanke in July 1917, he began to see her regularly. Their courtship consisted of regular telephone calls and evening meetings, as well as written correspondence. Their dates included trips to the county fair, as well as attractions in other locales, such as movie theaters. As he wrote in November 1917, "Ella & I to Janesville & had the bestest time."[50] After an engagement of nearly a year, the two married secretly. Seth had wanted to buy Ella a sewing machine, but she had refused the gift as improper, unless they were married. After a notice in the paper revealed their marriage, Seth's and Ella's parents insisted on a "real" wedding, which was held in May 1919. As with many young couples, marriage did not mean immediately setting up an independent household. Seth and Ella Adolphson lived with his parents for the first year of their marriage, with Seth working on his parents' farm. Only later would they establish their own tobacco farm.[51] Marriage, however, made them adults, eligible to make their own decisions and their own way in the world.

Social and sexual activities were only one part of the maturation process. Growing up also implied making decisions about the future—whether to continue on the farm or move into the cities. As the nineteenth century gave way to the twentieth, it was less and less of a given that youngsters would remain in the communities where they grew up, working the land as their parents had. Farm youngsters were being born into a world where the economic options were much wider than they had been for previous generations. The combination of economic change with the appeal of social change happening in America's cities made the choice to leave the farm an alluring one. Cities promised jobs, but they also promised new and exciting diversions. Turn-of-the-century St. Paul, for example, boasted movie theaters, dance halls, amusement parks, and public gardens.[52] Even something as simple as electric lighting in urban homes may have made cities and towns more attractive. Adulthood may be understood as a time when individuals become old enough and mature enough to understand and exercise their options. The late nineteenth and early twentieth centuries were a time when there were more options available than ever before for the countryside's dissatisfied, curious, or ambitious youth.

The work lives that farm children had endured often figured heavily in their decisions. Childhoods spent working long and arduous hours were not uncommon in the nineteenth century. Hundreds of thousands of farm children shared similar burdens. Additionally, many poor urban children toiled in factories, earning wages that would allow their families and themselves food, clothing, and shelter. In most cases, children's wages and children's efforts contributed to the well-being of the family as a whole, and not to the individual savings and spending of children. Legally, a child's wages and efforts belonged to his or her parents until he or she was twenty-one, and few farm families—or working-class families, for that matter—could afford to grant children the right to any significant portion of their wages. Studies done in the 1920s and 1930s showed that only the smallest minority of farm youth earned money for themselves rather than for their families, a situation that increasingly aggravated youngsters who wanted to experience the expensive amusements available in cities and towns.[53]

Leaving the rural community presented, too, the possibility of better pay for less arduous work. Wellington Clay, who in the 1890s left an Olmsted County, Minnesota, farm for a job in St. Paul, described in a letter to his sweetheart the benefits of working in this new urban location: "I am at work in the Leader [newspaper] office setting type. I am doing well this summer, and am having a pretty fair time too. I do not have to work as many hours a day as I would on a farm; only eight; so you see I have all the evenings after 5 O'Clock to my self, and a half holiday on Saturday, during the hot weather."[54] Clay found his new working situation far more appealing, especially during the oppressive heat of a midwestern summer, and would remain for the rest of his life in urban, rather than rural, Minnesota. Although the options were more limited for young women, the Twin Cities also beckoned to them. They could easily find work in homes, hotels, and restaurants, as well as in various manufacturing and retail outlets. Life in a city offered wages and a degree of independence often unavailable in rural areas.[55]

The same undercurrents were present in an anonymous farm boy's turn-of-the-century essay, entitled "Life on the Farm." In his essay, the youngster focused on the work involved in making a farm. He wrote, "Although I am only a young boy, I have some idea of the daily routine of such a life. It is work from early morning till late at night, with a few minutes set apart for each meal." He detailed the labors necessary to care for animals and crops and the uncertainty of the harvest. "When the time for reaping comes the farmer is anxious to know the fruits of his labor, whether it be thirty, sixty, or a hundred fold. Upon this depends their necessaries and pleasures of life." Although he acknowledged the "occasional holiday" that the farmer took, he emphasized that farming involved a never-ending round of work, writing, "Then comes Spring with the same duties as the year preceding." The young man's parting shot, perhaps tongue in cheek, perhaps not, expressed his preference for a future outside of agriculture. "But for my part I would rather be [Admiral] Dewey or president McKinley."[56] If this farm boy did choose to make a life outside of agriculture, he would have been one of thousands.

For others, the problem was not so much a desire to leave agriculture as much as the economic and personal tensions between fathers and sons. Young Bill Rendelman, working on his father's southern Illinois farm, seems to have accepted the premise that "boys weren't paid any money for their work." As he moved into his twenties and wanted to marry, however, working for his father became a less and less appealing option. After proposing to Edith Bradley, Bill approached his father about the possibility of renting one of the family's farms. His father said that "no, he could just go on working for him. In that day, the father kept all the money and gave it out to you as he wanted." A resolute Bill left his father a note, explaining his actions, and went to Granite City in search of a job. He found one in a steel mill. His father soon recognized the error of his ways because "Bill was his mainstay," and he offered his son a tenant farm and a share of the crop. Bill, not liking the city, accepted his offer and moved with his bride back to the farm.[57]

Bill Rendelman's story played out in farms across the midwest. By the turn of the century, a true "boy problem" existed in many locations. Any number of factors were contributing to the outflow of young males from farming communities: economic hardship, scarcity of land, and the perceived cultural insufficiency of rural areas as compared with urban centers. These pressures increased as the United States moved into the twentieth century.[58] Although the suggestions to keep boys on the farm were many, most amounted to giving the boys a stake, or a sense of ownership, in the family farm. A writer for the *Kansas Farmer* argued that the way for parents to keep boys on the farm was to give them as enjoyable a life as they could, make it financially possible for them to remain in agriculture, and teach them scientific agriculture. "Upon the parents," he wrote, "rests the responsibility for making the boy like or dislike farming. Let them make it attractive in a social, financial, and intellectual way."[59] Just as important, others claimed, was for parents, and particularly fathers, to "be square" with their sons. Being square meant allowing boys to make the decisions about, and keep the money generated by the sale of, the livestock they personally raised. Equally, it meant treating sons as the future inheritors of the family homestead, rather than as hired men. Henry Wallace, writing as the editor of *Wallace's Farmer,* recognized the tensions between farmer fathers and their sons and argued for greater understanding on the part of both. To sons he wrote encouragingly (and perhaps overly optimistically), "By and by he [the father] will come to trust you [the son] implicitly. First, he will be to you a sort of older brother; as the years go on he will learn to depend upon you, to lean on you, so to speak, and by and by he will be disposed, when he begins to lean heavily on his staff, to pay as much deference to your opinion as you did to his when you were a little boy."[60] Agricultural journals such as *Wallace's Farmer* encouraged fathers to take their sons into partnership and to share the decision making, as well as the rewards, with them. The writers hoped that these more equal arrangements would result in fewer embittered young men of twenty-one fleeing their parents' farms for the cities.[61] Writers were careful, however, not to assume that every farm-raised boy would make a good farmer. Parents were reminded that if their son "practised making pills of mud when he was a child, and extracted teeth from the jaws of dead horses with pincers when he got older, if he reads physiology while his brothers are deep in Robinson Crusoe, he will be far more likely to succeed with a lancet than with a scythe."[62] Only the properly inclined son, many argued, should be encouraged to stay.

Solving the "girl problem" on the farm was also important but not addressed with quite such regularity. After all, few girls were in line to inherit the family farm. But girls were important, too, as their parents' helpers and as future farm wives. If girls chose to leave the farm en masse, there was little chance that boys could be persuaded to remain as well. As a writer for the *Farmer's Wife* so aptly put it, "Too often a youth well started and thoroughly qualified by birth and training, abandons the farm for a city job with no promise in it, because the girl of his choice will not face the future of a

Are You Square With Your Boy?

In 1911, the Kansas Farmer *encouraged parents to be square with their boys because of the infinite services farm boys rendered. Kansas Farmer, June 10, 1911. By permission of the Kansas State Historical Society, Topeka, Kansas.*

farmer's wife."[63] Parents could encourage their daughters to remain on the farm not only by way of improved amenities, but also with a financial stake in farm life. In 1917, the *Farmer's Wife* suggested the installation of labor-saving machinery powered by electricity as an important incentive to keep daughters at home. The author also encouraged parents to allow their daughters sufficient leisure time, organized social activities, and a small amount of money to spend as they chose. If a family had little to spare, the author exhorted parents to allow what they could, claiming "lawn swings, porch rockers, croquet sets . . . cost little and they have great possibilities in pleasure-giving and home-making."[64] Other journals suggested even more forcefully that the way to keep girls on farms was to give them financial opportunities. "We girls are just as independent as our brothers. We possess just as good business qualities and it is just as humiliating for us to ask for our 'pin money' as it is for them."[65] Flora Bullock of the University of Nebraska argued that it was both unfair and stultifying to confine girls to the house, constantly telling them, "Mary, go into the house and help your mother." Too often, this bred resentment and a desire to leave the farm. One way to encourage girls to remain on the farm was through gardening, which would give girls healthy outdoor pursuits and the opportunity to earn an independent income. A parent's goal, Bullock argued, was to make a daughter "a responsible member of the firm."[66] Then, and only then, would girls be more attracted to rural life than to the growing American cities. None of the reformers suggested that girls seek employment, even temporarily, off the farm. Presumably they feared that employment in town might make young women even more discontented with their lot. Notice, too, that there was no suggestion that the way to keep girls on farms was to make them farmers and the inheritors of their families' land. From the perspective of 1890, 1920, or even 1960, this would have been too radical a means of giving girls a stake in the family farm.

Country Life reformer Martha Foote Crow, in her 1915 book *The American Country Girl,* painted a fairly rosy picture of the lives of farm daughters. On the basis of her analysis of a survey of farm daughters, the average country girl relished the "charms" of country and farm life: fresh air, good food, meaningful work, independence, and strong family ties. "No, the farm is not monotonous; one acquires a liberal education just by being alive; nature study, the work in the flower garden, affords constant variety; and there are new interests and adventures every day."[67] Crow could not, however, in good conscience deny that some farm daughters suffered through rural life, rather than enjoying it. They lacked "congenial companionship," faced a "woful [sic] lack of books, magazines, and papers," as well as other forms of entertainment, and struggled through a "dull weary succession of duties following each other day in and day out without rest or respite, and without any or with few of the modern conveniences to lighten the work."[68] Girls such as these looked beyond the farm for their futures. "Farming seems to them drudgery," Crow wrote, "which means labor without inspiration or acknowledgment. . . . They feel intensely the monotony of farm life, the stagnation of the rural community. The sameness, the humdrum tediousness of the every-day life drives them to the city."[69] The answer to this problem, reasoned Crow, was that farm girls be given "a share in the responsibility." Girls wanted, and should receive, some acres, some livestock, and some acknowledgment of their contributions to the family farm.[70] But Crow chided farm daughters and suggested that they be more realistic as well. By providing examples of the myriad tasks and burdens of the agricultural "super-women" of the past, Crow remonstrated that the country girls of her time should not to be discouraged by their duties but should instead appreciate the reduction in toil that modern appliances had afforded and incorporate those tools into their working lives.[71] More than three hundred pages of advice in Crow's book encouraged young women to improve their lives and commit their energies to the rural homes and communities they lived in.

But no matter how closely farm parents followed these and other suggestions in the agricultural press, they could not guarantee a child's decision to remain in agriculture. Some factors were well beyond the efforts and abilities of parents. Most parents could not manage their farms without the labors of their children, and children would continue to work at difficult tasks in all weathers. There was little parents could do to control the vagaries of the agricultural economy, and therefore little that they could do to guarantee their families a comfortable income; consequently, it was beyond the ability of many to reward older children financially for their contributions to the family enterprise. Many youngsters left agriculture in search of regular wages, which might be greater for a skilled laborer than for a farming family. Indeed, when in 1904 and 1905 Liberty Hyde Bailey, Country Life reformer and dean of the Agricultural College at Cornell University, surveyed students (overwhelmingly male) about why they planned to leave farming, 40 percent of them cited the lack of remuneration, and 20 percent cited the onerousness of the work. A respondent raised in Illinois commented, "No money in farming. I like the city and its pleasures. There is nothing 'doing' on a farm." A young man from Wisconsin wrote, "On a farm, especially dairy, a person is kept at work each day, no time to be away more than half a day at a time, as help on a farm is not always to be trusted. As compared with other occupations, farm life demands longer hours, harder work, and less pay."[72]

Farm children also grew up with the experience of uncertainty. Uncertainty remained, and remains, a constant feature of life in agriculture. Families simply had to expect ups and downs in prices from year to year, as well as variations in moisture and temperature. Uncertainty, however, could be far more extreme than a few cents' variation in the price of corn, or an inch or two of moisture. In the late nineteenth and early twentieth centuries, midwestern farm families experienced grasshopper plagues that decimated their crops for years running, leaving them literally starving. They experienced extreme drought that wrecked their fortunes. Families suffered through violent ups and downs in the agricultural markets that could raise their hopes and dash them within a few short years. The experience of these hardships did little to encourage youngsters to remain in agriculture, no matter how hard their parents tried to make farm homes and farm life not only palatable but pleasant. As a respondent to Bailey's survey commented, "Life is short and uncertain. Why spend it performing a painful task, which is at the same time a thankless one?"[73] And no matter how comfortable a parent could make the farm, it often could not compete with cities and their attractions, such as movie theaters, dance halls, and easy access to other social events.[74]

Not all parents worked to keep their children on the farm. For some, this was an acknowledgment of the practical difficulties of starting a farm in the late nineteenth and early twentieth centuries. Rising land prices and land scarcity, visible in increasing tenancy rates, made it less likely that midwestern farm parents would be able to locate their sons (daughters were rarely considered) on affordable, high-quality land. In Iowa, for example, land prices rose from $36.35 an acre in 1900 to $82.58 in 1910.[75] Another type of economic reality led parents to provide a life in agriculture for one of their children, but not the rest. Knowing that a farm split many ways could not adequately support anyone, some German American parents handed their land down to a single child and planned for the others to migrate to cities.[76] Yet other parents believed that, given the hardships and stress of farm life, their children might be better off out of agriculture. Frank Klingberg, who after a farm childhood became a professor at the University of California–Los Angeles, commented (presumably in reference to himself) that "the hardships of farm life caused parents to plot a professional life for their brighter children."[77] Henry Taylor, who also became a professor, credited his father with directing him away from agriculture when he told Henry that "you are well prepared for far more important work, and there are plenty of people to run farms."[78] Many a farm mother encouraged her daughters to marry men who were not farmers, telling them in word and example of the hours of work, the lack of a regular income, and "the drudgery, isolation and lack of time and opportunity for self-improvement."[79] Not all parents wanted farm life for their children. Other authority figures, such as teachers and ministers, might also counsel youngsters to seek their futures outside of agriculture.[80]

Parents, too, might disagree with each other about the proper futures for children. In the case of the Emery family, of Olmsted County, Minnesota, mother Helen and father Caleb had very different plans for their youngest son, Robert. By the time Robert Emery was sixteen, his father was seventy-two and in dire need of his son's help around the family's eighty-acre farm. While one older sister remained on the farm, his only brother had been gone for a decade and his three other sisters were either married or pursuing careers in other locations. Hands were short on the farm, and Caleb Emery wanted Robert to work. His mother, however, yearned for him to have a future outside of agriculture and resisted her husband's efforts to make a farmer out of Robert. As Helen Emery wrote in her diary, "Cale has groaned & worried until Robt has about given up his ambition to go to school & thinks he will work on the farm & work what he can for others until he is 18. If he gives up school now I am afraid he will never see the time & inclination to begin again & must drudge for a living—but one finds it hard to know just what is best."[81]

Although Helen Emery sounded somewhat equivocal about her intentions for her son, commenting, "It is hard to know just what is best," she expressed her opinions more forcefully in other passages. In February 1907, she wrote, "I may be mistaken but it seems a pity for a boy who can learn so easily or who likes to study to spend his days shoveling manure & digging on the farm & if I can manage he shall have his chance."[82] The elder Emerys worked out a compromise; Robert lived at home and worked on the farm in addition to attending school when he could. He also enrolled in correspondence courses in subjects he could not learn in the local country school, such as rhetoric and Latin. On an April day, his mother described the practical results of the compromise: "Robt has worked all day hauling manure & is studying Latin tonight."[83] Farm labor during the day and lessons at night helped to fulfill both parents' intentions for their son, although the correspondence school did cost the family money, something that would not have pleased Caleb Emery. Helen Emery's justification was that the supplemental material "costs some but is helping to make a fine man of my little boy."[84] Being fine, in her world, meant being educated. Helen Emery's intentions, and Robert Emery's ambitions, eventually triumphed. Robert Emery would become a journalist, and he made a career with various midwestern newspapers. Farming was not to be his future.

This, however, is not entirely a story of children leaving the farm. Some made life choices that brought them back to agriculture in spite of educational experiences that gave them options outside of agriculture. In 1888, sixteen-year-old Frisby Leonard Rasp left the family farm in Polk County, Nebraska, to attend Omaha Business College. Although his body was in Omaha, his heart and mind were often at home, on his parents' land. On a

May day he queried his parents, "How many sows have pigs and how many pigs how many new calves & colts are you raising any chickens. . . . I hope to be home in time to shock up the oats and help to stack & hay. How is the pasture is it good? Have you sold any cows."[85] Despite months and months of residence in Omaha, his ambitions were never in the city. His impressions of Omaha at least partially answer the question of why Frisby Rasp, after achieving a further education that would have allowed him to work in an urban location, returned home to marry and to farm. His wonderfully detailed letters describe his dismay with urban conditions. He wrote, "Every thing is Coal smoke and dirt and people." The people were as bad as the physical environment. The girls, he said, were "showy but pukey, and the boys are worse." His intentions were clear: "I wouldn't live in the City always for anything. Get an Education there and a good start in life and then let me have a farm. If I had to live in the City always the very thought would kill me."[86]

Frisby Rasp's objections to Omaha went far beyond the physical deficiencies of the place and the people. He believed that there was a moral gulf between himself and the urban residents around him. He observed drunkenness and people breaking the Sabbath. To his parents he wrote, "I saw three fellows drunk today the first I have seen. This is an awful wicked town the saloons run on sunday and most all work goes right on."[87] The poor children he saw in the streets violated his sensibilities as well. They put him "in mind of pups or a pet pig they set in the middle of the street and play in the dust and if there is a water puddle near they are sure to be in it They will step up to a man when they are just learning to talk and say gimme a chaw of Tobacky."[88] Omaha struck him as a more selfish place than the rural community he had left behind. "Every body looks out for himself in this cursed place."[89] Clean air, quiet, and an environment familiar in all ways pulled Frisby Rasp back to the land, as did his parents' promises. In a letter to Frisby, his mother wrote, "Pau says as soon as you are through your learning he will quit farming."[90] As the eldest son, destined to inherit the family farm, Frisby Rasp had more incentive than many sons to remain in agriculture. Not surprisingly, studies of persistence in late nineteenth-century farming communities have indicated that those young men most likely to remain in rural communities were those whose parents had chosen them to inherit the land.[91]

Mary Blair, of rural Arrowsmith, Illinois, also pursued other options, only to return to farming. In 1890, she traveled to one of the larger communities in central Illinois, Bloomington, to attend music school, presumably at Illinois Wesleyan University. Unlike Rasp, Blair's impressions of urban life were largely positive (although Bloomington, admittedly, was a much smaller place). She enjoyed buggy rides in Bloomington's shaded streets and claimed to be running the risk of being spoiled by city amenities. "But you know a rotten egg is hard to spoil." Her on-again, off-again, suitor, Lea Hutton, noted that she had become "somewhat stuck on Bloomington" but encouraged her to continue her studies. In 1894, after years of discussion about what her future should be and where she should use her newly developed skills, true love finally conquered all, and Blair married Hutton, settling on a farm in rural Belleflower. She filled her days with all of the usual chores of a farm wife and brought extra money into the family enterprise by teaching music lessons. In the course of four years, Mary Blair Hutton's education had brought her full circle, back to life on a family farm, albeit with new skills that allowed her to supplement the farm's income from agricultural products.[92]

Liberty Hyde Bailey's survey of farm-raised Cornell students also revealed that although some planned to use their education to escape the farm, others hoped to use their education in agriculture. These young men generally had more than one reason for choosing the farm, and most identified nonpecuniary reasons as the most important. Out of 193 respondents, 145 of them listed among their reasons for their choice "love of out-of-doors and of nature," "love of farm life and of the kind of work," "love for living and growing things," or "love of the free life of the farm." Another seventy-seven lauded farming as "an independent life," whereas forty-one called it "a healthful life," and twenty found it an "ideal place for home and rearing of children." Only thirty-nine claimed they were making their choice on the basis of farming as "a profitable occupation." As one young man wrote, "After living in the city for several years, while attending preparatory school, I have come to the conclusion that the farm is the only place to develop well-rounded, sturdy manhood. The farmer need not fear lest his children be led astray by the evil influences of an indolent city life; he is independent and, if temperate, sure of good health and long days."[93] Frisby Rasp was not alone in his assessment of the health and positive attributes of life on the family farm.

Education had presented youngsters such as Frisby Rasp and Mary Blair with choices. With a degree from a business college, Frisby Rasp could have remained in Omaha or moved to another town and worked as a clerk. It would have been steady employment, and clerking would have held the possibility of upward mobility. He could have escaped some of the uncertainties of life on a Nebraska farm. Instead, he chose that farm and the way of life that it represented. For him, getting an education was a means to return to farming better prepared to assume its operation. Mary Blair's education also presented her with choices. She had obtained the credentials to teach; the question was where to use those skills. When Mary Blair began her education, she may or may not have been thinking of music and teaching as lifelong careers. After all, if she chose to teach full-time, she would be choosing essentially to remain single, because turn-of-the-century Americans generally did not believe that careers and marriage were an appropriate combination for women. Her choice to marry Lea Hutton, a longtime suitor and a farmer, defined the way she would use her musical talents. She would give lessons to local children part-time while being a farm wife full-time, a solution that may or may not have been satisfying in the long run. Her music lessons would have brought a small but welcome amount of cash into the family coffers and would have allowed her to continue to indulge her love of music.

By making these choices, Frisby Rasp and Mary Blair were moving against the current. Increasingly, those who had the education and the opportunity were making their lives outside of agriculture, choosing the urban over the rural, choosing a paycheck over the uncertainty of farming. The absolute numbers of farmers rose until 1910 or shortly thereafter, but then began a long and generally unchecked descent. The relative numbers of farmers in the population had begun to decline long before. Between 1880 and 1910, the number of people in rural areas grew by fourteen million, while the number of people in urban centers grew by twenty-eight million. In 1920, the Census Bureau found that more than half the population, or 51.4 percent, was living in urban areas.[94] These well-established trends would continue, and even accelerate. In the decade of the 1920s, another 6.25 million individuals left the countryside, most of them young. By 1930, more than half of all farm operators were over the age of forty-five.[95] The economic fluctuations and national disruptions of the early twentieth century would only make choices such as those of Rasp and Blair more uncommon.

In 1907, President Theodore Roosevelt formed the Country Life Commission to study the problems of the countryside and to make suggestions for their solution. This was a response to the concerns of middle-class, generally urban, reformers who feared that the hemorrhage of population, and especially the population of intelligent young people, from rural areas into American's cities would debilitate, and perhaps even destroy, rural communities.[96] In 1909, when the Country Life Commission presented its report to President Theodore Roosevelt, the commissioners concluded their report with an appeal to the youth of the United States. Rural America, the Commission announced, needed "young people of quality, energy, capacity, aspiration, and conviction, who will live in the open country as permanent residents on farms, or as teachers, or in other useful fields."[97] Although the needs of the countryside were clear and the commission's appeal well intentioned, the needs of rural youth were just as pressing. In spite of what might be lost in habits of industry and the joys of country living, America was moving to the city. More rural youth were choosing what they perceived as the comforts and pleasures of the city over the stresses of rural life. Although these trends were well established by the early years of the twentieth century, the experience of World War I, the Great Depression, and World War II would more or less guarantee the impossibility of retaining the majority of America's farm-raised youth in the countryside. Increasingly, growing up meant choosing a new life in a town or city.

EPILOGUE

"We Are at Home with the Land"

Remembering Farm Childhood

We are at home with the land, secure in the midst of nature's bounty and in spite of its fury. We know that the land and the elements are kind although they may also be cruel. We recall that the now cold land can be warm and generous, and we consciously or unconsciously thank God for it all. The now quiet serenity of the land imparts a silent sermon to us—the world is beautiful, and we are part of it. This is the Prairie, breadbasket of our world, a new home for those who came in hope and trust and were willing to blend their toil with what they found to make it productive for man, a wholesome place for those willing to labor in its fields, live with its uncertainties, and guard its preciousness as best they could.
—William S. Miller, recalling the lessons of growing up in Goose Lake, Illinois

For many who grew up on turn-of-the-century farms, what remained, in the end, were only memories of the place in which they grew up and the lessons that they learned there. Increasingly, as the nineteenth century made its way into the twentieth, the children of America's farms became adults in its cities. The economics of farm life encouraged these individual decisions to migrate, as did the workloads and other stresses inherent in farm childhood. The economic ups and downs of the late nineteenth and early twentieth centuries did little to encourage youngsters raised in the country to become farmers as adults. The agricultural depression after World War I that continued to the opening guns of World War II was discouraging at best. The wars themselves gave farm-raised people an excellent excuse to leave, either to fight for their country or to take advantage of the economic opportunities presented by wartime production and labor shortages. Increasingly, roads led away from, rather than toward, the midwest's farms.

By the end of World War II, rural depopulation was well under way. In the five years between 1939 and 1944, 8.711 million people left the farm. In the generation between 1940 and 1970, the proportion of Americans living on farms fell from 23 percent to a mere 5 percent. Economic stress, increased productivity, and greater opportunities in urban areas had taken their toll.[1] The same trends were visible in the midwestern states. Between 1920 and 1960, the percentage of the population living in rural areas in each of the states studied fell below 50 percent. In 1920, the rural populations in Illinois, Iowa, Kansas, Minnesota, Nebraska, and Wisconsin were 32.1, 63.6, 65.2, 55.9, 68.7, and 52.7 percent of the total population, respectively. By 1960, the situation was much different, with 19.3, 47.9, 39.0, 37.8, 45.7, and 36.2 percent of the population living in rural areas.[2] Increasingly, growing up in the countryside, let alone on a farm, was only a distant national memory.

The memories of farm-raised adults, however, remained, memories that were now outside the American mainstream. As individuals raised on midwestern farms began to realize that their experiences would soon be part of a closing chapter of American history, they rushed to put pen to paper and commemorate their childhoods in print. The products of their writing range from John Ise's carefully researched history of family life in north-central Kansas, continuously available in print since the 1960s, to much more modest endeavors, available only in historical society manuscript collections, such as David Bruce Dill's "Boy Life on the Farm, Wyman, Iowa, 1896–1903," or Margaret Pike's "Remembrances of a Life."[3] Approximately seventy of these writings, between the published and unpublished, as well as a small number of oral histories, inform this discussion of memories of midwestern farm childhood.[4] The stories range from those of childhoods lived in terrible poverty to those lived in relative wealth, although most fall somewhere in between. Some of the writers chose as adults to remain on the land; many more lived out their lives in towns and cities, although most remained in the midwest. They are the stories of immigrant children, as well as the native born. Both men and women reflected on their earlier lives. Their memories were full of the stuff of childhood: chores completed, games played, holidays celebrated, meals eaten, and schools attended. Not all of these memories were pleasant. Siblings and parents died; parents responded to accidents and misadventures with beatings; failed crops resulted in cold and hungry winters. These writers, however, had the luxury of remembering these events from a distance. They were individuals who had survived farm childhood, and in a measure thrived. As adults, they had the time, energy, education, and inclination to put their memories on paper.

In gathering together these memories of farm childhood, I did not expect to find a single, objective, or definitive discussion of the realities of children's farm life in the late nineteenth and early twentieth centuries. The writers came from a variety of backgrounds, from impoverished to comfortable, and all points in between. They were immigrant and native, male and female. Their memoirs, just as their experiences, demonstrated a broad range of possible childhoods. Looking back over many decades, writers were unlikely to remember all of their experiences or to bring any degree of objectivity to what they remembered of life so long ago. Those events most vividly remembered and subsequently recorded were likely to be those accompanied by strong emotion, either good or bad. Good and bad memories, however, were unlikely to get equal treatment in written records of childhood. Those events committed to paper were often those that did not shame or embarrass the writer or reader, because many of the reminiscences were recorded for members of the writers' immediate families. As Maurice Minor wrote in the preface to *Three in a Hill,* his published memoir of a central Illinois boyhood, the book was most importantly written to help his grandchildren understand "what things were like when Grandpa was a boy."[5] Within the limitations of this framework, authors such as Minor were disinclined to include memories that might shock, horrify, or embarrass their readers. And equally, those who suffered the most horrific childhoods were reluctant to revisit those experiences and commit them to print as adults.[6]

This desire not to shock or horrify, however, did not prevent writers from presenting a child's life on the farm as hard. Many memoirs seem to have an underlying purpose of providing moral instruction to the young and of helping them to understand just what it was like to live "in those days." Whether their experience was good or bad, writers felt the need to demonstrate that life as a child on a midwestern farm demanded effort and character greater than that required in other, less rigorous environments, such as the nation's suburbs and cities. As much as any theme can be universalized from these seventy documents, the memory of a powerful, if often painful, formative relationship with the land remains. The land and their youth upon it shaped their characters and their futures.

Given the amount of time that farm children spent working, it is not surprising that reminiscences of those years devote much attention to that topic. Because of a wide range of family situations, the way in which farm-raised adults reflected upon their childhood duties varied enormously. Some people remembered their working lives being initiated by benevolent parents who slowly and carefully inculcated within them habits of industry. Maurice Minor wrote that he experienced a progression of work, from small chores such as weeding and carrying wood and water at age five and a half, to greater responsibilities, such as mowing the lawn, and finally working in the field with a team at age ten.[7] Charles Turner, too, commented on a progression of responsibilities assumed over time, supervised by a careful father. He wrote, "We did a good deal of farm work but never enough to hurt us in any way. And we always had gentle well trained horses to work with, if there were any partly broken, or wild horses father always used them. We never had to run reapers or mowers till we were old enough to handle them as they should be used."[8] Theresa Rickett, who worked alongside her father and brothers in the fields, commented, "I didn't often make mistakes and my father was patient if I did."[9] These descriptions represent an ideal: careful tutelage on the part of parents and supervision and progression of chores suited to a child's age.

Just as pervasive were memories of the demands of work unrelentingly pushing children, day in and day out. As Frank Klinberg opined, "Verily farm life was poetical for the outsider, but often child labor was a savage part of it. It was not how little a child could do but how early and how much."[10] Although the beneficiary of a gradual initiation into farm work, Maurice Minor also noted that the needs of a farm family were incessant. Preparing food was a year-long task, as was gathering fuel for fires. Family members faced continuous chores outside and inside the house. The necessity and pressure of it all was what Minor recalled in retrospect. "There was no other way in this society to maintain respect from one's peers and attain a reasonable degree of security than to work, sometimes almost to the limits of one's physical endurance. . . . there were days when my endurance was taxed to the limit, and I labored with considerable doubt as to whether I would be able to keep up the pace and avoid ignoble disgrace."[11] Oscar Hallam, once he had attained a sufficient age, had endured a similar regimen: "There was no time for the big boys to play until dark."[12] Predictably, such demanding work meant that children spent less time in school. In later years, farm boy Clare Thompson memorialized his experience in verse:

> But where is the boy at the age of nine,
> Who drove this team in so straight a line.
> On March, the first, from school he stayed
> That spring work might not be delayed.

Some forms of work, such as driving a goat cart, may have crossed the line from work to play. Photograph by Harry D. Ayer. By permission of the Minnesota Historical Society.

> He drove this team the whole spring through,
> As no one else in the world would do.[13]

For Marie Koberstein Guethlein, the demands did not come from the fields but from the family. As the oldest child and only girl in a large German Catholic family, her younger siblings were her responsibility. "And the diaper pail was always full of diapers and when Mother was sick having another baby I had to wash diapers, which I didn't appreciate." The diapers in particular soured her on the prospect of additional siblings. "One time when the fourth baby was born when I came home from school the midwife stood at the window with a baby in her arms and smiling—I just wouldn't look at it. Nor go in to see my Mother, another brother—what a feeling and it took a few days for it to wear off." She escaped as quickly as possible into the relative bliss (in her opinion) of hired domestic labor.[14] What those who had been raised on farms remembered about their working lives was very similar to what other youngsters recorded in their letters and diaries; field and household chores were central to a child's life in this time and place.

School, like work, received a varied treatment, but few neglected to mention its presence in their lives. Its significance can be measured, in part, by the pages and pages devoted to detailed descriptions of schoolhouses, schoolteachers, and the many varieties of devilment to which students aspired during school hours. Just like youngsters' diaries and letters, memoirs attested to the wide variety of meanings adults ascribed to their childhood experiences of school. For Augusta Thomas, school and shame were closely associated. Moving between schools, and experiencing poor, unsympathetic teaching, left her woefully behind in math. At age thirteen, she found that "I could not seem to catch up, and I grew sick with helplessness whenever arithmetic time came. . . . I persuaded [Mother] to let me stay home and take care of my baby brother." She tried to return to school at fifteen, was injured, and again fell behind. She left, never to return.[15] Charles Turner remembered the tension between play and school. "I remember how hurt I felt when I was attending school and a good snow would come and rabbit and quail hunting would be good that day and I would have to attend school that day." He overcame his tendency toward truancy, however, eventually being the first person from his district school to attend high school, followed by a career in teaching.[16] For Catharine Wiggins Porter, the dominating memory was one of disorder and teachers who were unable to control their students. "I can still recall the fearful disorder in that school; it was 'confusion worse confounded.' Some of the larger boys were utterly unmanageable." But it was also the place where she learned to play games such as Crack-the-Whip, London Bridge, and Drop the Handkerchief.[17] Nehemias Tjernagel, living in the Norwegian community of Sheldahl, in central Iowa, remembered the excitement and sense of purpose that the school imparted to the community. School events, such as exhibitions and spelling contests, focused the attention of adults and children on the joys of learning. "Thus, when the whole family turned out to the school exhibitions the air was so saturated with happy joyousness that it was a bit difficult to breathe, especially just before the curtain went up. And I doubt it the Roman gladiators ever held their honors in higher esteem than did the hero of the spelling match."[18] Perhaps befitting someone who became a minister and Chautauqua speaker as an adult, Hugh Orchard recognized the limitations of the country school but also praised it for its positive effect on his life. "We both hated and loved that district school. We cursed it and praised it. We starved and mistreated it. We thought of it as a necessary evil that had to be endured, and never half appreciated what it did for us. That school stirred our intellects, exercised our youthful imagination, taught us how to find out things for ourselves, and forced real knowledge into our heads."[19] School clearly mattered, if not always in the ways that parents, teachers, and school board members anticipated.

Others were sure to mention the importance of play to their young lives. Again, the value of play and toys can be measured, in part, in careful and loving descriptions of the many games that children played, such as Prisoner's Base and Anti-I-Over, in addition to detailed instructions for the creation of various toys, such as cornstalk fiddles and popguns.[20] If work was among the hardest parts of childhood remembered, play and leisure were times of relief and rejuvenation. Oscar Hallam believed that his best memories of childhood centered on family gatherings in the dining room on winter evenings. "We loved to sit around the old wood range. . . . We loved to pop corn, 'pull' candy, boil furmity at the big cook stove. We loved to play 'authors' around the big table in winter evenings."[21] The circus, for Margaret Pike, took pride of place as her favorite memory. Fortunately, her father was a great fan of the circus, and every time one came to town, he took the children. She found it "terrifically exciting. I would come home and try to copy some of the stunts I had seen. I don't know that I was very successful but it was the greatest entertainment for me."[22] Other favorite memories of play featured the schoolyard, where youngsters had the time and opportunity to exercise their imaginations. Wisconsin-raised Theresa Rickett could hardly wait for spring to come, so that she and her friends could really enjoy the wonders of the outdoors. "We could get permission from the teacher to go down in the woods at lunch time. There the boys chase around and blundered into thistles while the girls played games of make-believe. One of the things we liked most to do was to make little playhouses. . . . we played in quite imaginative ways."[23] Play offered a marvelous escape from the often hard realities of agricultural life.

The writers infused descriptions of the land on and around their farms

Students and their teacher stand in front of the Webster, Iowa, school, 1886. This is a somewhat unusual picture in that it is clearly summer (note the students' bare feet), but the teacher is a man. Most schools hired women in the summer term. By permission of the State Historical Society of Iowa.

with an equal degree of warmth and fervor. As youngsters, they had lived in close contact with nature and relished the sights, sounds, and smells that surrounded them. For many, enjoyment of nature and participation in play were intimately linked. Louisa Boylan reflected later in life, "The hill sides abounded with flowers, dutch mans breeches, spring beauties, Indian paint-brushes & many others. What joy we had roaming those hills & woods."[24] In Anna Stanley's memories, the Wisconsin woods of her childhood remained a source of wonder. The enormous roots of toppled pine trees had been her playhouses. "We gathered moss for carpeting; Princes pine, wild hops and other trailing vines formed attractive draperies; the trailing pigeon berry vines & wintergreen berry vines lent color to our draperies. Where there were niches and recesses we built up a soft mossy bed where we could lie comfortably."[25] Maurice Minor claimed to have been pleasantly over-whelmed as a small boy by the night sky and the sounds of the summer evening. The ground beneath his feet was equally evocative. "I can remember yet the soft, warm feel of the dust in the country road, the soothing sensation of burying one's feet ankle-deep in the soft, cool, oozing mud along the pasture stream."[26] In the absence of a church in their rural Kansas community, Frances Moore and her family spent Sundays taking in the countryside. "Up among the rocks in this canyon there grew the most beautiful Sweet William I have ever seen! . . . We all enjoyed wandering around over the rocks gathering flowers and ferns to carry home."[27] In some, it stirred a lifelong love of nature. Reflecting upon the lessons learned in childhood, William Miller wrote, "We are home with the land, secure in the midst of nature's bounty and in spite of its fury."[28]

Nature did not provide all of the texture of farm life as presented in these memoirs. People remembered the homes they had lived in and the clothing they had worn. An even more evocative subject was food, either because youngsters had known hunger and were overjoyed when it was abundant, or because food conjured up memories of special moments in farm childhood. In either case, the food that people remembered was not usually terribly exotic, but commonplace comfort food—food that made them feel good. Memories fostered by hunger could last a lifetime.[29] Frances Moore grew up in Kansas, and her family endured the ravages of grasshopper plagues. As a result, apples took on a special significance. "We children were not thriving very well as I remember, so my father and several men of the community went to Missouri and bought apples. We had had too much corn meal with no variety of diet. Those apples! To this day . . . a good juicy apple touches a spot in my stomach and mind that is untouched by other things. When I see people leave too much on the core of an apple or peel too deeply into its delicious crispness, I know they have never felt the deep indescribable need for an apple."[30] The ongoing lack of fresh fruit could translate into a passion for it, leading to raiding expeditions into orchards and berry patches. Eva Phelps's childhood cravings, never well enough fulfilled, resulted in a special love for apples, berries, crab apples, and rhubarb.[31] Bread, hot from the oven and smothered in butter, evoked pleasant memories of mothers working in the kitchen.[32] Hot bread and butter were strongly associated with all being right with the world, as were other homely dishes, such as chicken and noodles, hominy, and popcorn.[33] Those remembering celebrations almost inevitably mentioned ice cream, a great treat and a rarity in homes without electricity and mechanical refrigeration. As Clifford Merrill Drury recounted, "What a treat it was for us children to lick the dasher after it had been pulled from the two-gallon container. No ice cream has ever tasted so delicious to me as the rich, creamy, vanilla-flavored ice cream we made on the farm."[34] One of the most enduring characteristics of the food, whether it was everyday fare or extraordinary, was that it came from the land, and they as youngsters had played some role in its gathering and preparation.

For youngsters who worked hard and often had to wait a long time for, or be disappointed by, the fruits of their labor, food was the most immediate reward available. One mother recognized this function of food and used it to motivate her children. "Our mother used to come to the door and call us, and we never knew! We might have to bring in what seemed unlimited numbers of armfuls of wood or pails of water, *or* she might have just taken out of the oven warm bread. We could have the crusts off the loaf, sometimes from every facet the loaf had, all the crust with butter. There might be cinnamon rolls or fresh cookies."[35] From a distance of many years, this potential reward of food helped to soften the contours of days organized around labor. Although a mother's call might be a call to work, it might also be a call to the warm comfort of baked goods.

The above-mentioned topics were present in most, if not all, of the memoirs. The interpretations of work, school, play, and even food varied, but each was a topic with which writers were comfortable and willing to contend. Other topics received much more cursory treatment. Because of the aforementioned desire not to shock or embarrass, writers chose to censor a number of their childhood memories or omit them from mention altogether. Although farm people lived in an environment rich with animal reproduction, sexuality (either animal or human) received very little attention in printed and preserved memories of farm childhood. Milo Pitcher, recalling his childhood on a central Iowa farm, commented offhandedly. "There was no need to tell us about the birds and the bees. We knew all about that. With all the colts, calves, pigs, kittens and pups that were born on the farm we had plenty of first hand experience."[36] David Dill, also of Iowa, was somewhat more forthcoming about the limits of learning purely by observation. "Another aspect of farm life—the process of reproduction—I learned to understand by observation not by verbal explanation. The roles of roosters and of hens and the purpose of the mother hen's sitting on her eggs I saw repeated by birds: the end result was the propagation of the species. It was some time before I fully understood the relation between that biological sequence and the interaction between boar and sow, bull and cow and stallion and mare." The practical, human application of this knowledge was not always so clear. From a distance of many years, Dill admitted, "I was aware of at least the threat of such an interaction between boy and girl."[37] Molly Krutza, reflecting on her sexual education, commented upon the inadequacy of pigs and chickens as teachers. "Not until I surreptitiously read the family doctor book did I understand what it was all about."[38] By all accounts, sex education in this environment was neither systematic nor terribly complete.

William S. Miller, in *Growing Up in Goose Lake,* was one of the few to describe in any detail the sexual awakening of farm youngsters. Living in proximity to so much animal life, both domesticated and wild, ensured that farm youngsters would grow up aware that "animals, human and otherwise, depended on the preservation of their kind by their natural response to a biological urge and that the fulfillment of this sex urge is necessary for the continuation of life in its various forms." Although cows, horses, and pigs might be observed in the barnyard, much of what happened with young human animals seems to have occurred in the school and playground. Teachers demanded that male and female students seated together place both hands on the desk, for fear that "foreign lands were being explored." Secluded parts of the schoolyard provided the setting for "close bodily contact" between older boys and girls. For young men in their teens and twenties, the hired girl was a particular object of interest. Miller wrote, "Any new hired girl was studied by the neighborhood help, in terms of her comeliness, her build, her possible consent to a nocturnal proposition." Girls who responded "to some degree" increased their chances of continuing male attention.[39] Miller, however, left the likelihood of these responses and their possible repercussions for the young women to his readers' imaginations. He did not admit to any personal adventures.

Surely, farm-raised individuals had more memories of their sexual coming of age than what they later admitted to. As these few memoirs make clear, animal reproduction was an essential part of farm life and could hardly be hidden in its entirety from the inquisitive eyes of children. Puberty, a universal experience for those who survived to adulthood, was almost entirely evaded in print, although it could hardly be avoided in life. An awareness of human sexuality would have been difficult to avoid as well, given the cramped quarters of most farm homes. In homes with mothers and daughters, some knowledge of menstruation would have been inevitable.[40] Modesty, however, seems to have prevented open discussion of such topics as youngsters and even at a distance of many years. If memoirs and reminiscences are correct, youngsters practiced a great deal of avoidance when confronted with such matters. Slovie Kissin-Marver's brother never told his siblings what transpired when he was allowed to witness the mating of the family's cow with a neighbor's bull; nevertheless, his sister theorized, "upon their return from the 'Wilder Farm' Alfred must have felt taller, wiser."[41] The sexual attitudes of the time did not encourage the sharing of such wisdom with one's younger siblings. None of this, however, should be surprising. As previously mentioned, letters and diaries written by youngsters during this time (and written by adults, too) made very little mention of human sexuality. And even if youngsters had a greater degree of sexual awareness than they would later admit to as adults, this would be equally unsurprising. For individuals of their generation, admitting to too much youthful sexual knowledge or experimentation would not be considered "nice," or proper.

Illnesses, too, received relatively little comment, despite the near-constant presence of disease, and fear of disease, in rural communities. This seems to be a facet of farm childhood that many preferred to forget. Given the excruciating pain of diphtheria and its treatment, for example, this is not surprising. Augusta Thomas's memoirs are illuminating. Although her bout with diphtheria had occurred nearly sixty years before, when she was just seven, she remembered it vividly. It was one of the few times that a doctor treated her. "He proceeded to burn my throat with a vitriol pencil until the blood ran. . . . I knew no more for some days. But the horror of it all was very real and for months those dreams returned causing me to wake in a cold sweat." The effects of the illness never left her. "I had been a healthy child up to that time, never having been sick that I could remember, but that illness left its mark in my body to last the rest of my life: impaired eye-sight, digestion, teeth, throat and a weakened constitution. But I lived."[42] In the end, it was the survival that mattered more than the suffering endured.

Deaths also received sparse treatment, perhaps because of the aforementioned reason. These writers, as survivors, may not have wanted to dwell on the fate of those who did not make it to adulthood, and they may not have wanted to relive the pain of those losses. Although many remembered the deaths of parents and grandparents, it was the death of siblings that received the most attention, when deaths received mention at all. Lula Gillespie Lentz watched four siblings, three brothers and one sister, suffer with typhoid fever, and her sixteen-year-old brother, Iva, died. She remembered "seeing the doctor lead away a fine young heifer one day as payment for his services."[43] Minnie Ellingson Tapping's brother, as the result of a dare, took a kick to the head from a new horse. In spite of the doctor's assurances that he would recover, Willie died on the third day after the accident. In remembering the incident, her sorrow was for her parents: "Poor Poppy! Poor Mommy!"[44] As a ten-year-old, Gladys Trimble held her seven-month-old brother while he died and then sucked the milk out of her mother's breasts when they became engorged after the baby's death.[45] Augusta Thomas lost her beloved brother, Osseon, to an unnamed, lingering illness that the doctors could not diagnose or treat. She was alone with him when he died. "I have always been thankful I was there, saw him go through that transition. I believed he saw something not given human eyes to see. Whatever it was made him very happy. But even now, with half a century between me and that scene, it shakes me to the core to write of it, and tears blind my words." Given the realities of life in a sod house, Augusta Thomas had to sleep in the same room with her brother's body before its burial. Even more disturbing, her parents very nearly lost touch with reality in the weeks after Osseon's death. Eventually the family returned to some semblance of normality.[46] Particularly in the cases of Trimble and Thomas, what is most palpable in their accounts is an awareness of their parents' fragility in the face of the loss of a child. This had to have made the family tragedy all the more painful and bewildering for the remaining children, who may for the first time have become completely aware of their parents as beings with emotions, weaknesses, and fears just like their own. These family events would have been extremely difficult to remember and record.

Other situations that reduced parents to despair also received short shrift. A number of the writers lived through the grasshopper plagues that swept the midwest in the last half of the nineteenth century, but few dwelled on them. Ovoe Swartz and his family lived northeast of Great Bend and watched the grasshoppers devour their first crop in Kansas. A dark cloud came from the northwest: "It held a deluge, sure enough, but instead of raining, the cloud disgorged an ever remembered down-pour of voracious grasshoppers. . . . The entire region's gardens and grain crops furnished the ravenous hoppers scarcely a full dinner and supper." Swartz well remembered their effect on his parents and the whole community. "With the season for growing more grain offering no hope, most pioneers were saddened and heart-sick beyond describable words."[47] Families were left at a loss, in every possible way.

In spite of such stresses, most of these writers described family relationships that were close and loving. Fathers were tough but fair; strong but generous mothers were the rock upon which the family foundation was built.

Few were as forthcoming as Hugh Orchard about family strife. Orchard was born and raised in Iowa and suffered under the direction of an extremely demanding father. All of Orchard's brothers escaped the farm around the age of eighteen; only Hugh remained, determined not to make his mother cry as she had when her older sons ran away. He remembered, "And I made good at it too but it was kinda hard sledding sometimes." The problem was Orchard's father, who "was wonderful in amusing little children. . . . But when his own children got big he seemed to back off, and quit noticing them altogether and became boss." He pushed his children to work as hard and as fast as possible. This included limiting their social contacts with other youngsters, so that they would be ready for work every morning. Orchard reflected, "We almost hated him for this at times, and I do not like to think of it now. It was so useless for him to act that way." Only their mother "found time to console us and keep us from open rebellion." Nevertheless, only one son, Hugh, took enough consolation to remain on the farm until he came of age.[48] That accomplished, he left the farm to become a minister.

But even in his writings, Orchard was not entirely negative about his experience as a farm child. He admitted that even work, at times, could be satisfying. In spite of the mental strain of working for his demanding father, Orchard wrote that, "farm work never hurt anybody and we hadn't got to the worrying place yet. We were always having a good enough time in spite of our troubles."[49] As a small boy, taking water to the harvest hands working in the fields was a special treat. "Mounted on my charger, I made the rounds of these harvest hands with my jug of cool water. . . . There I was, guiding a big, strong horse all by myself, swatting a greenhead that lit on her shoulder or riding through a weed patch eight feet high. Talk about luxury, or heaven—it was all those with some to spare."[50] Only as a near-adult did he begin to understand his father's perspective on the farm, crops, and work.

> As a youngster, I never could understand Pap's talk about being glad for a bumper crop. I was always glad—especially after I got big enough to work steady in the fields—when there was a *short* crop of either small grain or corn. That made less work to do. Hard work and youngsters never did go well together, so I was always glad for a missing hill of corn at husking time and for the wet places where the grain had been drowned out. I was almost grown before I began to see that we had to depend on the crops for our living, our comforts and our food.[51]

Orchard's memories of, and reflections upon, his rural Iowa childhood demonstrate one of the realities of such reminiscences; writers often presented positive and negative memories between the same two covers of the book. The negative emotions surrounding his father's heavy hand existed side by side with Orchard's positive memories of his work and his adult understanding of the importance of that labor.

Orchard was not the only farm-raised adult to incorporate this contradiction into a memoir. Liahna Babener, in a chapter entitled "Bitter Nostalgia: Recollections of Childhood on the Midwestern Frontier," has argued that this is a common characteristic of such writings. According to Babener, the coexistence of nostalgic memories of the past beside the "dark obverse conditions" on farms reveals "an incipient strain of animosity toward their regional heritage." Those who grew up on midwestern farms felt an "indignation about the deprivations that attended a midwestern upbringing." She argues that these memoirs are essentially hypocritical, or "double minded," in their treatment of a farm childhood in that, on the one hand, the authors argued that their experiences deeply and positively shaped their values and mind-set, whereas on the other, they were left bitter about the pains they suffered as children.[52] My argument, however, is somewhat different. It is entirely possible for the experience of growing up, no matter what one's location, one's family's occupation, or one's social class, to leave a person feeling at the same time both glad for the experience and the lessons and bitter about the scars left by the same experiences and lessons. Only the most unusual individual leaves childhood without scars, sorrows, and bitterness. Childhood is a time of limits drawn by others, plans made by others, and often essential powerlessness in the face of adults. It is a time of enormous peer pressure and expectations. A memoir written without resentments and pain is a rare memoir indeed. Farm-raised adults could quite understandably walk away from the experience glad, in some ways, that they had grown up in that environment while at the same time never wishing to return.

These memoirs, clearly, are an interpretation of child life on the farm. The individual writers sifted through their memories and decided which ones to record, and how to record them. To paraphrase the words of historian David Thelen, constructing a memoir is a bit like creating a picture album: "People seek to freeze or preserve memories by taking pictures that remind them of shared moments or people from the past. In discussing which pictures to frame or place in albums, people literally decide what image of their pasts they want to show others. . . . In the course of taking a picture or creating an album they decide what they want to remember and how they want to remember it."[53] The pictures preserved in the memoirs of writers such as Augusta Thomas, David Dill, or Hugh Orchard were as carefully selected as those in their family albums. Although the grittiness of farm life was present in descriptions of such topics as work, disease, and death, clearly some of the texture was lost in the selectivity of writers.

Acknowledging that, the question then becomes, how did farm-raised midwestern adults interpret their experience of growing up, and what aspects of that experience did they choose to emphasize? Again and again, writers returned to the influence of farm childhood on their core values. Growing up on a farm shaped who they were: the skills they had, their perspectives on life, and their expectations of the world. For some, their place of origin and its intimate ties to nature meant, in turn, an intimate relationship with God. William Miller saw in the prairie a "silent sermon" that came from experiencing the land in all weathers.[54] Maurice Minor reflected that "there you felt a part of God's creation. Your life was ruled by Nature—the weather, the soil, the seasons, God's creatures. You had a ringside seat as Nature's laws were played out by the elements before your very eyes." Inevitably, he argued, this kind of life made a superior person. "There were lessons to be learned in all of these things. Only the most insensitive could have lived in this environment without becoming a better and wiser person for the experience."[55] In Anna Stanley's memory, a childhood lived on an isolated Wisconsin farm yielded enormous benefits. "Each day was brim full of interest and fun. We had no toys but I believe that developed the creative within us. We were forced to draw heavily upon our imaginations and make our own fun."[56] A childhood in agriculture, in their opinion, enriched the soul and spirit.

The training farm childhood offered, however, was not just spiritual, but practical as well. In picking over the navy beans, Samuel Goldenman learned an essential life lesson. "I never liked picking over beans. Of course, the option of refusing was not available to me. Dad would 'plunk down' a pile of beans on the table; games and other things had to wait until the evening's quota was met. Looking back, I know it was good training for life. Some things just have to get done—and they have priority."[57] Clifford Drury credited farm childhood with the development of practical skills and an acceptance of hard work. "I learned lessons and acquired habits which have been of inestimable value to me throughout my life." Henry Taylor characterized his entire Iowa childhood as "in-service training," beginning at age two and continuing throughout his apprenticeship at his father's side. What he learned from his father, most importantly, were "skills that required the coordination of hand and eye under the control of the mind," as well as an "ability to patiently observe and analyze."[58]

In spite of the agricultural change happening in the late nineteenth and early twentieth centuries, those raised on farms maintained that agriculture was still a truer and more honest way to earn a living. A strong strain of agrarianism ran through midwestern farming communities, coloring individuals' thinking about the place of agriculture in the life of the nation. Many farmers continued to believe, with Thomas Jefferson, that "those who labor in the earth are the chosen people of God" and that "corruption of morals in the mass of cultivators is a phenomenon of which no age nor nation has furnished an example." In the agrarian mind-set, independence, hard work, and honesty were intertwined and peculiarly the province of those who farmed.[59] In the mid- to late twentieth century, these beliefs found their way into the memoirs of farm-raised adults. Maurice Minor argued that

> there a day's work brought a day's pay, and the end result of the work lay in naked exposure for all to view and compare. There the consumer was for the most part also the producer and the producer the consumer. There family welfare was a function of family organization and industry. There a part of one's acquisitions was allocated for giving and share. There you felt a kinship with your neighbors and somehow everyone's welfare was everyone's concern. There your every act stood before the judgment of your fellow men and it was important that your deeds were acceptable to the society in which you lived before being reviewed by a Higher Power.[60]

J. Glenn Logan, raised on a Kansas farm, said the same thing, if in a somewhat simpler form: "Everything had to come from the soil, directly or indirectly. There were no wages, no salaries, no investments, except as stated, and while the soil in those days was rich and would produce any kind of crop when there was rainfall, there were years of drought."[61] Farmers, in their opinion, remained uncorrupted by creeping industrialization and commercialism.

The essential honesty of the farming life, others believed, carried over into other facets of the family and community experience. Bruce Bliven credited the lack of juvenile delinquency in his northwestern Iowa community to the industry of the young. Work in all its forms meant that "in our non-affluent society nobody ever had cause to complain that he had 'nothing to do.'"[62] For Frances Olsen Day, the benefits of labor went even further. Work, even

This early twentieth-century farm child's drawing illustrates youngsters'
fascination with the machinery involved in farming operations such as threshing.
McClary Collection. By permission of the Nebraska State Historical Society.

for small children, meant that they had a sense of purpose. "There was
plenty of hard work for everyone but there was a satisfaction even to a child
of knowing that ones efforts were needed in the general scheme of things.
That even the small daily chores faithfully done made life pleasant for us all
and what greater reward can one wish for than to feel you have done your
duty?"[63] If the work was hard, then the reward was a joy in simple things.
For boys, such as Bruce Bliven and Milo Pitcher, the simple thing that
brought a great thrill was a threshing machine. The contraption induced
"unforgettable alarm." "I'll never forget," Pitcher wrote, "the smell of hot
grease and coal smoke."[64] Growing up on a farm, according to these observers, created honest, hard working, purposeful people, able to see and
appreciate the wonder in their lives.

The lessons learned and the values inculcated, not to mention the thrill of
the threshing machine, however, were not always enough to convince
youngsters of the benefits of a lifelong commitment to agriculture. Although
some of the writers remained in rural areas and lived out their lives on
farms, more found their way into towns and cities, either because their parents abandoned agriculture or because they themselves did so as young
adults. Their emotions upon leaving the farm were decidedly upbeat. In
1915, when Clifford Drury's family moved from a Sac County, Iowa, farm
to town, Drury rejoiced. "There were no more cows to milk, no livestock to
feed, no stables to be cleaned out, and no need to go out-of-doors to do
chores in stormy weather. . . . We had moved into a new age!"[65] As an adult,

Drury chose to become a minister and missionary rather than a farmer. Lula Gillespie Lentz experienced many of the same emotions when her family abandoned its Illinois farm for the small town of Creal Springs. "I felt no remorse in leaving the farm. Town life had an appeal. It had board sidewalks that clicked under my feet."[66] Addie Thompson Sinclair, whose early years on a Kansas farm had provided her ample opportunity to observe the difficulties of her mother's life, spurned an otherwise acceptable suitor who wanted to farm. "I was determined never to marry a farmer and have to live on a farm."[67] As a teenager, Augusta Thomas began to question her place on the family farm. Although she was proud of the work she did in the family's fields and cherished her father's praise of her straight corn rows, she felt that it was not enough. "I could do with my hands. But would I ever be able to do with my head, as my cousins in town were doing? The long green rows of corn gave me no answer."[68] The answer came in the form of marriage to a minister and a farewell to the land. These were not mournful reflections upon a way of life left behind.

In a 1989 examination of the uses of oral history in agricultural history, Lu Ann Jones and Nancy Grey Osterud argued that only in two cases, the depths of the Great Depression and the farm crisis of the 1980s, were farm people comfortable with describing leaving the land "not as a personal moral failure but rather as the result of overwhelming economic pressures." Staying in farming, in spite of the hardships, was a virtue that many oral histories celebrated; leaving the farm, on the other hand, was not necessarily an occasion for rejoicing.[69] How, then, do we explain their celebratory tone, as farm-raised youngsters remembered leaving the farm for town? Oral histories were generally collected from adults who had lost their farms, rather than from individuals who had chosen as young adults not to enter farming. Consequently, in writing their memoirs, farm-raised adults took a somewhat different tone. Although some remained in agriculture, many left the farm to go to school, to teach, to become ministers, or to become urban housewives. The narratives they created about this experience allowed them to tell their childhood's stories, weigh their importance, and explain and legitimate for a later generation their reasons for abandoning their agrarian roots. In writing about their childhood experiences, they demonstrated a full understanding of the many facets of farm life, from work to school to play, and calculated both their cost and benefit. They claimed the positive aspects of their childhoods, such as the values learned from hard work, while asserting that they had lived through enough to last a lifetime. Even if farm-raised adults did not want to return to the farm, their memories formed an "ideological backdrop" against which they could understand and measure the choices that shaped their present.[70] No one argued that a childhood like their own, in spite of its virtues, was a requirement for his or her own children.

In *The Past Is a Foreign Country*, David Lowenthal writes, "As the past seems to recede from us, we seek to re-evoke it by multiplying paraphernalia *about* it—souvenirs, mementoes, historical romances, old photos—and by preserving and rehabilitating its relics."[71] Farm-raised adults did this by assembling and recording their reminiscences of a time they remembered vividly, but that was increasingly outside the mainstream. The vast majority of modern Americans, however, do not have this option. At the dawn of the twenty-first century, slightly less than 2 percent of people in the United States lived on farms. Few have milked a cow, gathered eggs, or even planted a vegetable garden large enough to provide significant resources for the winter. In the absence of a real rural experience, they consume enormous numbers of magazines exploiting country themes and providing decorating and culinary advice for recreating a homey, country atmosphere. A proliferation of living history farms makes it possible for us to visit our rural roots, even if just for an afternoon. A few of the truly hard-core have had the opportunity to take part in the creation of several historically based "reality series" on public television, such as *Pioneer House* and *Colonial House,* attempting to relive a time before the intrusion of automobiles, televisions, telephones, and tractors. The rest of us have the chance to watch, wonder, and evaluate.[72] As much as we try, however, we cannot go there. In this country, that place and time no longer exist. One-room schools disappeared from most locations in the immediate post–World War II period. Thanks to radio, television, the movies, and computers, the popular culture of urban childhood became increasingly accessible to those in even the most remote locations. Children continued (and continue) to work for their parents, but school became more and more the defining force in their lives. As historian David Danbom has written, farm children's lives as they existed a hundred years ago are thoroughly an artifact of the past. Although farm children still "help out," work is no longer the center of their lives. They go to school, participate in extracurricular activities, and often go to college. The farm is no longer "an educational institution in which boys and girls [learn] their future occupations by working with their parents. . . . The farm today is mainly a place where people grow up. When they have reached adulthood, they are more likely to leave and become accountants or computer programmers or retail clerks than they are to follow in their parents' footsteps."[73] The turn-of-the-previous-century's farm childhood is now, well and truly, another country.

The youngsters who grew up in that world made decisions and reacted to events in a way that remade childhood. In large numbers, they left the land and raised their own children in urban places. Aside from the small number of youngsters living in a few insular religious communities, such as the Amish or the Hutterites, childhoods such as those described in this book are gone, not to be recreated. How we feel about this social and cultural loss, I suspect, is much how those farm-raised adults, looking backward, felt about leaving the farm. On the one hand, the loss of certain traditions, practices, and experiences is a cause for mourning, or at the very least, reflection. Other facets of this experience have disappeared, much to the relief of the larger part of the population. A hundred years ago, farm children contributed in important ways to the ongoing economic health of their families. If the memoirs of the individuals cited in this chapter are correct, those contributions helped to create a sense of belonging and rootedness in farm children. In order to make these contributions, children had to work side by side with their parents, learning bit by bit the tasks that filled their days. Children took pride in those accomplishments, even if they chose not to make a lifetime out of plowing fields and planting corn. Unfortunately, however, hard work could stray into the realm of too hard, with children overtaxing their muscles and bones, experiencing frost-bitten fingers and toes, and missing out on an increasingly valuable facet of modern life—their education. Work was a mixed bag of opportunities and losses.

The same could be said of most children's experiences in school. Country schools provided an intimate environment where children could work at their own pace, often with the help of the older children around them. Their teachers knew them and their families, and the connection between school and community was a strong one. Parents built the school, hired the teachers, and formed the school board. Teachers often lived in family homes, with the children they taught. Millions of children were able to parlay their country school educations into the opportunity for higher education in high schools and colleges. But the youngest and least experienced teachers often taught in the country schools; some of those schools were also woefully overcrowded and undersupplied. Problems with discipline rendered many a classroom unfit for study—although this characteristic was certainly not unknown to schools in cities and towns. Most youngsters left school at the end of eighth grade, able to read, write, and figure, but not necessarily with the kind of skills that would offer them a broad range of opportunities in areas beyond the farm. If there was one area in farm children's lives that late nineteenth and twentieth century reformers insisted needed attention, this was it.

We may also mourn the loss of the kind of resourcefulness that was apparent in farm-raised teenagers, such as Rhoda Emery and Hermann Benke. Thousands of youngsters like them completed the eighth grade and took over schools, bringing education to other farm children. Teenagers today have few opportunities to display such levels of responsibility, both for the students they taught and the families they helped to support. The admiration and amazement that we have for such young people, however, may also be tempered by a sense of loss for them. Where Hermann Benke went after his stint of public school teaching is unknown. That he would have benefited from and greatly enjoyed a college education is readily apparent. Rhoda Emery was finally able to achieve a year of college education and to develop a career in education, but had she been born in different circumstances, she might have achieved so much more. Hard work and determination on the part of farm girls like her rarely took them as far as they could dream.

It is in play, perhaps, that we feel the greatest nostalgic pull for a past we have lost. These children played without the distractions of radios, televisions, and computers. Although they lived in a world that was becoming more consumer-oriented by the moment, their family's circumstances often precluded much in the way of store-bought toys, games, and books. Even youngsters from relatively well-to-do families, such as the Krueger twins, relied heavily on the homemade in the creation of their fun. The circumstances of life in midwestern farming communities forced youngsters to devise their own playthings, create their own games, and make the most of the physical environment, both built and natural. It is not surprising that the fondest memories of farm-raised adults centered on their pursuit of creative play in and around their parents' farms. Unlike modern children, their play, for the most part, was free-form and unscripted, and parents and other adults interfered as little as possible. It was their own. In that way, it was, perhaps, far more physically dangerous than the play allowed to many modern American children. Although it was not unusual for farm children to risk limbs (and sometimes their lives) in pursuit of entertainment, one of the greatest threats from the forms of entertainment pursued by modern

In April 1901, Hattie Pautz posed with her dolls and their lovingly made accessories. Photograph by Alex Krueger. By permission of the Wisconsin Historical Society.

children is obesity, brought on by sedentary pursuits. For most farm children, this was hardly a concern.

The harsh lives lived by the poorest of farm children, those who were so poor that they became wards of the state, are, I hope, less prevalent than they were a century ago. Since the 1930s, starvation and homelessness have been addressed more systematically than they were previously. Although the solutions that states found for their care were decidedly incomplete and prone to abuse, they were, unfortunately, probably as good as most state legislatures could have managed (or imagined) at that time. The problems experienced by the children indentured to the Wisconsin State Public School only serve to emphasize that as far as the nation has come in caring for the children of the poor, the mechanisms in use today (such as foster care) can be as flawed and prone to failure as they were a hundred years ago. The options open to the poor and disadvantaged, then as now, were severely limited, and even in the late twentieth century, the problems facing rural children were significant. Americans tended to perceive the problems of childhood to be confined largely to the inner cities. Rural children, who were more likely to be white, more likely to live in two-parent homes, and whose parents generally were employed (although often at very low wages) were rarely a topic of concern. However, rural child poverty exceeded that in urban areas. Rural children had less access to health care, and their schools, on average, were more poorly funded than those in urban areas.[74] Much like the rural and farm children of the previous century, their problems tended to be hidden by their location, and by stereotypes that place the concerns of the nation firmly in the dangerous cities and opposed to the seemingly more benign countryside.

Coming of age remains a painful experience, no matter where it takes place. The turn-of-the-century's farm children came to adulthood with a limited education about the physical transformations they were undergoing, and often with a limited understanding of what their opportunities might be beyond the communities in which they lived. Within those limitations, they forged their lives. As difficult as their beginnings often were, those who chose to write about their experiences as adults had come to terms with midwestern farm childhood. Their lives were not balanced in the same way as modern children's lives are. In their time, work took precedence over all, as opposed to lives devoted to school and play. It was hard and often painful work, but with a purpose. School, too, had a purpose. Parents often perceived that purpose as discipline and preparation for a life in agriculture. Youngsters often saw it as a time of relief from labor, putting its educational value second. Their play gave them wings that they often could not use in their working and school lives. Many reached legal adulthood with a lifetime's share of hard work, family tragedy, and responsibility. In the end, there was a decision to be made: life on the farm or a foray into the problems and possibilities of life in the nation's growing urban centers. What memoirs and reminiscences tell us of children's lives on the farm, and what the numbers equally tell us, is that in addition to giving them a desire for change, farm life had prepared them well enough (if not perfectly) to take the plunge and begin something new. Rural youngsters became urban and suburban adults, and with the nation, they embarked on a new chapter in its history.

Notes

Introduction

1. Department of Commerce, Bureau of the Census, *Thirteenth Census of the United States, 1910, Population* (Washington, DC: Government Printing Office, 1913), 1:56–57.

2. It was only in 1920 that nationwide the number of people working in manufacturing surpassed the number of people working in agriculture. Agriculture remained the single most important occupational category until 1920. Department of Commerce, Bureau of the Census, *Fourteenth Census of the United States, 1920, Population* (Washington, DC: Government Printing Office, 1923), 4:35–43.

3. Jon Gjerde argues that during these years, although changes in agricultural production were "dizzying," "meaningful continuities regarding the centrality of household labor endured." Jon Gjerde, *The Minds of the West: Ethnocultural Evolution in the Rural Middle West, 1830–1917* (Chapel Hill: University of North Carolina Press, 1997), 136.

4. The growing freedom and broad range of entertainment possibilities available to urban youth is well documented in studies such as Kathy Peiss, *Cheap Amusements: Working Women and Leisure in Turn-of-the-Century New York* (Philadelphia: Temple University Press, 1986). The problem that this presented to the parents of teenaged girls is also well documented in books such as Mary E. Odem, *Delinquent Daughters: Protecting and Policing Adolescent Female Sexuality in the United States, 1885–1920* (Chapel Hill: University of North Carolina Press, 1995); and Ruth M. Alexander, *The "Girl Problem": Female Sexual Delinquency in New York, 1900–1930* (Ithaca: Cornell University Press, 1995).

5. United States Census Office, *Twelfth Census of the United States, 1900, Census Reports, Population*, vol. 1, part 1 (Washington, DC: U.S. Census Office, 1901), clxxiii, 482–83, 491, 732–35.

6. Ning de Coninck-Smith, Bengt Sandin, and Ellen Schrumpf, eds., *Industrious Children: Work and Childhood in the Nordic Countries, 1850–1990* (Odense: Odense University Press, 1997).

7. Wisconsin has been chosen as a case study for this chapter because of the state's wealth of public records, as well as the existence of the Wisconsin State Public School, a remarkably well-documented public institution that had a particularly interesting relationship to the poor and neglected children of the state.

8. I became aware of the existence of these sources first in New Zealand, studying farm children there. Upon my return to the United States, I discovered the same types of letters in American farm papers.

CHAPTER 1.
"I Would Rather Live in the Country"

1. Ellen Schrumpf, "From Full-Time to Part-Time: Working Children in Norway from the Nineteenth to the Twentieth Century," in Ning de Coninck-Smith, Bengt Sandin, and Ellen Schrumpf, eds., *Industrious Children: Work and Childhood in the Nordic Countries, 1850–1990* (Odense: Odense University Press, 1997), 72–73.

2. Viviana Zelizer, *Pricing the Priceless Child: The Changing Social Value of Children* (Princeton: Princeton University Press, 1994), 11.

3. Michael Grossberg, "Changing Conceptions of Child Welfare in the United States, 1820–1935," in Margaret Rosenheim et al., eds., *A Century of Juvenile Justice* (Chicago: University of Chicago Press, 2002), 10.

4. Zelizer, 11–13.

5. Grossberg, 14.

6. Katherine Ann Tinsley, "Continuing Ties: Relations Between Middle Class Parents and Their Children in Midwestern Families, 1870–1920" (PhD diss., University of Wisconsin–Madison, 1995), 15–22.

7. Richard Bremner, "Other People's Children," *Journal of Social History* 16, no. 3 (Spring 1983): 85.

8. Charles Loring Brace, *The Dangerous Classes of New York and Twenty Years' Work Among Them* (New York: Wynkoop & Hallenbeck, 1872), 91–92.

9. Grossberg, 22–23.

10. Kriste Lindenmeyer, *"A Right to Childhood": The U.S. Children's Bureau and Child Welfare, 1912–1946* (Urbana: University of Illinois Press, 1997), 14.

11. United States Department of Labor, Children's Bureau, *State Child-Labor Standards* (Washington, DC: Government Printing Office, 1921), chart.

12. Zelizer, 6.

13. Grossberg, 29.

14. United States Department of Labor, Children's Bureau, *State Compulsory School Attendance Standards Affecting the Employment of Minors, January 1, 1921* (Washington, DC: Government Printing Office, 1921), 1.

15. Grossberg, 29.

16. Mats Sjoberg, "Working Rural Children: Herding, Child Labour and Childhood in the Swedish Rural Environment 1850–1950," in Ning de Coninck-Smith, Bengt Sandin, and Ellen Schrumpf, eds., *Industrious Children: Work and Childhood in the Nordic Countries, 1850–1990* (Odense: Odense University Press, 1997), 122.

17. E. L. Kirkpatrick, *The Farmer's Standard of Living: A Socio-Economic Study*

of 2886 White Farm Families of Selected Localities in 11 States, Department Bulletin No. 1466 (Washington, DC: United States Department of Agriculture, November 1926), 60.

18. Mary Neth, *Preserving the Family Farm: Women, Community, and the Foundations of Agribusiness in the Midwest, 1900–1940* (Baltimore: Johns Hopkins University Press, 1995), 17–19.

19. Jon Gjerde, *The Minds of the West: Ethnocultural Evolution in the Rural Middle West, 1830–1917* (Chapel Hill: University of North Carolina Press, 1997), 150, 162, 178.

20. Claire Toynbee, *Her Work and His: Family, Kin and Community in New Zealand, 1900–1930* (Wellington: Victoria University Press, 1995), 54–55.

21. United States Department of Labor, Children's Bureau, *Child Labor in the United States*, Bureau Publication No. 114 (Washington, DC: Department of Labor, 1921), 6; United States Department of Labor, Children's Bureau, *State Child-Labor Standards*, chart.

22. Nettie McGill, *Children in Agriculture*, Department of Labor, Children's Bureau, Bureau Publication No. 187 (Washington, DC: Government Printing Office, 1929), 22–29, 47.

23. Grossberg, 3.

24. John M. Gillette, "Rural Child Labor," *Child Labor Bulletin* 1, no. 1 (June 1912): 154–55.

25. "Senator Beveridge Declares Regulation of Child Labor a National Problem," in Grace Abbott, *The Child and the State* (Chicago: University of Chicago Press, 1938), 1:474; Zelizer, 77.

26. Hugh D. Hindman, *Child Labor: An American History* (Armonk, NY: M. E. Sharp, 2002), 13–16.

27. State of Iowa, Department of Public Instruction, *Hand-Book for Iowa Schools, 1900* (Des Moines: F. R. Conway, State Printer, 1900), 187.

28. Ibid.

29. William A. Bullough, "'It Is Better to Be a Country Boy': The Lure of the Country in Urban Education in the Gilded Age," *Historian* 35, no. 2 (February 1973): 184.

30. Charles W. Eliot, "An Appreciation of the Farm Boy," *Rural Manhood* 1 (January 1910): 15–16.

31. Bullough, 188.

32. Preston Willis Search, *An Ideal School, or Looking Forward* (New York, 1904), 104, in Bullough, 186–87.

33. John Dewey, *Democracy and Education: An Introduction to the Philosophy of Education* (New York: Macmillan, 1938), 139, 165–68, 229–30, 360–62.

34. Nettie McGill, *Children in Agriculture*, Bureau Publication No. 187 (Washington, DC: Government Printing Office, 1929), 42.

35. Charles Josiah Galpin, *Rural Life* (New York: Century, 1918), 120–23.

36. Ibid., 120–21.

37. Ibid., 120.

38. Hindman, 286–87.

39. Richard Wohl, "The 'Country Boy' Myth and Its Place in American Urban Culture: The Nineteenth-Century Contribution," *Perspectives in American History* 3 (1969): 95–96.

40. Edwin Osgood Grover, "The Country Boy's Creed," *Rural Manhood* 3, no. 4 (April 1912): 106.

41. For a much more detailed description of Roosevelt and his views, see Gail Bederman, "Theodore Roosevelt: Manhood, Nation, and 'Civilization,'" in *Manliness and Civilization: A Cultural History of Gender and Race in the United States, 1880–1917* (Chicago: University of Chicago Press, 1995), 170–216.

42. Michael Smith, "And They Say We'll Have Some Fun When It Stops Raining: A History of Summer Camp in America" (PhD diss., Department of History, Indiana University, 2002), 38.

43. Theodore Roosevelt, "The Strenuous Life," in *The Strenuous Life: Essays and Addresses* (New York: Century, 1901), 1–2.

44. See Gail Bederman, "'Teaching Our Sons to Do What We Have Been Teaching the Savages to Avoid': G. Stanley Hall, Racial Recapitulation, and the Neurasthenic Paradox," in *Manliness and Civilization*, 77–120.

45. Smith, 35–36.

46. David I. MacLeod, *Building Character in the American Boy: The Boy Scouts, YMCA, and Their Forerunners, 1870–1920* (Madison: University of Wisconsin Press, 1983), 32, 52, 227.

47. "The National Scope of County Work," *Rural Manhood* 1 (December 1910): 12.

48. Wayne E. Fuller, "Making Better Farmers: The Study of Agriculture in Midwestern Country Schools, 1900–1923," *Agricultural History* 60, no. 2 (Spring 1986): 154–68.

49. Wohl, 92.

50. Brace, 225.

51. Katharine P. Hewins, "The Development of Placing-out Work by Institutions," in *Foster Home Care for Dependent Children,* Children's Bureau Publication No. 136 (Washington, DC: Government Printing Office, 1926), 101.

52. Emelyn Foster Peck, "Summary of State 'Importation' and Exportation Laws," in *Laws Relating to the Interstate Placement of Dependent Children,* Children's Bureau Publication No. 139 (Washington, DC: Government Printing Office, 1924), 1–2.

53. Marilyn Irvin Holt, *The Orphan Trains: Placing Out in America* (Lincoln: Bison Books, 1992), 161.

54. Bernard Mergen, "The Discovery of Children's Play," *American Quarterly* 27, no. 4 (October 1975): 403.

55. National Child Labor Committee, *Rural Child Welfare: An Inquiry by the National Child Labor Committee Based upon Conditions in West Virginia* (New York: Macmillan, 1922), 1, 10.

56. Mergen, 416.

57. Brian Sutton-Smith, *A History of Children's Play: New Zealand, 1840–1950* (Philadelphia: University of Pennsylvania Press, 1981), 284–86.

58. Brace, 176, 318.

59. Jacob Riis, *How the Other Half Lives: Studies Among the Tenements of New York* (New York: Hill and Wang, 1957), 149.

60. Mergen, 412–13.

61. See Peter Monaghan, "A Child's Place in the World," *Chronicle of Higher Education*, April 7, 2000, A21.

62. Kenyon Butterfield, "Play and Recreation in Our Country Life," *Rural Manhood* 3, no. 5 (May 1912): 147–50.

63. Country Life Commission, *Report of the Country Life Commission* (Washington, DC: Government Printing Office, 1909), 50–52.

64. "Point Rows," *Nebraska Farmer*, June 5, 1912, 590.

65. "Recreation on the Farm," *Nebraska Farmer*, November 27, 1912, 1104.

66. "How to Make Farm Homes Attractive to the Young People," *Farmer's Family Journal* 1, no. 2 (September 1904): 12; Mrs. J. C. Banta, "How Can the Farmer Encourage His Children to Stay on the Farm," *Kansas Farmer*, February 21, 1901, 188–89.

67. Mrs. S. S. Stewart, "Social Life in Town and Country," *Nebraska Farmer*, February 19, 1913, 227.

68. "Home Life for Children," *Nebraska Farmer*, February 17, 1917, 214, 226.

69. M. H. Hancock, "Using Rural Churches," *Nebraska Farmer*, June 11, 1913, 652; Edith Raymond, "Our Young Folks," *Farmer's Wife*, November 1915, 150.

70. I. G. W. Tuttle, "Mischievous Idle Hands," *Farmer's Wife*, January 1919, 180.

71. Advertisement, "Don't Rob Your Family for Your Farm," *Nebraska Farmer*, January 24, 1912, 85.

72. de Coninck-Smith et al., introduction, 13.

73. Elizabeth Hampsten, *Settlers' Children: Growing Up on the Great Plains* (Norman: University of Oklahoma Press, 1991), 229.

74. Wisconsin Child Center, History of Children, Series 2271, vols. 1–6, 1886–1913, Archives Division, Wisconsin Historical Society, Madison, Wisconsin (hereafter WHS).

75. Sutton-Smith, 135.

CHAPTER 2.
"But What Kind of Work Do the Rest of You Do?"

1. Florence Brown Sherbon and Elizabeth Moore, *Maternity and Infant Care in Two Rural Counties in Wisconsin*, Rural Child Welfare Series No. 4, United States Department of Labor, Children's Bureau Publication No. 46 (Washington, DC: Government Printing Office, 1919), 39, 40, 45–48.

2. David Danbom, *Born in the Country: A History of Rural America* (Baltimore: Johns Hopkins University Press, 1995), 132–34, 152–54.

3. Elliott West found a child of less than three years fetching, carrying, and

generally being useful to his farming parents. Elliott West, *Growing Up with the Country: Childhood on the Far Western Frontier* (Albuquerque: University of New Mexico Press, 1989), 75.

4. Mrs. L.R.H., "Our Home Club," *Farmer's Wife*, April 1914, 368.

5. Lula Gillespie Lentz, "Illinois Commentary: The Reminiscences of Lula Gillespie Lentz, Part I," *Journal of the Illinois State Historical Society* 63, no. 3 (June 1975): 276; Frances Olsen Day, typescript reminiscence, "Pioneering," Archives, State Historical Society of Iowa, Iowa City, Iowa (hereafter SHSI), 4.

6. Jon Gjerde, *The Minds of the West: Ethnocultural Evolution in the Rural Middle West, 1830–1917* (Chapel Hill: University of North Carolina Press, 1997), 152; Mary Neth, *Preserving the Family Farm: Women, Community, and the Foundations of Agribusiness in the Midwest, 1900–1940* (Baltimore: Johns Hopkins University Press, 1995), 20; West, 93.

7. Neth, 27.

8. Sarah Gillespie Huftalen, MS diary, 1877–1879, Archives Collection, SHSI, November 6, 1879.

9. Ibid., February 6, February 7, March 2, July 10, 1877.

10. *Kansas Farmer* 9, no. 7 (April 1, 1872); *Kansas Farmer* 9, no. 20 (October 15, 1872); *Kansas Farmer* 9, no. 22 (November 15, 1872). For a more complete discussion of this topic in an international context, see Kathryn Hunter and Pamela Riney-Kehrberg, "Rural Daughters in Australia, New Zealand and the United States: An Historical Perspective," *Journal of Rural Studies* 18 (2002): 135–43.

11. Hamlin Garland, *Main-Travelled Roads* (1891; reprint, Lincoln: Bison Books, 1995). For an extensive discussion of Garland's stories, as well as other fictional depictions of women's field work, such as those in the writings of Herbert Quick, see Gjerde, 170–85.

12. Martha Foote Crow, *The American Country Girl* (New York: Frederick A. Stokes, 1915), 90.

13. Ibid., 90–91.

14. Helen Mary Emery, Diaries, 1894–1907, Rhoda J. Emery and Family Papers, Manuscripts Collection, Minnesota Historical Society, St. Paul, Minnesota (hereafter MHS), July 16, November 9, December 13, 1897.

15. Neth, 21.

16. Norton Family Diaries, 1879–1880.

17. August Schulz, manuscript diary, Manuscripts Division, Kansas State Historical Society, Topeka, Kansas (hereafter KSHS), July 11, 1877.

18. Neth, 25.

19. Ibid., 21.

20. John J. Stilson and Sadie Stilson, manuscript diary, 1871, Archives, SHSI, April 18, 1871; Mary Elizabeth Pascoe, manuscript diary, 1871, Wisconsin Historical Society, Madison, Wisconsin (hereafter WHS), May 8, 9, 1871.

21. Mary Van Zante, typescript diary, 1889, Iowa Women's Archives, Univer-

sity of Iowa Libraries, Iowa City, Iowa, November 25, 27, December 2, 1889; Mary Eleanor Armstrong Peet, typescript diary, 1891–1897, Archives, SHSI, October 19, 20, 29, November 2–19, 1891.

22. Peet, November 19, 1891.

23. Mollie Krutza, typescript reminiscence, "Memories of Childhood on an Iowa Farm by Mollie Krutza nee Mary Ellen Harbold Written in 1952," Archives, SHSI, 17; Peet, March 15, 1892; Genevieve M. Regan, typescript reminiscence, "The Story of My Childhood." Archives, SHSI, 3.

24. Mrs. Raymond Millbrook, ed., "Mrs. Hattie E. Lee's Story of Her Life in Western Kansas," *Kansas Historical Quarterly* 22, no. 2 (summer 1956): 117; Carrie Dean Pruyn, typescript autobiography, "Out of the Dusk: Memories of a Girl of the Gay Nineties," Archives, SHSI, Iowa City, Iowa, 1; Neth, 24–25.

25. Oscar Hallam, "The Farmer Boy's Day—Or Days," Manuscript Collection, MHS, 35–37.

26. Norton Family, Norton Diaries, 1876–1895, copied and annotated by Helen Norton Starr, with permission of Henry L. Norton, Manuscripts Division, KSHS, March 28, 1879, April 29, 1879.

27. John Talcott Norton, manuscript diary, ibid., October 27, 1877.

28. Ibid., January 12, 1878.

29. Ibid., January 1878.

30. Jon Gjerde has argued for a more rigid gender division of labor between boys and girls, but I have found quite a bit of evidence that these boundaries were somewhat permeable. Boys did in fact help their mothers when it became necessary, although it was the rare boy who would do household labor and readily admit to the fact. Gjerde, 152–53.

31. John and Sadie Stilson, April 24, 1871, October 21, 1874.

32. Clifford Merril Drury, "Growing Up on an Iowa Farm, 1897–1915," *Annals of Iowa* 42, no. 3 (winter 1974): 178; William Graf, *Growing Up on a Farm* (New York: Vantage Press, 1970), 93–94; William S. Miller, *Growing Up in Goose Lake* (N.p.: William S. Miller, 1974), 50.

33. Hallam, 111.

34. James Lincoln Wood, manuscript diary, 1879, Wood Family Papers, Eau Claire Area Research Center, Wisconsin Historical Society, Eau Claire, Wisconsin, January 25, 1879, March 10, 1879, August 14, 1879.

35. Ibid., July–August, 1879.

36. Wood Family Papers, Finding Aid, Eau Claire Area Research Center, Wisconsin Historical Society, Eau Claire, Wisconsin.

37. Ralph Wood, manuscript diaries, 1879–1880, Wood Family Papers, Eau Claire Area Research Center, Wisconsin Historical Society, Eau Claire, Wisconsin, January 9, 1889, February 3, 1889, March 23, 1889, January 7, 1890, January 16, 1889, July 23, 1889.

38. Ibid., July 19 to November 11, 1889.

39. Ibid., July 20, 1889.

40. While processing milk seems to have been a woman's job on most farms, doing the actual milking might be considered men's or women's work, depending on family traditions.

41. Ralph Wood, January 25, 1893, April 8, 1893, April 19, 1893.

42. Trimble Family Papers, "Stories Told by Gladys," Iowa Women's Archives, University of Iowa Libraries, Iowa City, Iowa, 2.

43. Neth, 25–31.

44. Ben S. Gitchel to Mother, July 13, 1892, Gitchel-Larsen Family Correspondence, MS 3622, Manuscripts Collection, Nebraska State Historical Society, Lincoln, Nebraska (hereafter NSHS).

45. Ibid., October 15, 1894.

46. Ibid., January 21, 1897.

47. Willie Swain, Sun Prairie, Wisconsin, to Manzo Swain, July 21, 1881, Mary Swain Collection, WHS.

48. Mary Swain to Manzo Swain, October 26, 1881.

49. "What a Girl Can Do," *Kansas Farmer* 9, no. 7 (April 1, 1872): 111.

50. "What Uncle Frank Says," *American Young Folks* 2, no. 7 (July 1876): 52.

51. John Campbell Bailey, typescript diary, 1867–1923, Manuscripts Collection, Illinois State Historical Library, Springfield, Illinois (hereafter ISHL), February 13 and 17, 1873.

52. It is impossible to calculate the same information for youths over fifteen, since the Census Office put all workers aged sixteen to fifty-nine in the same category. Department of the Interior, Census Office, *Ninth Census, the Statistics of Population of the United States* (Washington, DC: Government Printing Office, 1872), 1:719–804.

53. James Ivins, manuscript diary, 1900–1901, Manuscripts Division, KSHS, March 9, 1900.

54. Peter S. Petersen, manuscript reminiscence, MS 4021, Manuscripts Collection, NSHS, 94–98.

55. Ibid., 102–4, 115.

56. Andrejs Plakans, "Intergenerational Ambivalences in the Past—A Social-Historical Assessment," in *Intergenerational Ambivalences: New Perspectives on Parent-Child Relations in Later Life,* ed. Karl Pillemer and Kurt Luscher (Amsterdam: Elsevier, 2004), 67–69.

57. Floyd Miles, "Autobiography," typescript autobiography, MS 1080, Manuscripts Collection, NSHS, 15–29.

58. Wisconsin Child Center, Agency Records, "Outside Placement Application Register, 1889–1906," vol. A, Archives, WHS.

59. Hugh Orchard, *Old Orchard Farm: The Story of an Iowa Boyhood* (Ames: Iowa State University Press, 1952), 8–9.

60. Gjerde, 136, 150.

61. Neth, 20.

62. Ibid., 20–22.

63. "Work and Play Club," *Nebraska Farmer,* March 6, 1907, 249.

64. Ibid., February 13, 1907, 167; "Young People," *Nebraska Farmer*, June 12, 1912, 613.

65. Steven R. Hoffbeck, *The Haymakers: A Chronicle of Five Farm Families* (St. Paul: Minnesota Historical Society Press, 2000), 11–12.

66. Henry C. Taylor, *Tarpleywick: A Century of Iowa Farming* (Ames: Iowa State University Press, 1970), 80.

67. Stephen M. Frank, *Life with Father: Parenthood and Masculinity in the Nineteenth-Century American North* (Baltimore: Johns Hopkins University Press, 1998), 58–69, 67–68.

68. Oliver Perry Myers, manuscript diary, 1872–1874, Oliver Perry Myers Papers, Archives Collection, SHSI.

69. Peet, April 18, 1892.

70. Louisa Sophia H. Gelhorn Boylan, manuscript reminiscence, January 1938, "My Life Story," Archives, SHSI, 12–13.

71. One of the few historical works to acknowledge the positive emotions inspired in children by their work is Ning de Coninck-Smith, Bengt Sandin, and Ellen Schrumpf, eds., *Industrious Children: Work and Childhood in the Nordic Countries, 1850–1990* (Odense: Odense University Press, 1997).

72. "Young People," *Nebraska Farmer*, February 7, 1912, 161.

73. Ibid., January 17, 1912, 65.

74. For work as play in a frontier context, see West, 104–7.

75. Elma Barnes Bamberg, typescript reminiscence, "My Home on the Smoky," Manuscripts Division, KSHS, 134; Frances Olsen Day, typescript reminiscence, "More About Life on the Prairie," Archives, SHSI, 5.

76. Bruce Bliven, "A Prairie Boyhood," *Palimpsest* 49, no. 8 (August 1968): 324; Milo Pitcher, *My Heritage on Hominyridge* (Marshalltown, IA: Milo Pitcher, 1977), 39–40.

77. John M. Inman, manuscript diary, 1870, John M. Inman Collection, Archives, SHSI, September 12–14, 1870.

78. Washington Lafayette McClary, manuscript diaries, 1892–1938, October 3, 1910, MS 3775, Manuscripts Collection, NSHS.

79. "Young People," *Nebraska Farmer*, March 27, 1912, 381.

80. Story, March 5, 1880.

81. "Carl Beck Killed Run Over by a Disc," *Audubon County Journal*, April 16, 1914, 1.

82. "Young People," *Nebraska Farmer*, May 27, 1914, 603.

83. As the local paper described it, Mr. and Mrs. Lewis Hansen's four- and eight-year-old daughters were alone in the house while Mr. Hansen was in town and Mrs. Hansen was driving the cows to pasture. Mrs. Hansen heard the explosion but could not get to the house in time to save the girls. "Two Girls Burn to Death," *DeForest Times*, October 15, 1915, 5.

84. Charles M. Turner, typescript reminiscence, 12, RS 1478.AM, Box 1, Manuscripts Collection, NSHS.

85. Department of Labor, Bureau of the Census, *Twelfth Census of the United*

States, 1900, Vital Statistics, Part 1 (Washington, DC: U.S. Census Office, 1901), 288.

86. Charles King, *Children's Health in America: A History* (New York: Twayne, 1993), 101.

87. Isaac G. Haycraft, typescript reminiscences, P 1441, Manuscripts Collection, MHS, 63.

CHAPTER 3.
"We Have Splendid Times at School"

1. Louise Bailey's diaries indicate that she sometimes had fifty or more students in class in the spring of 1895. Louise Bailey, manuscript diaries, 1893–1897, Archives Division, Wisconsin Historical Society, Madison, Wisconsin (hereafter WHS), May–June 1895.

2. The description of toddlers being deposited in classrooms for a day or a term appears in several places but most eloquently in Mary Van Zante's diary. "The girls of Van Woerkum brought their little sister Ella along with them to school. She behaved very well untill after the last recess and then she just talked and laughed and made the whole school laugh and teacher would take her and put her in her chair and she would have to hold her for she would want to get out so bad and she would tell teacher to let her go till she got loose and as soon as her was free she would commence again." Mary Van Zante, manuscript diary 1889, Van Zante and De Cook Family Papers, Iowa Women's Archives, University of Iowa Libraries, University of Iowa, Iowa City, Iowa, April 17, 1889.

3. Frances Olsen Day, "School Days at Elm Grove in Calhoun County, Iowa (1880's)," Archives, State Historical Society of Iowa, Iowa City, Iowa (hereafter SHSI), 1–2; Paul Theobald, *Call School: Rural Education in the Midwest to 1918* (Carbondale: Southern Illinois University Press, 1995), 106–7.

4. Kansas State Department of Education, *Standard Rural Schools: Requirements and Suggestions of the State Board of Education* (Topeka: Kansas State Printing Plant, 1916); Lorraine Elizabeth Wooster, State Superintendent of Public Instruction, *Kansas Rural-School Bulletin, 1922* (Topeka: Kansas State Printing Plant, 1922), 44–48.

5. William S. Miller, *Growing Up in Goose Lake* (N.p.: William S. Miller, 1974), 15–16.

6. A. J. Ingli, "Rural School Program," *Wisconsin Journal of Education* 36, no. 2 (February 1904): 46–47.

7. Mary Elizabeth Pascoe, manuscript diary, 1871, WHS, February 7, 1871.

8. Theresa Baughman Rickett, typescript of tape-recorded reminiscences, 1974–1976, WHS, 41.

9. Oliver Perry Myers, manuscript diary, 1872–1874, Oliver Perry Myers Papers, Archives Collection, SHSI, February 27, March 20, 1874.

10. E. May Lacey Crowder, "Pioneer Life in Palo Alto County," *Iowa Journal of History and Politics* 46, no. 2 (April 1948): 186.

11. Day, 3.

12. Ibid., 4.

13. Mamie Griswold, manuscript diaries, 1878–1883, 1883–1894, Henry A. Griswold Family Papers, Illinois State Historical Society, Springfield, Illinois (hereafter ISHS), May 28–30, 1878.

14. Fred A. Lacey, *The Public Schools of North Des Moines, Iowa, 1898* (Des Moines: Talbott-Koch, 1898), 5, 6.

15. Country Life Commission, *Report of the Country Life Commission* (Washington, DC: Government Printing Office, 1909), 53.

16. Ibid., 53–56; Ellwood P. Cubberly, *Rural Life and Education: A Study of the Rural School Problem as a Phase of the Rural-Life Problem* (New York: Houghton Mifflin Company, 1914), 83–103.

17. E. T. Fairchild, *Bulletin of Information Regarding Consolidation of Rural Schools* (Topeka: State Printing Office, 1908), 5.

18. In 1910, Kansas had 7,859 one-teacher schools; 2,344 of them were taught by teachers in their first year. [Kansas] State Superintendent of Public Instruction, *Seventeenth Biennial Report of the State Superintendent of Public Instruction of Kansas* (Topeka: State Printing Office, 1910), 66, 69.

19. David Danbom, "Rural Education Reform and the Country Life Movement," *Agricultural History* 53, no. 2 (April 1979): 467–68.

20. Some scholars, such as Paul Theobald, are quite critical of the rural public schools, while others, such as Wayne Fuller, find much of value in the rural school experience. Paul Theobald, *Call School;* Wayne E. Fuller, *The Old Country School: The Story of Rural Education in the Middle West* (Chicago: University of Chicago Press, 1982).

21. Shirley Mollett Webb, "Reminiscences of School Days," Manuscripts Division, Kansas State Historical Society, Topeka, Kansas (hereafter KSHS).

22. Reformers in urban areas sometimes went so far as to remove children from urban homes that they perceived as inadequate and send them to the countryside to begin lives as children in farm families. See Marilyn Irvin Holt, *Orphan Trains: Placing Out in America* (Lincoln: Bison Books, 1992); Linda Pollock, *Forgotten Children: Parent-Child Relations from 1500 to 1900* (Cambridge: Cambridge University Press, 1983), 81–82.

23. See, for example, Jacob Riis, *How the Other Half Lives: Studies Among the Tenements of New York* (New York: Hill and Wang, 1957).

24. United States Department of Labor, Children's Bureau, *Child Labor in the United States*, Bureau Publication No. 114 (Washington, DC: Department of Labor, 1921), 1.

25. Fred E. Haynes, *Child Labor Legislation in Iowa* (Iowa City: State Historical Society of Iowa, 1914), 11.

26. United States Bureau of Education, Department of the Interior, *Report of*

the Commissioner of Education, 1888–1889 (Washington, DC: Government Printing Office, 1891), 1:503–4.

27. [Kansas] State Superintendent of Public Instruction, *Fifteenth Biennial Report of the State Superintendent of Public Instruction of Kansas for the Year Ending June 30, 1905, and June 30, 1906* (Topeka: State Printing Office, 1906), 207–10.

28. *Child Labor in the United States*, 1.

29. Conrad E. Patzer, *Public Education in Wisconsin* (Madison, WI: State Superintendent of Schools, 1924), 458.

30. Forest Chester Ensign, *Compulsory School Attendance and Child Labor: A Study of the Historical Development of Regulations Compelling Attendance and Limiting the Labor of Children in a Select Group of States* (Iowa City, IA: Athens Press, 1921), 208.

31. Patzer, 472, 475.

32. United States Department of Labor, Children's Bureau, *State Compulsory School Attendance Standards Affecting the Employment of Minors, January 1, 1921* (Washington, DC: Government Printing Office, 1921), 3.

33. *Report of the Commissioner of Education*, 1:504–5; *Child Labor in the United States*, 1.

34. *Report of the Commissioner of Education*, 1:522.

35. *Child Labor in the United States*, 2.

36. Ibid. *History of Olmsted County, Together with Biographical Matter, Statistics, Etc.* (Chicago: H. H. Hill, 1883), 738–39.

37. *Report of the Commissioner of Education*, 1:523–24.

38. State of Nebraska, Department of Public Welfare, *Report of the Nebraska Children's Code Commission 1920* (Lincoln: Department of Public Welfare, State Capitol, 1920), 12.

39. Ella Arvilla Merritt, United States Department of Labor, Children's Bureau, "Important Changes Made by the State Legislatures of 1921, and of 1922 so far as Available Nov. 1, 1922, in Child Labor Standards and in Compulsory School Attendance Standards Affecting the Employment of Minors" (Washington, DC: U.S. Department of Labor, Children's Bureau, 1922), summary of changes for Nebraska.

40. *Report of the Commissioner of Education*, 2:711.

41. Carroll Engelhardt, "Compulsory Education in Iowa, 1872–1919," *Annals of Iowa* 49, no. 1–2 (summer/fall 1987): 66.

42. Keach Johnson, "Elementary and Secondary Education in Iowa, 1890–1900: A Time of Awakening," parts 1 and 2. *Annals of Iowa* 45, no. 2–3 (fall 1979/winter 1980): 109; *Child Labor in the United States*, 1.

43. Engelhardt, 71.

44. John M. Gillette, "Rural Child Labor," *Child Labor Bulletin* 1, no. 1 (June 1912): 160.

45. Johnson, 103.

46. Crowder, 176.

47. This was not just the case in the United States. New Zealand, with its more strict compulsory school attendance laws, also experienced similar problems. Pamela Riney-Kehrberg, "The Limits of Policy: Rural Children and Work in the United States and New Zealand, 1870–1920," *History of the Family* 6 (2001): 51–67.

48. William Converse, manuscript diaries, 1882, 1883, 1887, Effie Elsie Converse Papers, 1882–1932, Wisconsin Historical Society, Eau Claire Area Research Center, Eau Claire, Wisconsin, 1883.

49. Cedar County, Iowa Township, School District No. 2 (North Liberty School), Records, Teacher's General Register, Spring 1877, and Teacher's Term Reports, 1887–1891, Archives Collection, SHSI.

50. "Without Latin," *Nebraska Farmer*, June 19, 1907, 555; "Keep the Boy in School," *Nebraska Farmer*, May 12, 1915, 562.

51. Augusta Thomas, who grew up in Iowa, Kansas, and Nebraska, switched between town and rural school and fell behind in her studies as a result. She then convinced her mother, who was herself a teacher, to allow her to stay at home and help take care of her new baby brother. Consequently, she fell even further behind, and she "begged Mother to let me stay home and care for the baby while she accepted another offer to school." Augusta Thomas, "Prairie Children," Kenetha Merrill Collection, Manuscripts Division, KSHS, 117–18.

52. "Our Post Office," *American Young Folks* 6, no. 5 (May 1880): 77. Diphtheria was one of the most serious diseases of childhood and killed up to 90 percent of those infected with it. Antitoxin was available as early as 1894, but parents did not always inoculate their children. Charles King, *Children's Health in America: A History* (New York: Twayne, 1993), 78–79.

53. "What Uncle Frank Says," *American Young Folks* 2, no. 7 (July 1876): 52.

54. Mollie Krutza, typescript reminiscence, "Memories of Childhood on an Iowa Farm by Mollie Krutza nee Mary Ellen Harbold Written in 1952," Archives Collection, SHSI, 5.

55. Louise Bailey, April 4–5, 1893.

56. Ralph Wood, manuscript diaries, 1889–1893, Wood Family Papers, Eau Claire Area Research Center, Wisconsin Historical Society, Eau Claire, Wisconsin, January 7, January 14, January 21, 1889.

57. Louise Bailey, December 1, 1893.

58. Ibid., January 10, 1893.

59. Clara S. Conron, typescript diary, 1884–1885, Manuscripts Division, KSHS, January 17, February 16, April 22, 1885; Sarah Gillespie Huftalen, manuscript diary, 1877–1879, Sarah Gillespie Huftalen Collection, Archives, SHSI, January 2, 1877; Lois Tucker Orr, typescript diaries, 1897–1936, Box 3, transcriptions, ISHS, February 17–18, 1910; Oliver Perry Myers, March 16, 1874; Lucy Van Voorhis White, Papers, 1866–1932, Iowa Women's Archives, University of Iowa Libraries, University of Iowa, Iowa City, Iowa, manuscript diary, May 5, 1882.

60. Louise Bailey, June 12, 1893.

61. "Barbarism in Rural Schools," *Wisconsin Journal of Education* 22, no. 4 (April 1892): 74–75.

62. Theobald, 106, 128–29, 136–37; Louisa Sophia H. Gelhorn Boylan, manuscript reminiscence, January 1938, "My Life Story," Archives Collection, SHSI, 10.

63. "The Big Boy in the Country School," *Nebraska School Journal,* reprinted in *Wisconsin Journal of Education* 19, no. 12 (December 1889): 494–95.

64. Kenneth W. Porter, ed., "A Little Girl on an Iowa Forty, 1873–1880—Catherine Wiggins Porter," *Iowa Journal of History and Politics* 51, no. 2 (April 1953), 147–48.

65. Huftalen, April 24, October 10, October 13, October 14, 1879.

66. Effie Elsie Converse, manuscript diaries, 1884, 1885, 1890, Effie Elsie Converse Papers, 1882–1932, Wisconsin Historical Society, Eau Claire Area Research Center, Eau Claire, Wisconsin, January 25, 1884, January 27, 1884.

67. George H. Van Horne, manuscript diary, 1875, MS 3629, Manuscripts Collection, Nebraska State Historical Society, Lincoln, Nebraska (hereafter NSHS), January 5, 1875; February 2, 1875.

68. Boylan, 10–11, 21.

69. Ibid., 10–11.

70. "Barbarism in Rural Schools," 74.

71. Lucy Van Voorhis White, manuscript diary, February 18, 1884.

72. Rhoda J. Emery, manuscript diaries, 1889–1890, 1892, 1893–1894, Rhoda J. Emery Collection, Manuscripts Division, Minnesota Historical Society, St. Paul, Minnesota (hereafter MHS), November 26, December 3, December 4, December 5, 1889.

73. Ibid., October 24, November 28, and December 28, 1893.

74. Crowder, 187.

75. Ada Carroll Wortman, "Schools Fail to Fit," *Nebraska Farmer,* October 1, 1913, 964.

76. John Ise, *Sod and Stubble: The Story of a Kansas Farm* (Lincoln: Bison Books, 1967).

77. Minnesota farm woman Helen Emery actively campaigned against her youngest child, Robert, remaining on the farm. On August 8, 1904, she wrote in her diary, "Cale [her husband, Caleb Emery] went to Oronoco & left Rob to help load all the manure & the little boy is tired. I will try to get Rob educated so that he need not stay here to be chore boy." Helen Mary Emery, manuscript correspondence and diaries, 1894–1907, Rhoda J. Emery and Family Papers, Manuscripts Collection, MHS, St. Paul, Minnesota, August 8, 1904.

78. This same concern is apparent in the Amish population in modern America. Amish children only attend school through the eighth grade. Amish parents reason that their children only need an eighth-grade education to undertake their preferred occupation, farming. They also fear that the additional exposure to worldly ideas that education would bring might cause their children to leave the faith and leave their rural communities, either of which would be, in their opinion, disastrous. See Dorothy and Elmer Schwieder, *A Peculiar*

People: Iowa's Old Order Amish (Ames: Iowa State University Press, 1975); and John Hostetler, *Amish Society* (Baltimore: Johns Hopkins University Press, 1993).

79. Crowder, 188–89.

80. Gene Harrison, "Our School 'System,'" *Nebraska Farmer,* May 1, 1912, 510–11.

81. "Work and Play Club," *Nebraska Farmer,* February 6, 1907, 136.

82. Miller, 20, 25. Brian Sutton-Smith noted this same phenomenon in New Zealand's rural schools. "For the first time the children in every district had a definite place for games. Before that there was seldom a community center where all could—and did—play regularly." Brian Sutton-Smith, *A History of Children's Play, New Zealand, 1840–1950* (Philadelphia: University of Pennsylvania Press, 1981), 18.

83. Crowder, 187.

84. Louise Bailey, May 21, 1894.

85. Webb, n.p.

86. Miller, 20–24.

87. Elliott West, *Growing Up in Twentieth Century America: A History and Reference Guide* (New York: Garland, 1996), 22.

88. Miller, 22–23.

89. Lucy Van Voorhis White, manuscript diary, April and May 1882.

90. Miller, 15.

91. Ibid., 20, 25.

92. Van Zante, typescript diary, April 4–5, 1889.

93. Thomas, 87–88.

94. Crowder, 187.

95. Dr. Rosa Armentrout Butterfield, typescript diary, 1876–1877, Archives, SHSI, February 4, 1877.

96. Ibid., February 6, 1876.

97. Ibid., February 7, 1876.

98. Ibid., March 1876.

99. Ibid., August 4, 1877.

100. Ibid., September 17, 1877.

101. Ibid., September 19, 1877.

102. West, 44, 45.

103. David R. Reynolds, *There Goes the Neighborhood: Rural School Consolidation at the Grass Roots in Early Twentieth-Century Iowa* (Iowa City: University of Iowa Press, 1999), 64.

104. Celestia Lee Barker, manuscript diary, 1885, MS 246, Box 1/5, Special Collections, Parks Library, Iowa State University, Ames, Iowa, April 23, 1885.

105. Krutza, 20–21.

106. Justine Norton Johnson to Justus Johnson, November 12, 1905, Johnson Family Manuscript Letters, Johnson Family Collection, Iowa Women's Archives, University of Iowa Libraries, Iowa City, Iowa.

CHAPTER 4.
"Today Is the First School-Day"

1. There was considerable variation in schoolteachers' salaries on the basis of factors such as location, school size, gender, and experience, but reports from Iowa, Kansas, and Nebraska indicate that in the years from 1870 to 1895 a monthly salary of $25 to $35 was not an unreasonable goal. Mary Hulbert Cordier, *Schoolwomen of the Prairies and Plains: Personal Narratives from Iowa, Kansas, and Nebraska* (Albuquerque: University of New Mexico Press, 1992), 20.

2. On the other hand, this pattern of hiring could be very hard on male teachers, who often could not find employment during summer terms because school boards believed that women teachers, who could be paid a lower salary, could manage the classroom. Paul Theobald, *Call School: Rural Education in the Midwest to 1918* (Carbondale: Southern Illinois University Press, 1995), 128–29, 136–37.

3. Ibid., 121–22.

4. Louise Bailey, manuscript diaries, 1893–1897, Archives Division, Wisconsin Historical Society, Madison, Wisconsin (hereafter WHS), January 18, 1893.

5. Rhoda J. Emery, manuscript diary, Rhoda J. Emery and Family Papers, manuscript correspondence and diaries, 1842–1963, Manuscripts Collection, Minnesota Historical Society, St. Paul, Minnesota (hereafter MHS), October 30, 1889. All Emery Family materials quoted in this chapter are to be found in the Rhoda J. Emery and Family Papers.

6. Bertha Benke, microfilm copy of manuscript diary, Manuscripts Division, Kansas State Historical Society, Topeka, Kansas (hereafter KSHS), September 3, 9, 11, 1886.

7. Ibid., January 18, 20, 21, 1886.

8. Ibid., August 8, 16, 1886.

9. Hermann C. Benke, microfilm of manuscript diary, Manuscripts Division, KSHS, June 30, July 1, 1886.

10. Bertha Benke, August 14, 1886.

11. Hermann C. Benke, January 2, 1886.

12. Ibid., January 12, 19, 27, 1886.

13. Ibid., March 31, April 1, April 28, 1886.

14. Ibid., January 29, 1886.

15. Bertha Benke, July 17, 27, August 13, 1886; Hermann Benke, September 4, 1886.

16. Bertha Benke, August 23, August 25, 1886, January 16, 1887.

17. Hermann C. Benke, January 15, 1887.

18. Ibid., January 13, 1887.

19. Ibid., January 26, 1887.

20. Ibid., January 15, 1887.

21. Ibid., April 8, 1887.

22. Ibid., July–August 1887, and appended materials.

23. Rhoda J. Emery, October 21, 1889.

24. *History of Olmsted County, Together with Biographical Matter, Statistics, Etc.* (Chicago: H. H. Hill, 1883), 911–12.

25. Mary Neth, *Preserving the Family Farm: Women, Community, and the Foundations of Agribusiness in the Midwest, 1900–1940* (Baltimore: Johns Hopkins University Press, 1995), 25.

26. On November 9, 1897, Helen Emery wrote in regard to her two younger daughters, Mary and Nell, "Cale & the girls cleaned wheat in the forenoon & moved the corn am sorry they have to work so." There is no reason to expect that work patterns, or Helen Emery's attitudes about girls' work, had been any different when Clara and Rhoda were young. Helen Emery, manuscript diary, November 9, 1897.

27. James Emery, West Concord, Minnesota, to Rhoda J. Emery, Winona, Minnesota, October 22, 1895; Cordier, 17–19.

28. Although being a hired girl did not have the same social connotations as being a servant, Helen Emery was probably responding to the social inferiority implied by cleaning and cooking in another family's home. This comment, too, may have been indicative of Helen Emery's discomfort with other local families and the social distance she believed existed between her family and others. Many residents of nineteenth-century farming communities perceived mutual aid in times of illness as a social duty. Faye E. Dudden, *Serving Women: Household Service in Nineteenth-Century America* (Hanover, NH: Wesleyan University Press, 1983), 18, 108; Nancy Grey Osterud, *Bonds of Community: The Lives of Farm Women in Nineteenth-Century New York* (Ithaca: Cornell University Press, 1991), 193–94.

29. Helen Emery, manuscript diary, November 12, 1897.

30. Olmsted County, Superintendent of Schools, Teacher's Annual Reports, District 97, 1892, 1893, State Archives Collection, MHS.

31. Rhoda Emery, manuscript diary, October 24, 1889.

32. Ibid., October 29, 1889.

33. Ibid., November 12, 1889.

34. Ibid., November 18, 1889.

35. Ibid., November 20, 1889.

36. Ibid., October 27, November 26, 1889.

37. Emery's experiences boarding were probably quite common to most young teachers. As Paul Theobald commented in *Call School*, "There were frequently problems and prejudices to overcome" (122). To read about the similar experiences of another young teacher, see Laura Ingalls Wilder, *These Happy Golden Years* (New York: Harper & Row, 1981).

38. Rhoda Emery, manuscript diary, January 13, 1890.

39. Ibid., June 18, 1894. Emery's handwriting is much more shaky than usual in this entry, seeming to indicate that she was quite disturbed by this development.

40. Ibid., June 19, 1894.

41. For an excellent discussion of duty and single farm women's lives, see Kathryn M. Hunter, *Father's Right-Hand Man: Women on Australia's Family Farms*

in the Age of Federation, 1880s–1920s (Melbourne: Australian Scholarly Publishing, 2004), 126–36.

42. Louise Bailey also gave large sums of money to her parents—and was not always happy with the results. She wrote, "I find that papa is not going to do with the money I let him take yesterday as I told him to. . . . I don't like it I'll let papa have no more money if that is the way he is going to do." However, she loaned him another $30 the next month. Louise Bailey, November 18, 1895, and Memoranda, 1895.

43. Annette Atkins describes the obligations binding siblings to each other in *We Grew Up Together: Brothers and Sisters in Nineteenth Century America* (Urbana: University of Illinois Press, 2001), 108–12.

44. Clara Emery, Stewartville, Minnesota, to Rhoda Emery, April 21, 1892.

45. Family legend alleged that as a result of this great disappointment, Rhoda never married, and that her suitor, Wellington Clay, never married either. In Clay's case, however, this is clearly untrue, because a letter to Rhoda Emery written by Clay on July 19, 1948, indicated that he had a wife and children. Wellington Clay to Rhonda Emery, July 19, 1948.

46. James Emery, West Concord, Minnesota, to Rhoda J. Emery, Winona, Minnesota, October 22, 1895.

47. Rhoda Emery, manuscript diary, October 19, 1894.

48. Ibid., February 1, 2, 1892.

49. Ibid., May 27, 1890.

50. Rhoda Emery, Wasioja, Minnesota, to Helen and Caleb Emery, undated.

51. This same tension and lamentation is visible in the diary of Lucy Van Voorhis, another farm daughter turned public schoolteacher. In 1891, after teaching for several years, she wrote: "How can I live without going to college! I want to go *so* much, and yet, it appears I am not willing to make the necessary sacrifices. I certainly am not advancing in my profession. Ah, well, that which is nearest must be done first, and it is better to be qualified for a higher place and not get it than it is to secure a position and not be prepared to fill it." Van Voorhis never attained a college education, instead attending teachers' institutes at "the Normal." At the age of twenty-six, she left teaching to marry. Lucy Van Voorhis White, diary, July 5, 1891. Lucy Van Voorhis White Papers, 1866–1932, Iowa Women's Archives, University of Iowa, Iowa City, Iowa.

52. *History of Olmsted County*, 738–39.

53. Ibid.

54. State Normal School at Winona, Minnesota, *Annual Catalogue of the Officers and Students of the State Normal School, at Winona, Minnesota, for the Year 1895–1896, with Annual Circular for 1896–1897* (Winona: D. Sinclair, 1896), 8, 19.

55. Ibid., 48.

56. State Normal School at Winona, Minnesota, "Enrollment and Attendance Record, 1889–1899," A-85-3-123. Archives, Winona State University Library, Winona State University, Winona, Minnesota.

57. Emery was not alone in facing family stresses that threatened her college

degree. Other students in her class were forced to leave their studies because of the illness of family members. Ibid.

58. Clara Emery, West Concord, Minnesota, to Helen Emery, January 20, 1896.

59. State Normal School at Winona, Minnesota, *Annual Catalogue,* 58–59.

60. Olmsted County, Superintendent of Schools, Teacher's Annual Reports, District 8, Rochester, State Archives Collection, MHS.

61. George F. Howard, Rochester, Minnesota, to Rhoda Emery, November 3, 1905.

62. J. W. Olsen, Superintendent, Minnesota Department of Public Instruction, to Rhoda J. Emery, May 6, 1907; Cordier, 53.

63. Superintendent, Board of School Inspectors, St. Paul, Minnesota, to Rhoda J. Emery, September 11, 1908.

64. Superintendent, Board of School Inspectors, St. Paul, Minnesota, to Rhoda J. Emery, February 18, 1909; Octave Savard, Secretary, Board of School Inspectors, St. Paul, Minnesota, to Rhoda J. Emery, June 15, 1909.

65. A survey made in Pittsburgh in 1906–1907 revealed that more than 60 percent of all working women in that city earned less than $7 a week. Studies show that in Massachusetts in 1900, women generally earned weekly wages of less than $10. For example, shop workers earned $7.52, textile mill workers earned $8.32, shoe factory workers earned $10.45, restaurant workers earned $5.38, and domestics earned $3.99. If Emery's salary is divided out over a fifty-two-week year, rather than the school year, her wages were approximately $14.42 per week. Divided over a thirty-six-week school year, she would have earned $20.83 per week. Mary P. Ryan, *Womanhood in America: From Colonial Times to the Present,* 2nd ed. (New York: New Viewpoints, 1979), 123; David M. Katzman, *Seven Days a Week: Women and Domestic Service in Industrializing America* (Urbana: University of Illinois Press, 1981), 142.

66. Joan Jensen, "Out of Wisconsin: Country Daughters in the City, 1910–1925," *Minnesota History* 59, no. 2 (summer 2004): 55–56.

67. Transcript, College of Education and General Extension Division, University of Minnesota, Minneapolis, Rhoda J. Emery and Family Papers.

68. Rhoda Emery and Grace Emery, *The Story of Minnesota* (Rochester, MN: N.p., 1916).

69. Rhoda J. Emery and George F. Howard, *Outline of Study of U.S. History for Use in Junior High Schools and Senior American History Classes,* 12th ed. (1912; St. Paul: Howard's Outlines, 1928), 73.

70. In the standard history texts of the 1920s, it is quite unusual to find references to social history. For example, Willis Mason West's 1928 text contains many references to political, economic, diplomatic, and constitutional history but only approaches social history very gingerly in a brief discussion of immigration. James Woodson and Thomas Moran's *Elementary American History and Government,* published in 1929, very briefly addresses health and education in addition to all of the standard, traditional subjects. Willis Mason West, *The American People: A New History for High Schools* (New York: Allyn and Bacon, 1928); James

Albert Woodburn and Thomas Francis Moran, *Elementary American History and Government* (New York: Longmans, Green, 1929).

71. Emery and Howard, 79–80.

72. Rhoda J. Emery, Rochester, Minnesota, to James Emery, Stewartsville, Minnesota, June 20, 1893.

73. Robert Emery, Bismarck, North Dakota, to Rhoda Emery, St. Paul, Minnesota, October 19, 1913.

74. James Wood, "Yes, Virginia, There Was Really an Aunt Rhody," typescript essay, Rhoda J. Emery and Family Papers.

PHOTOGRAPHIC ESSAY.
Growing Up in Dodge County, Wisconsin

1. Marjorie L. McLellan, ed., *Six Generations Here: A Farm Family Remembers* (Madison: State Historical Society of Wisconsin Press, 1997), 13.

2. Ibid., 16.

3. Shirley Krueger Oestreich, as quoted in McLellan, 65.

4. McLellan, 129.

5. Ibid., 62.

6. Ibid., 65–66.

7. Ibid., 66.

8. Ibid., 17–21.

9. Ibid., 96–97.

10. Ibid., 38, 125.

11. Ibid., 115, 121.

12. Ibid., 129.

CHAPTER 5.
"It Surely Pays to Go to a Circus"

1. Brian Sutton-Smith's fine work on child's play in New Zealand, *A History of Children's Play: New Zealand, 1840–1950* (Philadelphia: University of Pennsylvania Press, 1981), suggests the universality of these conditions among children in rural and farming environments (3–6).

2. E. Anthony Rotundo asserts that by the early twentieth century, boys' play in an urban environment was increasingly scripted and controlled by adults, such as mothers in the home, teachers in the schools, and fathers who attempted to mold their sons through organizations such as the Boy Scouts. E. Anthony Rotundo, "Boy Culture: Middle-Class Boyhood in Nineteenth-Century America," in *Meanings for Manhood: Constructions of Masculinity in Victorian America,* ed. Mark C. Carnes and Clyde Griffen (Chicago: University of Chicago Press, 1990), 33–36.

3. Elliott West, *Growing Up with the Country: Childhood on the Far Western Frontier* (Albuquerque: University of New Mexico Press, 1989), 102–3.

4. Barbara Hanawalt, *Growing Up in Medieval London: The Experience of Childhood in History* (Oxford: Oxford University Press, 1993), 78–80, 114–18.

5. Sears, Roebuck and Company, *The 1902 Edition of the Sears, Roebuck Catalogue* facsimile edition (New York: Gramercy Books, 1993), 912–16.

6. Gary Cross's excellent study of American children's toys notes that in the period before 1900, fantasy toys were quite rare, and most toys "reflected conventional work roles and the tools that went with them." Manufacturers marketed toys to adults rather than children, and toys reflected parents' ideas about what was appropriate children's play. Gary Cross, *Kids' Stuff: Toys and the Changing World of American Childhood* (Cambridge: Harvard University Press, 1997), 24–26.

7. Miriam Formanek-Brunell, *Made to Play House: Dolls and the Commercialization of American Girlhood, 1830–1930* (New Haven: Yale University Press, 1993), 28, 30–31, 70–71, 166–67; Marilyn Irvin Holt, *Children of the Western Plains: The Nineteenth Century Experience* (Chicago: Ivan R. Dee, 2003), 133–34.

8. As Cross notes, the revolution in the type, variety, and number of toys largely affected children of the "comfortable classes," rather than working-class, African American, and rural children. "Relatively unorganized play" remained the norm in many rural areas. Cross, 36.

9. Maurice E. Minor, *Three in a Hill* (New York: Carlton Press, 1979), 121.

10. Theresa Baughman Rickett, typescript of tape-recorded reminiscences, 1974–1976, Wisconsin Historical Society, Madison, Wisconsin (hereafter WHS), 26.

11. Addie M. Thompson Sinclair, "My Story: An Autobiography of Addie M. Thompson Sinclair Covering the Years 1880 to 1961," Manuscripts Division, Kansas State Historical Society, Topeka, Kansas (hereafter KSHS), 34–35; Agnes Mary Kolshorn, "Kolshorn Family History," typescript genealogy and reminiscence, Manuscripts Collection, Minnesota Historical Society, St. Paul, Minnesota (hereafter MHS), section entitled "Children's Life on the Valley Farm, 1882–1902."

12. Anna Leona Lansworth Stanley, "Autobiography of Anna Leona Lansworth Stanley," Archives Division, WHS, 3; Mollie Krutza, typescript reminiscence, "Memories of Childhood on an Iowa Farm by Mollie Krutza nee Mary Ellen Harbold Written in 1952," Archives, State Historical Society of Iowa, Iowa City, Iowa (hereafter SHSI), 10; Louisa Sophia H. Gelhorn Boylan, "My Life Story," manuscript reminiscence, Archives, SHSI, 18.

13. Sinclair, 34–35.

14. Maude Keene Gill, "Reminiscences," Archives Division, WHS, 15, 24–25.

15. Minor, 121–26.

16. Kolshorn, "Children's Life on the Valley Farm, 1882–1902."

17. See diaries such as that of Mary Eleanor Armstrong Peet, typescript diary, 1891–1897, Archives, SHSI, March 26, 1892, and April 2, 1892, for descriptions of evenings spent with dominoes and checkers.

18. Ibid.; Sadie Stilson, manuscript diaries of John J. and Sadie Stilson, 1870–1878, Archives, SHSI, April–May, 1873.

19. Sadie Stilson, April–May, 1873; James Lincoln Wood, manuscript diary, 1879, Wood Family Papers, Eau Claire Area Research Center, Wisconsin Historical Society, Eau Claire, Wisconsin, May 24, June 12, July 4, 1879.

20. Ralph Wood, manuscript diary, 1893, Wood Family Papers, Area Research Center, Wisconsin Historical Society, Eau Claire, Wisconsin, May–July 1893.

21. "How Girls Can Learn to Be Housekeepers," *American Young Folks* 2, no. 10 (October 1876): 74; "A Smart Iowa Girl," *American Young Folks* 4, no. 10 (October 1878): 158; "Chore Boys," *American Young Folks* 2, no. 1 (January 1876): 14.

22. " 'Tis Only a Grasshopper," *American Young Folks* 3, no. 3 (March 1877): 38.

23. E. May Lacey Crowder, "Pioneer Life in Palo Alto County," *Iowa Journal of History and Politics* 46, no. 2 (April 1948): 191. The *Oxford Companion to Children's Literature* comments that in spite of modern wonderment at the appeal of moralistic literature to children, many moralistic tales went into multiple printings, and surviving copies are, in fact, well thumbed, indicating children's enjoyment of this type of literature. "Moral Tales," in *Oxford Companion to Children's Literature* (New York: Oxford University Press, 1984), 359.

24. "What Uncle Frank Says," *American Young Folks* 2, no. 4 (April 1876): 31; "What Uncle Frank Says," *American Young Folks* 3, no. 11 (November 1877): 172; "Our Post Office," *American Young Folks* 5, no. 3 (March 1879): 43; "Our Post Office," *American Young Folks* 4, no. 5 (May 1878): 75; "Our Post Office," *American Young Folks* 5, no. 8 (August 1879): 124; "Our Post Office," *American Young Folks* 7, no. 1 (January 1881): 6; "What Uncle Frank Says," *American Young Folks* 2, no. 9 (September 1876): 71; "Our Post Office," *American Young Folks* 6, no. 5 (May 1880): 77.

25. A religious publication, the *Youth's Companion* was published weekly from 1827 until 1927 and continued as a monthly until 1929. Circulation reached half a million before 1900. "*Youth's Companion, The*," in *Oxford Companion to Children's Literature*, 586.

26. Minnie Ellingson Tapping, selection entitled "Home," in typescript reminiscence, "Eighty Years at the Gopher Hole, 1867–1947," Manuscripts Collection, MHS.

27. Ralph Wood, manuscript diary, January 11, January 18, January 28, February 10, February 17, February 22, 1889.

28. Frances Olsen Day, "More About Life on the Prairie," Archives, SHSI, 5.

29. *Oxford Companion to Children's Literature*, 5–8, 249–50, 358–60.

30. Sears Catalogue, 255–60.

31. Minnie Mae Moon, manuscript diaries, 1892–1893, Moon Family Collection, Box 3, Archives Collection, McLean County Historical Society, Bloomington, Illinois, June 27, 1892.

32. Rhoda J. Emery, manuscript diary, 1889, Rhoda J. Emery and Family Papers, Correspondence and Diaries, 1842–1963, Manuscripts Collection, MHS, November 3, December 15, 1889.

33. Rhoda J. Emery, January 23, 1892, February 1–2, 1892.

34. *The American Boy's Book of Sports and Games: A Practical Guide to Indoor and*

Outdoor Amusements (New York: Dick and Fitzgerald, 1864; reprint edition, New York: Lyons Press, 2000).

35. "Work and Play Club," *Nebraska Farmer,* July 3, 1907, 593; "What Uncle Frank Says," *American Young Folks* 3, no. 11 (November 1877): 172; "Our Post Office," *American Young Folks* 4, no. 12 (December 1878): 188; "Our Post Office," *American Young Folks* 5, no. 2 (February 1879): 28; Milo Pitcher, *My Heritage on Hominyridge* (Marshalltown, IA: Milo Pitcher, 1977), 6, 8–9; Bruce Bliven, "A Prairie Boyhood," *Palimpsest* 49, no. 8 (August 1968): 326–27; "Our Post Office," *American Young Folks* 5, no. 9 (September 1879): 139.

36. Curtis Hoppin Norton, Norton Family Diaries, 1876–1895, diary of Curtis Norton, March 31, 1878. The transcriber noted that Norton used the term *cowturd* in the original manuscript, but it had been crossed out and *cowdropping* substituted. I have used Curtis's original term.

37. "Work and Play Club," *Nebraska Farmer,* March 20, 1907, 299; "Young People," *Nebraska Farmer,* February 7, 1912, 161; "Work and Play Club, *Nebraska Farmer,* March 27, 1907, 327; "Work and Play Club," *Nebraska Farmer,* December 25, 1907, 1115; "Young People," *Nebraska Farmer,* April 30, 1913, 539; "Young People," *Nebraska Farmer,* April 15, 1914, 481, "Young People," *Nebraska Farmer,* July 8, 1914, 701.

38. "Young People," *Nebraska Farmer,* May 1, 1912, 511; "Young People," *Nebraska Farmer,* May 8, 1912, 533; "Young People," *Nebraska Farmer,* April 2, 1913, 437; "Young People," *Nebraska Farmer,* May 7, 1913, 563; "Young People," *Nebraska Farmer,* November 11, 1916, 1181.

39. "Our Post Office," *American Young Folks* 5, no. 2 (February 1879): 28; "Young People," *Nebraska Farmer,* May 19, 1915, 583; "Young People," *Nebraska Farmer,* January 5, 1916, 17; "Work and Play Club," *Nebraska Farmer,* March 13, 1907, 279; "Young People," *Nebraska Farmer,* April 14, 1915, 469; "Young People," *Nebraska Farmer,* March 15, 1916, 381; "Young People," *Nebraska Farmer,* May 3, 1916, 564; Krutza, 5.

40. "Young People," *Nebraska Farmer,* February 21, 1912, 223; "Young People," *Nebraska Farmer,* February 24, 1915, 261; "Young People," *Nebraska Farmer,* July 19, 1916, 787.

41. Walker D. Wyman, "Boyhood Recollections of Dogs, Ponies, Trapping, Even Flying Off the Hen House Roof," from the personal collection of, and by permission of, Mark Wyman, Normal, Illinois.

42. Peter Monaghan, "A Child's Place in the World: Modern Play Spaces May Be Safe, but They're Stultifying, Some Experts Say," *Chronicle of Higher Education,* April 7, 2000, A21. This article is a more concise statement of Stuart C. Aitken's argument that modern playgrounds and other adult-constructed play spaces are an attempt to "put children in their place." Stuart C. Aitken, *Putting Children in Their Place* (Washington, DC: Association of American Geographers, 1994), 2.

43. "Young People," *Nebraska Farmer,* January 15, 1913, 69; June 19, 1912, 629; March 3, 1915, 293; January 24, 1912, 97; September 17, 1913, 913; October 1, 1913, 953; May 28, 1913, 615; March 15, 1916, 381; May 17, 1916, 613.

44. Charles Augustus Story Jr., manuscript diary, 1879–1884, Film MS 62, Manuscripts Collection, Nebraska State Historical Society, Lincoln, Nebraska (hereafter NSHS), December 25, 1879, November 25, December 25, 1880.

45. Sarah Gillespie Huftalen, manuscript diary, 1877–1879, Sarah Gillespie Huftalen Collection, Archives, SHSI, December 25, 1877, December 25, 1878, December 25, 1879.

46. Rosa Armentrout Butterfield, typescript diary, 1876–1877, Archives, SHSI, February 4, 1877.

47. "Work and Play Club," *Nebraska Farmer,* January 2, 1907, 11, and January 23, 1907, 73.

48. Mary Van Zante, typescript diaries, 1888–1890, Van Zante and De Cook Family Papers, Iowa Women's Archives, University of Iowa Libraries, Iowa City, Iowa, December 25, 1889.

49. Today, Pella, Iowa, is well known for its parade and celebration of Sinterklaas Day. Personal communication from David Timmer, Department of Philosophy/Religion, Central College, Pella, Iowa, July 1, 2004; Geoffrey D. Reynolds, Joint Archives of Holland, Hope College, Holland, Michigan, July 2, 2004; and Murt Kooi, Pella, Iowa. See Sjoerd Sipma, letter to Friesland, September 26, 1848, in Pella Historical Society, *History of Pella, Iowa, 1847–1987* (Dallas: Curtis Media, 1988), 27.

50. Robert Ostergren, *A Community Transplanted: The Trans-Atlantic Experience of a Swedish Immigrant Settlement in the Upper Middle West, 1835–1915* (Madison: University of Wisconsin Press, 1988), 228.

51. Mamie Griswold, manuscript diaries, 1878–1883, Henry A. Griswold Family Papers, Box 4, Illinois State Historical Library, Springfield, Illinois (hereafter ISHL), July 4, 1879; Ralph Wood, July 4, 1891; John Stilson, July 4, 1870.

52. Butterfield, July 5, 1877.

53. Moon, December 30, 1892.

54. Ralph Wood, January 1, 1889; Peet, December 31, 1892.

55. "Young People," *Nebraska Farmer,* November 19, 1913; January 28, 1914; December 2, 1916.

56. Trick-or-treating only became a part of American youth culture in the period after World War I, although the pranks associated with Halloween had a long history. In 1939, the *Oxford English Dictionary* first defined the term. Anthony F. Aveni, *The Book of the Year: A Brief History of Our Seasonal Holidays* (Oxford: Oxford University Press, 2003), 124–25.

57. Bliven, 322.

58. Rhoda J. Emery, June 21, 1894.

59. "Young People," *Nebraska Farmer,* November 25, 1916, 1229; Krutza, 3; Myers, June 3, 1876.

60. Krutza, 3–4; Boylan, 3; Genevieve M. Regan, typescript reminiscence, "The Story of My Childhood," Archives, SHSI, 2.

61. Peet, November 26, 1891.

62. John J. and Sadie Stilson, manuscript diaries, June 26, 1870, November 3, 1872.

63. Crowder, 192–93.

64. Moon, January 15, May 19, May 21, June 16, 1893.

65. Hudson Baptist Church, Records, Program of the Baptist Young People's Union, 1891, and Prayer Meeting Topics, July 1896–January 1897, McLean County Historical Society, Bloomington, Illinois.

66. Jane M. Pederson, *Between Memory and Reality: Family and Community in Rural Wisconsin, 1870–1970* (Madison: University of Wisconsin Press, 1992), 137–38.

67. Peet, January 23, 1892.

68. Oliver Perry Myers, manuscript diary, 1872–1876, Archives, SHSI, November 8, 1873, January 26, 1874.

69. Mary Norton, Norton Diaries, 1876–1895, copied and annotated by Helen Norton Starr, by permission of Henry L. Norton, Manuscripts Division, KSHS, February 7, 1879.

70. Norton, January 20, 1880, January 23, 1880, February 21, 1880.

71. Hermann C. Benke, manuscript diary, Manuscripts Division, KSHS, March 2, 1886.

72. Clara M. Johnson, transcript of oral history interview, February 16, 1985, Rural Women's Oral History Project, Manuscripts Collection, Archives Division, WHS, 3–6.

73. Griswold, January 3, January 12, January 26, August 29, October 3, October 10, 1878; January 7, September 23, 1879; July 29, 1883; January 23, 1885.

74. Stilson, October 16, 1872.

75. Peet, November 10, December 4, December 11, December 29, 1891, January 14, February 5, February 6, February 19, March 12, 1892.

76. Krutza, 12.

77. Peet, October 16, 1896.

78. Vivian C. Hopkins, ed., "Diary of an Iowa Farm Girl: Josephine Edith Brown, 1892–1901," *Annals of Iowa* 42, no. 2 (fall 1973): 139.

79. Norton Family Diaries, January 23, 1880, January 28, 1880, February 7, 1880.

80. Seth Adolphson, manuscript diaries, 1913–1919, Seth Adolphson Papers, 1913–1982, Whitewater Area Research Center, Wisconsin Historical Society, Whitewater, Wisconsin, April 29, 1917, June–November, 1917, January 2, 1918. Adolphson was not the only farm youngster whose life was made more interesting by the telephone. Several girls wrote to *Nebraska Farmer* about using the phone to talk to friends. "Work and Play Club," *Nebraska Farmer,* March 13, 1907, 279; May 22, 1907, 495.

81. Helen Mary Emery, manuscript diary, 1904, Rhoda J. Emery and Family Papers, June 30, 1904.

82. Ibid., September 14, 1896, November 5, 1904, September 9, 1906.

83. Rhoda J. Emery, December 29, 1889.

84. Ibid., June 9, 1890.

85. Ibid., June 1, 1890.

86. Ibid., June 16, 1890.

87. Helen Mary Emery, September 14, 1896.

88. Helen Mary Emery, March 4, 1907.

89. Ibid., June 21, 1904.

90. Ibid., September 9, 1906.

91. Ibid., September 8, 1906.

92. Although fictional, Hamlin Garland's short story, "The Creamery Man," is descriptive of the social superiority some native born individuals felt toward young women of immigrant extraction who labored in the fields. Hamlin Garland, *Main-Travelled Roads* (1891; reprint, Lincoln: Bison Books, 1995), 145–61.

93. Ostergren, 233; Pederson, 42.

94. Effie Elsie Converse, manuscript diary, January 25, February 10, August 4, August 22, October 28, November 17, December 19, December 29, 1884, Effie Elsie Converse Papers, 1882–1932, Wisconsin Historical Society, Eau Claire Area Research Center, Eau Claire, Wisconsin.

95. "Young People," *Nebraska Farmer*, February 7, 1912, 161; June 26, 1912, 645.

CHAPTER 6.
"This Case Is a Peculiarly Hard One"

1. Among the forms of public records useful to such a study, but not used extensively in this chapter, are divorce records. One such divorce record, that of Anna and Albert Bigalke, of Waupaca County, Wisconsin, details such issues as nonsupport, domestic abuse, and sexual abuse of children. Anna Bigalke, trial transcript, divorce proceedings, 1906–1907, Archives Division, Wisconsin Historical Society, Madison, Wisconsin (hereafter WHS).

2. United States Department of Labor, Children's Bureau, *Foster-Home Care for Dependent Children* (Washington, DC: Government Printing Office, 1926), 101, 105.

3. United States Department of Labor, Children's Bureau, *Laws Relating to Interstate Placement of Dependent Children* (Washington, DC: Government Printing Office, 1924), 1–11.

4. Emma O. Lundberg, "Dependent Wards of the State of Wisconsin: A Study of Children Indentured into Family Homes by the State Public School," United States Department of Labor, Children's Bureau, draft report, 1924, Series 1401, Boxes 7 and 8, Archives Division, WHS, 125–26.

5. Polk County, Wisconsin, Superintendent of the Poor, County Home Records, 1876–1934, Polk Series 17, Box 3, vol. 7, Ledger, 1882–1885, 32, 51, 75, 45, 58, 88, 57, Wisconsin Historical Society, River Falls Area Research Center, River Falls, Wisconsin.

6. City of Eau Claire, Wisconsin, Commissioner of the Poor, Case Record

Book, 1911–1917, Eau Claire Series 83, 34, Wisconsin Historical Society, Eau Claire Area Research Center, Eau Claire, Wisconsin. By permission of the Eau Claire County Department of Human Services.

7. Lundberg, 491.

8. Polk County, Wisconsin, Superintendent of the Poor, County Home Records, 1876–1934, Polk Series 17, Box 3, vol. 8, Ledger, 1885–1887.

9. Lundberg, 1.

10. Polk County, Wisconsin, Criminal Docket, 1874–1926, 16–25. Wisconsin Historical Society, River Falls Area Research Center, River Falls, Wisconsin.

11. The records of the Wisconsin Child Center are restricted by Wisconsin state law. However, state law allows those records generated more than seventy-five years ago to be examined by scholars and others. No records generated after 1920 were examined for this study.

12. Wisconsin Child Center, Agency History Record, Children Received, 1886–1906, Series 2271, vol. 18. Archives Division, WHS.

13. Lundberg, 89.

14. Ibid., 276.

15. Ibid., 117.

16. Eau Claire County, Wisconsin, County Court Record of Admission to State Public School, 1887–1901, Eau Claire Series 59, Wisconsin Historical Society, Eau Claire Area Research Center, Eau Claire, Wisconsin.

17. Lundberg, 8, 33.

18. Ibid., 8.

19. Ibid., 210.

20. Ibid., 466.

21. Wisconsin Child Center, Agency History Record, "Adopted, Returned to Counties, Marriages, Deaths," Series 2271, 15:49; Lundberg, 10, 15, 22.

22. Lundberg, 19–20, 50–57.

23. First Biennial Report of the State Board of Control of Wisconsin Reformatory, "Charitable and Penal Institutions for the Two Fiscal Years Ending September 30, 1892," 17, in Lundberg, 48.

24. One of the most important reasons for the Children's Aid Society to begin placing out was to avoid the disease environment of orphanages, hospitals, and other children's institutions. Charles R. King, *Children's Health in America: A History* (New York: Twayne, 1993), 58, 107.

25. Lundberg, 186.

26. Ibid., 203, 44.

27. Wisconsin Child Center, Agency History Record, "Outside Placement Application Register, 1889–1906," A:2, 26.

28. Ibid., 6; Wisconsin Child Center, Agency History Record, "Outside Placement Application Register, 1889–1906," B:48, 52, 120.

29. Wisconsin Child Center, Agency History Record, "Outside Placement Application Register, 1889–1906," A:32; B:51, 59, 70, 147.

30. Wisconsin Child Center, Agency History Record, "Outside Placement Application Register, 1889–1906," B:62, 147, 156, 180.

31. Ibid., A:2, 6, 16; B:148.

32. Wisconsin Child Center, Agency History Record, History of Children, Series 2271, 4:2351.

33. Polk County, Wisconsin, Record of the Criminal Court, 207, Wisconsin Historical Society, River Falls Area Research Center, River Falls, Wisconsin.

34. Lundberg, 277.

35. Wisconsin Child Center, Agency History Record, History of Children, Series 2271, 1:93.

36. Ibid., 1:117, 3:1814.

37. Ibid., 2:913.

38. Ibid., 3:1530.

39. Julie Berebitsky, *Like Our Very Own: Adoption and the Changing Culture of Motherhood, 1851–1950* (Lawrence: University Press of Kansas, 2000), 28–29; Karin Calvert, "Patterns of Childrearing in America," in *Beyond the Century of the Child: Cultural History and Developmental Psychology,* ed. Willem Koops and Michael Zuckerman (Philadelphia: University of Pennsylvania Press, 2003), 71.

40. Berebitsky, 34–35.

41. Ibid., 40–45.

42. United States Census Office, *Twelfth Census of the United States, 1900* (Washington, DC: U.S. Census Office, 1901), 2:cxxxv.

43. Eau Claire County, Wisconsin, County Court Record of Admission to State Public School, 1887–1901, Eau Claire Series 59.

44. Wisconsin Child Center, Agency History Record, History of Children, vols. 1–6.

45. Lundberg, 125–26, 130.

46. Wisconsin Child Center, Agency History Record, History of Children, 2:1376–79.

47. Ibid., 4:2798–800.

48. Ibid., 4:2496.

49. Kenneth L. Kusmer, *Down and Out, on the Road: The Homeless in American History* (Oxford: Oxford University Press, 2002), 105.

50. *Foster-Home Care for Dependent Children.*

51. Lundberg, 133–37.

52. Ibid., 142–44.

53. Ibid., 216, 222–23.

54. Ibid., 473.

55. Ibid., 292.

56. Ibid., 295–97.

57. Ibid., 286.

58. Ibid., 287, 289.

59. Ibid., 306–7.

60. Ibid., 312.

61. Ibid., 316.

62. Ibid., 306.

63. For example, one family took in three state school children between 1913 and 1917, all for the purpose of being hired boys and girls. "All these children were obliged to work very hard; all were deprived of schooling, and neighbors complained bitterly about the abuse which the children received in this home." Ibid., 260.

64. Lundberg, 229–30.

65. Berebitsky, 28–29.

66. Lundberg, 231.

67. Ibid., 421.

68. Ibid., 312.

69. Ibid., 313.

70. Ibid., 263–64.

71. Ibid., 265–67.

72. Ibid., 429.

73. Ibid., 371.

74. Ibid., 414–16, 484.

75. Ibid., 355–61.

76. Ibid., 474.

CHAPTER 7.
"I Wouldn't Live in the City Always for Anything"

1. Martha Foote Crow, *The American Country Girl* (New York: Frederick A. Stokes, 1915), 8.

2. Fourteen-year old John Talcott Norton understood that mortgages put the family enterprise in peril. "Pa borrowed $100 yesterday of Cassat and Mortgaged [word outlined in black] Dick, Pet and Fannie. It is too bad." John Talcott Norton, manuscript diary, February 15, 1877, Norton Family Diaries, Manuscripts Division, Kansas State Historical Society, Topeka, Kansas (hereafter KSHS).

3. Oliver Perry Myers, manuscript diary, 1872–1874, Oliver Perry Myers Papers, Archives Collection, State Historical Society of Iowa, Iowa City, Iowa (hereafter SHSI), March 20, 1874.

4. Mamie Griswold, manuscript diaries, 1878–1883, 1883–1884, Henry A. Griswold Family Papers, Box 4, Manuscripts Department, Illinois State Historical Society, Springfield, Illinois (hereafter ISHS), September 10, November 19, 1884, January 2, October 18, 1885.

5. Mary J. Aberle, microfilm of typescript diary, 1874–1876, Manuscripts Division, KSHS, June 18, 1875, January 3, 1876.

6. Lucy Van Voorhis White, "Biography," May 8, 1884, Lucy Van Voorhis White Papers, 1866–1932, Iowa Women's Archives, University of Iowa, Iowa City, Iowa.

7. Linda Peavy and Ursula Smith, *Frontier Children* (Norman: University of Oklahoma Press, 1999), 137–41.

8. The White Shield Pledge for Girls was found in Lucy Van Voorhis White, undated notebook from Hardin County Normal School, Lucy Van Voorhis White Papers. Information about Frances Willard and the Social Purity movement may be found in Frances E. Willard, "Social Purity Work for 1887," *Union Signal* 13, January 1887, 12, in "Women and Social Movements in the United States, 1775–2000," available at http://womhist.binghamton.edu/index.html (accessed March 22, 2004).

9. Mary Norton, Norton Family Diaries, January 26, 1880.

10. Ibid., February 2, 1880.

11. Ibid., January 21, 1881.

12. Helen Emery, manuscript correspondence and diaries, 1894–1907, Rhoda J. Emery and Family Papers. Manuscripts Collection, Minnesota Historical Society, St. Paul, Minnesota (hereafter MHS), November 30, 1905.

13. Helen Emery, December 3, 1905.

14. Kathy Peiss, *Cheap Amusements: Working Women and Leisure in Turn-of-the-Century New York* (Philadelphia: Temple University Press, 1986), 12–16, 34.

15. Ibid., 60, 61, 68–69.

16. Addams feared particularly that the transplantation of unsupervised young people from the countryside into the cities would lead to the spread of immorality and vice among young women, seeking easy access to funds and fashionable clothing. Jane Addams, *A New Conscience and an Ancient Evil* (New York: Macmillan, 1912), 212–15; Jane Addams, *Twenty Years at Hull-House* (New York: Macmillan, 1960), 239–56.

17. Mary Neth, *Preserving the Family Farm: Women, Community, and the Foundations of Agribusiness in the Midwest, 1900–1930* (Baltimore: Johns Hopkins University Press, 1995), 254–58.

18. John Ise, *Sod and Stubble: The Story of a Kansas Farm* (Lincoln: Bison Books, 1967), 246–51.

19. Ibid., 251.

20. John A. Hostetler, *Amish Society* (Baltimore: Johns Hopkins University Press, 1993), 146, 349–51.

21. Neth, *Preserving the Family Farm*, 22.

22. Rolf Johnson, *Happy as a Big Sunflower: Adventures in the West, 1876–1880,* edited by Richard E. Jensen (Lincoln: University of Nebraska Press, 2000), 92–93. Johnson's frank discussion of his relationship with Thilda Danielson is unusual. I have yet to locate an equally frank discussion by a young woman.

23. Ibid., 96.

24. Ibid., xxvii.

25. Neth, *Preserving the Family Farm*, 252, 256–58.

26. Beth L. Bailey, *From Front Porch to Back Seat: Courtship in Twentieth-Century America* (Baltimore: Johns Hopkins University Press, 1989), 13–18.

27. Mary E. Odem, *Delinquent Daughters: Protecting and Policing Adolescent Female Sexuality in the United States, 1885–1920* (Chapel Hill: University of North Carolina Press, 1995), 187–88.

28. Steven Mintz and Susan Kellogg, *Domestic Revolutions: A Social History of American Family Life* (New York: Free Press, 1989), 112.

29. See Odem; see Ruth M. Alexander, *The "Girl Problem": Female Sexual Delinquency in New York, 1900–1930* (Ithaca: Cornell University Press, 1995).

30. Mamie Griswold, manuscript diary, 1883.

31. Edith Bradley Rendleman, *All Anybody Ever Wanted of Me Was to Work*, ed. Jane Adams (Carbondale: Southern Illinois University Press, 1996), 116, 134.

32. Wisconsin Child Center, History of Children, Series 2271, 4:2486, 5:3090, 6:3758, Agency History Record, Archives Division, Wisconsin Historical Society, Madison, Wisconsin (hereafter WHS).

33. Joan Jensen, "The Death of Rosa: Sexuality in Rural America," *Agricultural History* 67, no. 4 (fall 1993): 6. Kenneth L. Kusmer has argued that the rise of child-saving institutions such as the State School was a boon to young women who could not afford to raise their children. The organizations took the children off their hands, and they were free to seek employment, usually as domestics. Kenneth L. Kusmer, *Down and Out, on the Road: The Homeless in American History* (Oxford: Oxford University Press, 2002), 113.

34. See David B. Danbom, "Rural Girls in Fargo During the 1930s," *Agricultural History* 76 (fall 2002): 659–68. Note, too, Jane Addams's concerns for rural girls, newly migrated to the city and seduced by its charms. Addams, *A New Conscience*, 212–15.

35. In relation to premarital pregnancy in southern Illinois, Jane Adams, anthropologist and editor of Edith Bradley Rendleman's memoir, comments that "if a couple got married the child bore no stigma of illegitimacy," and the community accepted the situation relatively easily. Children born outside of wedlock, however, were heavily stigmatized. Rendleman, 15.

36. Dane County, Wisconsin, coroner's inquest, December 27, 1915, testimony of Dr. J. H. Bertrand, Dane Series 71, Box 5, 1912–1915, 3.

37. Ibid., testimony of Mrs. William Paulman, 27.

38. *DeForest Times*, December 10, 1915, 1.

39. Dane County, Wisconsin, coroner's inquest, testimony of Christina Christiansen, 17.

40. Ibid., testimony of Alma Christiansen, 11–12.

41. Ibid., 14.

42. Ibid., testimony of Christina Christiansen, 16.

43. Ibid., testimony of Oscar Heisig, Ferd Rademacher, and Josephine Rademacher, 21, 25, 30.

44. Examination of the *Brooklyn Teller* from December 1, 1915, to January 12,

1916, revealed no stories about Alma Christiansen's child's death, the inquest, or the verdict.

45. Dane County, Wisconsin, coroner's inquest, verdict, January 7, 1916.

46. Dane County, Wisconsin, coroner's inquest, testimony of Rasmus Christiansen, 19; Manuscript Census of Population, Dane County, Wisconsin, 1920, Volume 13, District 23, Sheet 1, Line 82.

47. Historian Joan Jensen's research uncovered a similar story, ending in young Rosa Petrusky's death due to complications from an illegal abortion in rural Waushara County, Wisconsin. Jensen, "Death of Rosa."

48. "Laws of Sex Education and Country Girls," *Rural Manhood* 3, no. 9 (November 1912): 325–29.

49. Seth Adolphson, manuscript diary, 1917, Seth Adolphson Papers, 1913–1982, Whitewater Area Research Center, Wisconsin Historical Society, Whitewater, Wisconsin, January 14, 1917.

50. Ibid., August 16, November 25, 1917.

51. Seth Adolphson, "From My Diary," typescript reminiscences, 1981, 5–6.

52. Joan Jensen, "Out of Wisconsin: Country Daughters in the City, 1910–1925," *Minnesota History* 59, no. 2 (summer 2004): 57–58.

53. Mary Neth, "Leisure and Generational Change: Farm Youths in the Midwest, 1910–1940," *Agricultural History* 67, no. 2 (spring 1993): 182–83.

54. Wellington S. Clay to Rhoda Emery, July 5, [1893–1894], Rhoda J. Emery and Family Papers, manuscript correspondence and diaries, 1842–1953, Manuscripts Collection, MHS.

55. Jensen, "Out of Wisconsin," 52–54.

56. Anonymous, manuscript essay, "Life on the Farm," John E. Brown Papers, Archives, SHSI.

57. Rendleman, 128, 133–34.

58. Neth, *Preserving the Family Farm*, 263–66.

59. Edgar G. Menizer, "How to Keep the Boy on the Farm," *Kansas Farmer*, April 9, 1910, 1.

60. Henry Wallace, "The Farm Boy and His Father," *Letters to the Farm Boy* (New York: Macmillan, 1918), 7.

61. "That Boy," *Farmer's Family Journal* 2, no. 6 (June 1905): 4; Frank Boyd O'-Connell, "Why the Boys Leave," *Nebraska Farmer*, December 18, 1912, 1162; "Are You Square With Your Boy?" *Kansas Farmer*, June 24, 1911, 3; Mary Barrett, "Why Roger Stayed on the Farm," *Nebraska Farmer*, September 8, 1915, 855.

62. "Boys Who Will Not Make Good Farmers," *Kansas Farmer* 13, no. 40 (October 6, 1875): 317; "The Boy on the Farm," *Farmer's Family Journal*, August 1904, 10.

63. Annie P. Searing, "In Dollars and Cents: The Monetary Value of the Farm Woman Needs Definite Recognition," *Farmer's Wife*, November 1914, 171.

64. Katharine Henry, "Daughter Chooses the Farm," *Farmer's Wife*, June 1917, 8.

65. Hestella Carothers, "How May a Farmer's Daughter Enjoy an Income Without Teaching School and Yet Live at Home," *Kansas Farmer*, March 31, 1904, 353.

66. Flora Bullock, "Girls' Interest in Farm Life," *Nebraska Farmer,* July 28, 1915, 739.

67. Crow, 48–49.

68. Ibid., 78–79.

69. Ibid., 80.

70. Ibid., 86.

71. Ibid., 89–95.

72. Liberty Hyde Bailey, *The Training of Farmers* (New York: Century, 1909), 108, 111, 113.

73. Ibid., 99.

74. David B. Danbom emphasizes the inability of rural communities to provide the same amenities as urban communities in his discussion of the rural to urban exodus of the late nineteenth and early twentieth centuries. David B. Danbom, *Born in the Country: A History of Rural America* (Baltimore: Johns Hopkins University Press, 1995), 161–84.

75. Dorothy Schwieder, *Iowa: The Middle Land* (Ames: Iowa State University Press, 1996), 146.

76. Jensen, "Out of Wisconsin," 50.

77. Frank J. Klingberg, "The Education of a Kansan," Manuscripts Division, KSHS, 9.

78. Henry C. Taylor, *Tarpleywick: A Century of Iowa Farming* (Ames: Iowa State University Press, 1970), 99–100.

79. "Would You Marry a Farmer? Answers of Women Who Speak From Experience," *Nebraska Farmer,* November 19, 1913, 1099. Similar articles, some with titles such as "Would You Want Your Daughter to Marry a Farmer?," appeared in farm journals throughout the midwest. The answers were decidedly mixed.

80. Bailey, *Training of Farmers,* 97.

81. Helen Mary Emery, manuscript diaries, 1894–1907, June 24, 1906.

82. Ibid., February 17, 1907.

83. Ibid., April 13, 1907.

84. Ibid., December 7, 1906.

85. Frisby Leonard Rasp to John and Lavina Rasp, May 25, 1888, in Frisby Leonard Rasp, manuscript letters, 1888, MS 0635, Manuscripts Collection, Nebraska State Historical Society, Lincoln, Nebraska (hereafter NSHS).

86. Rasp, May 6, 1888, May 9, 1888, May 13, 1888, May 16, 1888.

87. Rasp to parents, May 13, 1888.

88. Ibid., June 5 [?], 1888.

89. Ibid., May 19, 1888.

90. Lavina Rasp to Frisby Leonard Rasp, May 9, 1888.

91. Francesca A. Florey and Avery M. Guest, "Coming of Age Among U.S. Farm Boys in the Late 1800s: Occupational and Residential Choices," *Journal of Family History* 13, no. 2 (1988): 247.

92. Mary Blair to Lea Hutton, September 21, 1890, September 30, 1890, and Lea Hutton to Mary Blair, November 20, 1890, Hutton Family Correspondence,

VIIf-1-a (1884–89), Archives Collection, McLean County Historical Society, Bloomington, Illinois.

93. Bailey, *Training of Farmers,* 124–25, 132–33.

94. Gilbert Fite, *American Farmers: The New Minority* (Bloomington: Indiana University Press, 1981), 7–9.

95. Danbom, *Born in the Country,* 196.

96. Ibid., 167–69.

97. Country Life Commission, *Report of the Country Life Commission,* U.S. Senate Document No.705 (Washington, DC: Government Printing Office, 1909), 65.

EPILOGUE.
"We Are at Home with the Land"

1. David B. Danbom, *Born in the Country: A History of Rural America* (Baltimore: Johns Hopkins University Press, 1995), 244–45.

2. U.S. Census Bureau, "Urban and Rural Population: 1900 to 1990," data released October 1995, available at: http://www.census.gov/population/censusdata/urpop0090.txt (accessed May 2004).

3. John Ise, *Sod and Stubble: The Story of a Kansas Farm* (Lincoln: Bison Books, 1967); David Bruce Dill, typescript memoir, "Boy Life on the Farm, Wyman, Iowa, 1896–1903," Archives, State Historical Society of Iowa, Iowa City, Iowa (hereafter SHSI); Margaret Pike, "Remembrances of a Life," Eau Claire Area Research Center, Wisconsin Historical Society, Eau Claire, Wisconsin.

4. Twenty-seven published and forty-two unpublished memoirs are the core of the research material for this chapter. This does not include memoirs and reminiscences of those who wrote exclusively as farm parents or rural schoolteachers.

5. Maurice Minor, *Three in a Hill* (New York: Carlton Press, 1979), preface.

6. A possible exception to this rule was Mari Sandoz, author of *Old Jules* and many other literary and historical works, who survived a horrendous childhood in rural Nebraska. Her father, Jules Sandoz, for whom she had a grudging admiration, was, by her account, an extremely abusive husband and father, meting out barbed-wire beatings to his wife and children when the spirit moved him. Because Sandoz's tale is about the Sand Hills and western Nebraska, it is not part of this analysis of children's lives in the midwest. Mari Sandoz, *Old Jules* (Lincoln: Bison Books, 1962).

7. Minor, 14.

8. Charles M. Turner, typescript reminiscence, RG 1478.AM, Box 1, Manuscripts Collection, Nebraska State Historical Society, Lincoln, Nebraska (hereafter NSHS), 14.

9. Theresa Baughman Rickett, typescript of tape-recorded reminiscences, 1974–1976, Archives Division. Wisconsin Historical Society, Madison, Wisconsin (hereafter WHS), 55.

10. Frank J. Klingberg, "The Education of a Kansan," Manuscripts Division, Kansas State Historical Society, Topeka, Kansas (hereafter KSHS), 9.

11. Minor, 15–17.

12. Oscar Hallam, typescript reminiscences, Manuscripts Collection, Minnesota Historical Society, St. Paul, Minnesota (hereafter MHS), 35.

13. Clare Thompson, "Kate and Ned and Jim," in Addie M. Thompson Sinclair, "My Story: An Autobiography of Addie M. Thompson Sinclair Covering the Years 1880 to 1961," Manuscripts Division, KSHS, 82–83.

14. Marie Sophia Koberstein Guethlein, typescript reminiscences, Archives Division, WHS, 6, 13, 15.

15. Augusta Thomas, typescript memoir, "Prairie Children," Kenetha Merrill Collection, Manuscripts Division, KSHS, 117–25.

16. Turner, 11, 18.

17. Kenneth W. Porter, ed., "A Little Girl on an Iowa Forty, 1873–1880—Catherine Wiggins Porter," *Iowa Journal of History and Politics* 51, no. 2 (April 1953): 147–51.

18. Nehemias Tjernagel, typescript reminiscence, "The Sheldall School," Tjernagel Papers, Archives, SHSI, 163.

19. Hugh Orchard, *Old Orchard Farm: The Story of an Iowa Boyhood* (Ames: Iowa State University Press, 1952), 212–13.

20. For particularly detailed descriptions of playground games, see William S. Miller, *Growing Up in Goose Lake* (N.p.: William S. Miller, 1974), 20–25; for toys, see Minor, 121–26.

21. Furmity was a dessert somewhat like rice pudding, but made with wheat. Hallam, 11–12.

22. Margaret Pike, typescript reminiscence, "Remembrances of a Life," Eau Claire Area Research Center, Wisconsin Historical Society, Eau Claire, Wisconsin, 3.

23. Rickett, 44–45.

24. Louisa Sophia H. Gelhorn Boylan, "My Life Story," manuscript reminiscence, January 1938, SHSI, 4.

25. Anna Leona Lansworth Stanley, "Autobiography of Anna Leona Lansworth Stanley," Archives Division, WHS, 3.

26. Minor, 126–27.

27. Frances E. (Gilmer) Moore, "Memories of a Pioneer in Kansas Since 1873," Manuscripts Division, KSHS, 25.

28. Miller, 81.

29. Barbara Walker, using Laura Ingalls Wilder's descriptions of food in her children's series, beautifully explains how a lack of food in childhood might affect an adult's writing about the topic. Barbara M. Walker, *The Little House Cookbook: Frontier Foods from Laura Ingalls Wilder's Classic Stories* (New York: Harper-Collins, 1995), 3–4.

30. Moore, 2–3.

31. Eva Phelps, *East by the Big Bridge* (N.p.: n.p., 1951), 22–23.

32. Walker D. Wyman, "Memories of 'Old Hen and Noodles' and Other Foods on the Illinois Farm," in *At the Wyman Table on the Eight Mile,* by Grace Conn McConnell (Nashville: Grace Conn McConnell, 1987), iii–iv; Rickett, 4.

33. Wyman, iv; Lula Gillespie Lentz, "Illinois Commentary: The Reminiscences of Lula Gillespie Lentz, Part II," *Journal of the Illinois State Historical Society* 63, no. 4 (September 1975): 280; Hallam, 11–12.

34. Clifford Merril Drury, "Growing Up on an Iowa Farm, 1897–1915," *Annals of Iowa* 42, no. 3 (winter 1974): 175.

35. Rickett, 4.

36. Milo Pitcher, *My Heritage on Hominyridge* (Marshalltown, IA: Milo Pitcher, 1977), 6.

37. Dill, 11.

38. Mollie Krutza, typescript reminiscence, "Memories of Childhood on an Iowa Farm by Mollie Krutza nee Mary Ellen Harbold Written in 1952," Archives, SHSI, 11.

39. Miller, 15, 25, 69–72.

40. For a history of menstruation, see Joan Jacobs Brumberg, *The Body Project: An Intimate History of American Girls* (New York: Vintage Books, 1997).

41. Slovie Kissin-Marver, typescript reminiscences, "Mamma and Papa's Legacy," Manuscripts Collection, MHS, 18.

42. Thomas, 66.

43. Lentz, 357.

44. Minnie Ellingson Tapping, "Willie," in "Eighty Years at the Gopher Hole, 1867–1947," Manuscripts Collection, MHS.

45. "Stories Told by Gladys," Trimble Family Papers, Iowa Women's Archives, University of Iowa Libraries, Iowa City, Iowa, 5.

46. Thomas, 96–104.

47. Ovoe Swartz, "Pioneer Kid's Midwestern Lore," Manuscripts Division, KSHS, 5–6.

48. Orchard, 8–9, 18–19, 92–93.

49. Ibid., 150–51.

50. Ibid., 102.

51. Ibid., 156.

52. Liahna Babener, "Bitter Nostalgia: Recollections of Childhood on the Midwestern Frontier," in *Small Worlds: Children and Adolescents in America, 1850–1950,* ed. Elliott West and Paula Petrik (Lawrence: University Press of Kansas, 1992), 302–5.

53. David Thelen, "Memory and American History," *Journal of American History* 75, no. 4 (March 1989): 1122.

54. Miller, 81.

55. Minor, 128.

56. Stanley, 3.

57. Samuel Goldenman, typescript reminiscence, "My Pilgrimage," Manuscripts Collection, MHS, 2.

58. Henry C. Taylor, *Tarpleywick: A Century of Iowa Farming* (Ames: Iowa State University Press, 1970), 80–85.

59. Excerpts from Thomas Jefferson, *Notes on Virginia,* in Everett E. Edwards, *Jefferson and Agriculture,* Agricultural History Series No. 7 (Washington, DC: U.S. Department of Agriculture, 1943), 23–25.

60. Minor, 127–28.

61. J. Glenn Logan, typescript reminiscence, "Stories of My Early Life, Compiled and Printed April, 1980," Manuscripts Division, KSHS, 72.

62. Bruce Bliven, "A Prairie Boyhood," *Palimpsest* 49, no. 8 (August 1968): 322.

63. Frances Olsen Day, typescript reminiscences, "More About Life on the Prairie," Archives, SHSI, 11.

64. Bliven, 324; Pitcher, 39.

65. Drury, 194.

66. Lentz, 361.

67. Sinclair, 117.

68. Thomas, 115–16.

69. Lu Ann Jones and Nancy Grey Osterud, "Breaking New Ground: Oral History and Agricultural History," *Journal of American History* 76, no. 2 (September 1989): 553.

70. Thelen, 1125.

71. David Lowenthal, *The Past Is a Foreign Country* (Cambridge: Cambridge University Press, 1985), 259.

72. Susan Sessions Rugh, "American Pastoral: The Family Farm and the Making of the Nation," presented at the Organization of American Historians Midwestern Regional Conference, Ames, Iowa, August 3–6, 2000.

73. Danbom, 251.

74. Arloc Sherman, *Falling by the Wayside: Children in Rural America* (Washington, DC: Children's Defense Fund, 1992), 1–5. See also Janet M. Fitchen, "Why Rural Poverty Is Growing Worse: Similar Causes in Diverse Settings," in *The Changing American Countryside: Rural People and Places,* ed. Emery N. Castle (Lawrence: University Press of Kansas, 1995), 261–66.

Bibliography

Newspapers and Periodicals

American Child
American Young Folks
Brooklyn Teller, Brooklyn, Wisconsin
Child Labor Bulletin
DeForest Times, DeForest, Wisconsin
Farmers Family Journal
Farmer's Wife
Kansas Farmer
Kansas Magazine
Nebraska Farmer
Prairie Farmer
Rural Manhood
Wisconsin Journal of Education

Manuscript and Archival Sources

Aberle, Mary J. *See* Eberle, Mammie.
Adolphson, Seth. Manuscript diaries, 1913, 1915–1919. Whitewater Area Research Center, Wisconsin Historical Society, Whitewater, Wisconsin.
Alden Family Papers. Family scrapbooks. Special Collections, Parks Library, Iowa State University, Ames, Iowa.
Anonymous. Manuscript essay, "Life on the Farm." John E. Brown Papers, Archives, State Historical Society of Iowa, Iowa City, Iowa.
Bailey, John Campbell. Typescript diary, 1867–1923. Manuscripts Collection, Illinois State Historical Library, Springfield, Illinois.
Bailey, Louise. Manuscript diaries, 1893–1897. Archives Division, Wisconsin Historical Society, Madison, Wisconsin.
Bamberg, Elma Barnes. Typescript reminiscence, "My Home on the Smoky." Manuscripts Division, Kansas State Historical Society, Topeka, Kansas.
Barker, Celestia Lee. Manuscript diary, 1885. MS 246, Box 1/5, Special Collections, Parks Library, Iowa State University, Ames, Iowa.

Benke, Bertha Mary Emily. Microfilm of manuscript diary. Manuscripts Division, Kansas State Historical Society, Topeka, Kansas.

Benke, Hermann C. Microfilm of manuscript diary. Manuscripts Division, Kansas State Historical Society, Topeka, Kansas.

Bigalke, Anna. Trial transcript, divorce proceedings, 1906–1907. Archives Division, Wisconsin Historical Society, Madison, Wisconsin.

Boylan, Louisa Sophia H. Gelhorn. "My Life Story." Manuscript reminiscence, January 1938. Archives, State Historical Society of Iowa, Iowa City, Iowa.

Butterfield, Dr. Rosa Armentrout. Typescript diary, 1876–1877. Archives, State Historical Society of Iowa, Iowa City, Iowa.

City of Eau Claire, Wisconsin. Commissioner of the Poor. Case Record Book, 1911–1917. Eau Claire Series 83. Wisconsin Historical Society, Eau Claire Area Research Center, Eau Claire, Wisconsin. By permission of Eau Claire County Department of Human Services.

Conron, Clara S. Typescript diary, 1884–1885. Manuscripts Division, Kansas State Historical Society, Topeka, Kansas.

Converse, Effie Elsie. Manuscript diaries, 1884, 1885, 1890. Effie Elsie Converse Papers, 1882–1932. Wisconsin Historical Society, Eau Claire Area Research Center, Eau Claire, Wisconsin.

Converse, William. Manuscript diaries, 1882, 1883, 1887. Effie Elsie Converse Papers, 1882–1932. Wisconsin Historical Society, Eau Claire Area Research Center, Eau Claire, Wisconsin.

Dane County, Wisconsin. Coroner's inquests, 1915. Dane Series 71, Box 5, 1912–1915. Archives Division, Wisconsin Historical Society, Madison, Wisconsin.

———. Manuscript Census of Population, 1920, Volume 13, District 23, Sheet 1, Line 82. Archives Division, Wisconsin Historical Society, Madison, Wisconsin.

Day, Frances Olsen. Typescript reminiscences, "Pioneering," "More About Life on the Prairie," "Prairie Flowers," and "School Days at Elm Grove in Calhoun County, Iowa (1880's)." Archives, State Historical Society of Iowa, Iowa City, Iowa.

Dill, David Bruce. Typescript memoir, "Boy Life on the Farm, Wyman, Iowa, 1896–1903." Archives, State Historical Society of Iowa, Iowa City, Iowa.

Eau Claire County, Wisconsin. County Court Record of Admission to State Public School, 1887–1901. Eau Claire Series 59. Wisconsin Historical Society, Eau Claire Area Research Center, Eau Claire, Wisconsin.

Eberle, Mammie, also listed as Mary J. Aberle. Manuscript diary, 1874–1875. Manuscripts Division, Kansas State Historical Society, Topeka, Kansas.

Emery, Helen Mary. Manuscript correspondence and diaries, 1894–1907. Rhoda J. Emery and Family Papers. Manuscripts Collection, Minnesota Historical Society, St. Paul, Minnesota.

Emery, Rhoda J. Manuscript diaries, 1889–1890, 1892, 1893–1894. Rhoda J. Emery and Family Papers. Manuscripts Collection, Minnesota Historical Society, St. Paul, Minnesota.

Gablemann Collection. Archives, State Historical Society of Iowa, Iowa City, Iowa.

Gill, Maude Keene. "Reminiscences." Archives Division, Wisconsin Historical Society, Madison, Wisconsin.

Gitchel-Larsen Family. Correspondence. MS 3622, Manuscripts Collection, Nebraska State Historical Society, Lincoln, Nebraska.

Goldenman, Samuel F. Typescript reminiscence, "My Pilgrimage." Manuscripts Collection, Minnesota Historical Society, St. Paul, Minnesota.

Grinnell, De Witt Clinton. Manuscript diary, 1867–1877. Manuscripts Division, Kansas State Historical Society, Topeka, Kansas.

Griswold, Mamie. Manuscript diaries, 1878–1883, 1883–1894. Henry A. Griswold Family Papers, Box 4. Manuscripts Department, Illinois State Historical Library, Springfield, Illinois.

Guethlein, Marie Sophia Koberstein. Typescript reminiscences. Archives Division, Wisconsin Historical Society, Madison, Wisconsin.

Hallam, Oscar. Typescript reminiscences. Manuscripts Collection, Minnesota Historical Society, St. Paul, Minnesota.

Haycraft, Isaac G. Typescript reminiscences. P 1441, Manuscripts Collection, Minnesota Historical Society, St. Paul, Minnesota.

Hudson Baptist Church. Records. McLean County Historical Society, Bloomington, Illinois.

Huftalen, Sarah Gillespie. Manuscript diary, 1877–1879. Sarah Gillespie Huftalen Collection. Archives, State Historical Society of Iowa, Iowa City, Iowa.

Hutton Family Correspondence, VIIf-1-a (1884–1889). Archives Collection, McLean County Historical Society, Bloomington, Illinois.

Inman, John M. Manuscript diary, 1870. John M. Inman Collection. Archives, State Historical Society of Iowa, Iowa City, Iowa.

Ivins, James. Manuscript diary, 1900–1901. Manuscripts Division, Kansas State Historical Society, Topeka, Kansas.

Johnson, Clara M. Transcript of oral history interview, February 16, 1985, Rural Women's Oral History Project. Manuscripts Collection, Archives Division, Wisconsin Historical Society, Madison, Wisconsin.

Johnson Family Manuscript Letters, Johnson Family Collection. Iowa Women's Archives, University of Iowa Libraries, Iowa City, Iowa.

Kissin-Marver, Slovie. Typescript reminiscences, "Mamma and Papa's Legacy." Manuscripts Collection, Minnesota Historical Society, St. Paul, Minnesota.

Klingberg, Frank J. "The Education of a Kansan." Manuscripts Division, Kansas State Historical Society, Topeka, Kansas.

Kolshorn, Agnes Mary. "Kolshorn Family History." Typescript genealogy and reminiscence. Manuscripts Collection, Minnesota Historical Society, St. Paul, Minnesota.

Krueger Collection. Photographic files. Archives division, Wisconsin Historical Society, Madison, Wisconsin.

Krutza, Mollie. Typescript reminiscence, "Memories of Childhood on an Iowa Farm by Mollie Krutza nee Mary Ellen Harbold Written in 1952." Archives, State Historical Society of Iowa, Iowa City, Iowa.

Logan, J. Glenn. Typescript reminiscence, "Stories of My Early Life, Compiled and Printed April, 1980." Manuscripts Division, Kansas State Historical Society, Topeka, Kansas.

Lundberg, Emma O. "Dependent Wards of the State of Wisconsin: A Study of Children Indentured into Family Homes by the State Public School." United States Department of Labor, Children's Bureau, draft report, 1924. Series 1401, Boxes 7 and 8. Archives Division, Wisconsin Historical Society, Madison, Wisconsin.

McClary, Washington Lafayette. Manuscript diaries, 1892–1938. MS 3775, Manuscripts Collection, Nebraska State Historical Society, Lincoln, Nebraska.

Miles, Floyd. "Autobiography." Typescript autobiography. MS 1080, Manuscripts Collection, Nebraska State Historical Society, Lincoln, Nebraska.

Moon, Minnie Mae. Manuscript diaries, 1892, 1893, 1895. Moon Family Collection, Box 3. Archives Collection, McLean County Historical Society, Bloomington, Illinois.

Moore, Frances E. (Gilmer). Typescript memoir, "Memories of a Pioneer in Kansas Since 1873." Manuscripts Division, Kansas State Historical Society, Topeka, Kansas.

Myers, Oliver Perry. Manuscript diary, 1872–1874. Oliver Perry Myers Papers. Archives, State Historical Society of Iowa, Iowa City, Iowa.

Norton Family. Norton Diaries, 1876–1895. Copied and annotated by Helen Norton Starr. By permission of Henry L. Norton. Manuscripts Division, Kansas State Historical Society, Topeka, Kansas.

Olmsted County, Minnesota, Superintendent of Schools. Teacher's Annual Reports, District 97, 1892, 1893. State Archives Collection, Minnesota Historical Society, St. Paul, Minnesota.

Orr, Lois Tucker. Typescript diaries, 1897–1936, Box 3, transcriptions. Illinois State Historical Library, Springfield, Illinois.

Pascoe, Mary Elizabeth. Manuscript diary, 1871. Archives Division, Wisconsin Historical Society, Madison, Wisconsin.

Peet, Mary Eleanor Armstrong. Typescript diary, 1891–1897. Archives, State Historical Society of Iowa, Iowa City, Iowa.

Petersen, Peter S. Manuscript reminiscence. MS 4021, Manuscripts Collection, Nebraska State Historical Society, Lincoln, Nebraska.

Pike, Margaret. Typescript reminiscence, "Remembrances of a Life." Eau Claire Area Research Center, Wisconsin Historical Society, Eau Claire, Wisconsin.

Polk County, Wisconsin. Criminal Docket, 1874–1926. Wisconsin Historical Society, River Falls Area Research Center, River Falls, Wisconsin.

————. Record of the Criminal Court. Wisconsin Historical Society, River Falls Area Research Center, River Falls, Wisconsin.

————. Superintendent of the Poor. County Home Records, 1876–1934. Wisconsin Historical Society, River Falls Area Research Center, River Falls, Wisconsin.

Pruyn, Carrie Dean. Typescript autobiography, "Out of the Dusk: Memories of a Girl of the Gay Nineties." Archives, State Historical Society of Iowa, Iowa City, Iowa.

Rasp, Frisby Leonard. Manuscript letters, 1888. MS 0635, Manuscripts Collection, Nebraska State Historical Society, Lincoln, Nebraska.

Regan, Genevieve M. Typescript reminiscence, "The Story of My Childhood." Archives, State Historical Society of Iowa, Iowa City, Iowa.

Rickett, Theresa Baughman. Typescript of tape-recorded reminiscences, 1974–1976. Archives Division, Wisconsin Historical Society, Madison, Wisconsin.

Schulz, August. Manuscript diary. Manuscripts Division, Kansas State Historical Society, Topeka, Kansas.

Sinclair, Addie M. Thompson. Typescript autobiography, "My Story: An Autobiography of Addie M. Thompson Sinclair Covering the Years 1880 to 1961." Manuscripts Division, Kansas State Historical Society, Topeka, Kansas.

Stanley, Anna Leona Lansworth. "Autobiography of Anna Leona Lansworth Stanley." Archives Division, Wisconsin Historical Society, Madison, Wisconsin.

State Normal School at Winona, Minnesota. *Annual Catalogue of the Officers and Students of the State Normal School, at Winona, Minnesota, for the Year 1895–1896, with Annual Circular for 1896–1897.* Winona, MN: D. Sinclair, 1896.

————. "Enrollment and Attendance Record, 1889–1899," A-85-3-123. Archives, Winona State University Library, Winona State University, Winona, Minnesota.

Stilson, John J. and Sadie. Manuscript diaries, 1870–1878. Archives, State Historical Society of Iowa, Iowa City, Iowa.

Story, Charles Augustus, Jr. Manuscript diary, 1879–1884. Film MS 62. Manuscripts Collection, Nebraska State Historical Society, Lincoln, Nebraska.

Swain, Mary. Manuscript letters, 1881. Archives Division, Wisconsin Historical Society, Madison, Wisconsin.

Swain, Willie. Manuscript letter, 1881. Archives Division, Wisconsin Historical Society, Madison, Wisconsin.

Swartz, Ovoe. "Pioneer Kid's Midwestern Lore." Manuscripts Division, Kansas State Historical Society, Topeka, Kansas.

Tapping, Minnie Ellingson. Typescript reminiscence, "Eighty Years at the Gopher Hole, 1867–1947." Manuscripts Collection, Minnesota Historical Society, St. Paul, Minnesota.

Thomas, Augusta. Typescript memoir, "Prairie Children." Kenetha Merrill Collection, Manuscripts Division, Kansas State Historical Society, Topeka, Kansas.

Tjernagel, Nehemias. Typescript reminiscence, "The Sheldall School." Tjernagel Papers. Archives, State Historical Society of Iowa, Iowa City, Iowa.

Trimble Family Papers. "Stories Told by Gladys." Iowa Women's Archives, University of Iowa Libraries, Iowa City, Iowa.

Turner, Charles M. Typescript reminiscence. RG 1478.AM, Box 1, Manuscripts Collection, Nebraska State Historical Society, Lincoln, Nebraska.

Van Horne, George H. Manuscript diary, 1875. MS 3629, Manuscripts Collection, Nebraska State Historical Society, Lincoln, Nebraska.

Van Zante and De Cook Families. Papers. Iowa Women's Archives, University of Iowa Libraries, Iowa City, Iowa.

Webb, Shirley Mollett. Typescript reminiscence, "Reminiscence of School Days." Manuscripts Division, Kansas State Historical Society, Topeka, Kansas.

White, Lucy Van Voorhis. Papers, 1866–1932. Iowa Women's Archives. University of Iowa, Iowa City, Iowa.

Wisconsin Child Center. Agency History Record. Archives Division, Wisconsin Historical Society, Madison, Wisconsin.

Wood, James Lincoln. Manuscript diaries, 1879, 1888. Wood Family Papers. Eau Claire Area Research Center, Wisconsin Historical Society, Eau Claire, Wisconsin.

Wood, Ralph. Manuscript diaries, 1889–1893. Wood Family Papers. Eau Claire Area Research Center, Wisconsin Historical Society, Eau Claire, Wisconsin.

Wyman, Walker D. Manuscript reminiscences. Collection of Mark Wyman, Normal, Illinois.

Published Primary Sources

Abbott, Edith, and Sophonisba P. Breckinridge. *The Administration of the Aid-to-Mothers Law in Illinois.* Washington, DC: Government Printing Office, 1921.

Addams, Jane. *A New Conscience and an Ancient Evil.* New York: Macmillan, 1912.

———. *Twenty Years at Hull-House.* New York: Macmillan, 1960.

American Boy's Book of Sports and Games: A Practical Guide to Indoor and Outdoor Amusements. New York: Dick and Fitzgerald, 1864; reprint edition, New York: Lyons Press, 2000.

Bailey, Liberty Hyde. *The Training of Farmers.* New York: Century, 1909.

Baldwin, Bird T., Eva Fillmore, and Lora Hadley. *Farm Children: An Investigation of Rural Child Life in Selected Areas of Iowa.* New York: D. Appleton, 1930; reprint, New York: Arno Press, 1972.

"Barbarism in Rural Schools." *Wisconsin Journal of Education* 22, no. 4 (April 1892): 74–75.

"The Big Boy in the Country School." *Nebraska School Journal,* reprinted in *Wisconsin Journal of Education* 19, no. 12 (December 1889): 494–95.

Bliven, Bruce. "A Prairie Boyhood." *Palimpsest* 49, no. 8 (August 1968): 308–52.

Burke, Dorothy May Williams, and Mary Elizabeth Skinner. *Work of Children on Illinois Farms.* Washington, DC: Government Printing Office, 1926.

Brace, Charles Loring. *The Dangerous Classes of New York and Twenty Years' Work Among Them.* New York: Wynkoop & Hallenbeck, 1872.

Children's Bureau. *Child Labor in North Dakota.* Washington, DC: Government Printing Office, 1923.

Country Life Commission. *Report of the Country Life Commission.* U.S. Senate Document No. 705. Washington, DC: Government Printing Office, 1909.

Crow, Martha Foote. *The American Country Girl.* New York: Frederick A. Stokes, 1915.

Crowder, E. May Lacey. "Pioneer Life in Palo Alto County." *Iowa Journal of History and Politics* 46, no. 2 (April 1948): 156–98.

Cubberly, Ellwood P. *Rural Life and Education: A Study of the Rural School Problem as a Phase of the Rural-Life Problem.* New York: Houghton Mifflin, 1914.

Department of Commerce. Bureau of the Census. *Children in Gainful Occupations in the Fourteenth Census of the United States.* Washington, DC: Government Printing Office, 1924.

———. *Thirteenth Census of the United States, 1910.* Washington, DC: Government Printing Office, 1913.

———. *Fourteenth Census of the United States, 1920.* Washington, DC: Government Printing Office, 1923.

Department of the Interior. Census Office. *Ninth Census, the Statistics of Population of the United States.* Washington, DC: Government Printing Office, 1872.

Dewey, John. *Democracy and Education: An Introduction to the Philosophy of Education.* New York: Macmillan, 1938.

Drury, Clifford Merril. "Growing Up on an Iowa Farm, 1897–1915." *Annals of Iowa* 42, no. 3 (winter 1974): 161–97.

Emery, Rhoda, and Grace Emery. *The Story of Minnesota.* Rochester, MN: N.p., 1916.

Emery, Rhoda J., and George F. Howard. *Outline of Study of U.S. History for Use in Junior High Schools and Senior American History Classes.* 12th ed. 1912; St. Paul: Howard's Outlines, 1928.

Fairchild, E. T. *Bulletin of Information Regarding Consolidation of Rural Schools.* Topeka: State Printing Office, 1908.

Galpin, Charles Josiah. *Rural Life.* New York: Century, 1918.

Garland, Hamlin. *Boy Life on the Prairie.* New York, Macmillan, 1899.

———. *A Pioneer Mother.* Chicago: Bookfellows, 1922.

———. *A Daughter of the Middle Border.* New York: Grossett and Dunlap, 1926.

———. *A Son of the Middle Border.* New York: Grosset and Dunlap, 1927.

———. *Main-Travelled Roads.* 1891; reprint, Lincoln: Bison Books, 1995.

Gillette, John M. "Rural Child Labor." *Child Labor Bulletin* 1, no. 1 (June 1912): 154–60.

Graf, William. *Growing Up on a Farm*. New York: Vantage Press, 1970.

Hewins, Katharine P. "The Development of Placing-out Work by Institutions." In *Foster Home Care for Dependent Children*. Children's Bureau Publication No. 136. Washington, DC: Government Printing Office, 1926.

Hopkins, Vivian C., ed. "Diary of an Iowa Farm Girl: Josephine Edith Brown, 1892–1901." *Annals of Iowa* 42, no. 2 (fall 1973): 126–46.

Ingli, A. J. "Rural School Program." *Wisconsin Journal of Education* 36, no. 2 (February 1904): 46–47.

Ise, John. *Sod and Stubble: The Story of a Kansas Farm*. Lincoln: Bison Books, 1967.

Jefferson, Thomas. *Notes on Virginia*. In *Jefferson and Agriculture*, by Everett E. Edwards. Agricultural History Series No. 7. Washington, DC: U.S. Department of Agriculture, 1943.

Johnson, Rolf. *Happy as a Big Sunflower: Adventures in the West, 1876–1880*. Edited by Richard E. Jensen. Lincoln: University of Nebraska Press, 2000.

Kansas State Department of Education. *Standard Rural Schools: Requirements and Suggestions of the State Board of Education*. Topeka: Kansas State Printing Plant, 1916.

[Kansas] State Superintendent of Public Instruction. *Fifteenth Biennial Report of the State Superintendent of Public Instruction of Kansas for the Year Ending June 30, 1905, and June 30, 1906*. Topeka: State Printing Office, 1906.

———. *Seventeenth Biennial Report of the State Superintendent of Public Instruction of Kansas*. Topeka: State Printing Office, 1910.

Kirkpatrick, E. L. *The Farmer's Standard of Living: A Socio-Economic Study of 2886 White Farm Families of Selected Localities in 11 States*. Washington, DC: United States Department of Agriculture, Department Bulletin No. 1466, November 1926.

Lacey, Fred A. *The Public Schools of North Des Moines, Iowa, 1898*. Des Moines: Talbott-Koch, 1898.

Lentz, Lula Gillespie. "Illinois Commentary: The Reminiscences of Lula Gillespie Lentz, Part I." *Journal of the Illinois State Historical Society* 63, no. 3 (June 1975): 267–88.

———. "Illinois Commentary: The Reminiscences of Lula Gillespie Lentz, Part II." *Journal of the Illinois State Historical Society* 63, no. 4 (September 1975): 353–67.

McGill, Nettie P. *Children in Agriculture*. United States Department of Labor, Children's Bureau, Publication No. 187. Washington, DC: Government Printing Office, 1929.

Merritt, Ella Arvilla. "Important Changes Made by the State Legislatures of 1921, and of 1922 so far as Available Nov. 1, 1922, in Child Labor Standards and in Compulsory School Attendance Standards Affecting the Employment of Minors." Washington, DC: U.S. Department of Labor, Children's Bureau, 1922.

Millbrook, Mrs. Raymond, ed. "Mrs. Hattie E. Lee's Story of Her Life in Western Kansas." *Kansas Historical Quarterly* 22, no. 2 (summer 1956): 114–37.

Miller, William S. *Growing Up in Goose Lake.* N.p.: William S. Miller, 1974.

Minor, Maurice E. *Three in a Hill.* New York: Carlton Press, 1979.

Moore, Elizabeth. *Maternity and Infant Care in a Rural County in Kansas.* Washington, DC: Government Printing Office, 1917.

National Child Labor Committee. *Rural Child Welfare: An Inquiry by the National Child Labor Committee Based upon Conditions in West Virginia.* New York: Macmillan, 1922.

Nebraska, State of, Department of Public Welfare. *Report of the Nebraska Children's Code Commission 1920.* Lincoln: Department of Public Welfare, State Capitol, 1920.

Orchard, Hugh. *Old Orchard Farm: The Story of an Iowa Boyhood.* Ames: Iowa State University Press, 1952.

Peck, Emelyn Foster. "Summary of State 'Importation' and Exportation Laws." *Laws Relating to the Interstate Placement of Dependent Children.* Children's Bureau Publication No. 139. Washington: Government Printing Office, 1924.

Phelps, Eva. *East by the Big Bridge.* N.p.: N.p., 1951.

Pitcher, Milo. *My Heritage on Hominyridge.* Marshalltown, IA: Milo Pitcher, 1977.

Porter, Kenneth W., ed. "A Little Girl on an Iowa Forty, 1873–1880—Catherine Wiggins Porter." *Iowa Journal of History and Politics* 51, no. 2 (April 1953): 131–55.

Rendleman, Edith. *All Anyone Ever Wanted of Me Was to Work.* Edited by Jane Adams. Carbondale: Southern Illinois University Press, 1996.

Riis, Jacob. *How the Other Half Lives: Studies Among the Tenements of New York.* New York: Hill and Wang, 1957.

Roosevelt, Theodore. *The Strenuous Life: Essays and Addresses.* New York: Century, 1901.

Sandoz, Mari. *Old Jules.* Lincoln: Bison Books, 1962.

Sears, Roebuck and Company. *The 1902 Edition of the Sears, Roebuck Catalogue* facsimile edition. New York: Gramercy Books, 1993.

Sherbon, Florence Brown, and Elizabeth Moore. *Maternity and Infant Care in Two Rural Counties in Wisconsin.* Rural Child Welfare Series No. 4, United States Department of Labor, Children's Bureau Publication No. 46. Washington, DC: Government Printing Office, 1919.

Sipma, Sjoerd. Letter, September 26, 1848. Pella Historical Society. *History of Pella, Iowa, 1847–1987.* Dallas: Curtis Media, 1988, 27.

State of Iowa. Department of Public Instruction. *Hand-Book for Iowa Schools, 1900.* Des Moines: F. R. Conway, State Printer, 1900.

Svendsen, Gro. *Frontier Mother: The Letters of Gro Svendsen.* Northfield, MN: Norwegian-American Historical Association, 1950.

Taylor, Henry C. *Tarpleywick: A Century of Iowa Farming.* Ames: Iowa State University Press, 1970.

United States Bureau of Education. Department of the Interior. *Report of the Commissioner of Education, 1888–1889.* Vol. 1. Washington, DC: Government Printing Office, 1891.

United States Census Office. *Twelfth Census of the United States, 1900.* Washington, DC: U.S. Census Office, 1901.

United States Department of Labor. Children's Bureau. *Child Labor in the United States.* Bureau Publication No. 114. Washington, DC: Department of Labor, 1921.

———. *Foster-Home Care for Dependent Children.* Washington, DC: Government Printing Office, 1926.

———. *Laws Relating to Interstate Placement of Dependent Children.* Washington, DC: Government Printing Office, 1924.

———. *State Child-Labor Standards.* Washington, DC: Government Printing Office, 1921.

———. *State Compulsory School Attendance Standards Affecting the Employment of Minors, January 1, 1921.* Washington, DC: Government Printing Office, 1921.

United States Senate. *Report of the Country Life Commission: Special Message from the President of the United States Transmitting the Report of the Country Life Commission.* Washington, DC: Government Printing Office, 1909.

Wallace, Henry. "The Farm Boy and His Father." *Letters to the Farm Boy.* New York: Macmillan, 1918.

———. *Uncle Henry's Letters to the Farm Boy.* New York: Macmillan, 1918.

West, Willis Mason. *The American People: A New History for High Schools.* New York: Allyn and Bacon, 1928.

Wilder, Laura Ingalls. *These Happy Golden Years.* New York: Harper & Row, 1981.

Woodburn, James Albert, and Thomas Francis Moran. *Elementary American History and Government.* New York: Longmans, Green, 1929.

Wooster, Lorraine Elizabeth, State Superintendent of Public Instruction. *Kansas Rural-School Bulletin, 1922.* Topeka: Kansas State Printing Plant, 1922.

Wyman, Walker D. "Memories of 'Old Hen and Noodles' and Other Foods on the Illinois Farm." In *At the Wyman Table on the Eight Mile,* by Grace Conn McConnell, iii–ix. Nashville: Grace Conn McConnell, 1987.

Secondary Sources

Abbott, Grace. *The Child and the State.* 2 vols. Chicago: University of Chicago Press, 1938.

Adams, Jane. *The Transformation of Rural Life: Southern Illinois, 1890–1990.* Chapel Hill: University of North Carolina Press, 1990.

Aitken, Stuart C. *Putting Children in Their Place.* Washington, DC: Association of American Geographers, 1994.

Alexander, Ruth M. *The "Girl Problem": Female Sexual Delinquency in New York, 1900–1930.* Ithaca: Cornell University Press, 1995.

Aries, Philippe. *Centuries of Childhood: A Social History of Family Life.* New York: Alfred A. Knopf, 1962.

Ashby, LeRoy. *Endangered Children: Dependency, Neglect, and Abuse in American History.* New York: Twayne Publishers, 1997.

Atkins, Annette. *We Grew Up Together: Brothers and Sisters in Nineteenth Century America.* Urbana: University of Illinois Press, 2001.

Aveni, Anthony F. *The Book of the Year: A Brief History of Our Seasonal Holidays.* Oxford: Oxford University Press, 2003.

Babener, Liahna. "Bitter Nostalgia: Recollections of Childhood on the Midwestern Frontier." In *Small Worlds: Children and Adolescents in America: 1850–1950,* edited by Elliott West and Paula Petrik, 301–20. Lawrence: University Press of Kansas, 1992.

Bailey, Beth L. *From Front Porch to Back Seat: Courtship in Twentieth-Century America.* Baltimore: Johns Hopkins University Press, 1989.

Barron, Hal. *Mixed Harvest: The Second Great Transformation in the Rural North, 1870–1930.* Chapel Hill: University of North Carolina Press, 1997.

Bederman, Gail. *Manliness and Civilization: A Cultural History of Gender and Race in the United States, 1880–1917.* Chicago: University of Chicago Press, 1995.

Berebitsky, Julie. *Like Our Very Own: Adoption and the Changing Culture of Motherhood, 1851–1950.* Lawrence: University Press of Kansas, 2000.

Bogue, Allan G. *The Farm on North Talbot Road.* Lincoln: University of Nebraska Press, 2001.

———. *From Prairie to Cornbelt: Farming on the Illinois and Iowa Prairies in the Nineteenth Century.* Chicago: University of Chicago Press, 1963.

Bremner, Richard. "Other People's Children." *Journal of Social History* 16, no. 3 (spring 1983): 83–103.

Brumberg, Joan Jacobs. *The Body Project: An Intimate History of American Girls.* New York: Vintage Books, 1997.

Bullough, William A. "'It Is Better to Be a Country Boy': The Lure of the Country in Urban Education in the Gilded Age." *Historian* 35, no. 2 (February 1973): 183–95.

Cable, Mary. *The Little Darlings: A History of Child Rearing in America.* New York: Scribner, 1975.

Calvert, Karin. "Patterns of Childrearing in America." In *Beyond the Century of the Child: Cultural History and Developmental Psychology,* edited by Willem Koops and Michael Zuckerman, 62–81. Philadelphia: University of Pennsylvania Press, 2003.

Carnes, Mark C., and Clyde Griffen, eds. *Meanings for Manhood: Constructions of Masculinity in Victorian America.* Chicago: University of Chicago Press, 1990.

Clement, Priscilla Ferguson. *Growing Pains: Children of the Industrial Age, 1850–1890.* London: Twayne, 1997.

Cordier, Mary Hulbert. *Schoolwomen of the Prairies and Plains: Personal Narratives from Iowa, Kansas, and Nebraska.* Albuquerque: University of New Mexico Press, 1992.

Cross, Gary. *Kids' Stuff: Toys and the Changing World of American Childhood.* Cambridge: Harvard University Press, 1997.

Danbom, David B. *Born in the Country: A History of Rural America*. Baltimore: Johns Hopkins University Press, 1995.

———. "Rural Education Reform and the Country Life Movement." *Agricultural History* 53, no. 2 (April 1979): 462–74.

———. "Rural Girls in Fargo During the 1930s." *Agricultural History* 76, no. 4 (fall 2002): 659–68.

de Coninck-Smith, Ning, Bengt Sandin, and Ellen Schrumpf, eds. *Industrious Children: Work and Childhood in the Nordic Countries, 1850–1990*. Odense: Odense University Press, 1997.

Degler, Carl N. *At Odds: Women and the Family in America from the Revolution to the Present*. Oxford: Oxford University Press, 1980.

Dudden, Faye E. *Serving Women: Household Service in Nineteenth-Century America*. Hanover, NH: Wesleyan University Press, 1983.

Engelhardt, Carroll. "Compulsory Education in Iowa, 1872–1919." *Annals of Iowa* 49, no. 1–2 (summer/fall 1987): 58–76.

Ensign, Forest Chester. *Compulsory School Attendance and Child Labor: A Study of the Historical Development of Regulations Compelling Attendance and Limiting the Labor of Children in a Select Group of States*. Iowa City: Athens Press, 1921.

Faragher, John. *Sugar Creek: Life on the Illinois Prairie*. New Haven: Yale University Press, 1986.

Fitchen, Janet M. "Why Rural Poverty Is Growing Worse: Similar Causes in Diverse Settings." In *The Changing American Countryside: Rural People and Places*, ed. Emery N. Castle, 247–67. Lawrence: University Press of Kansas, 1995.

Fite, Gilbert. *American Farmers: The New Minority*. Bloomington: Indiana University Press, 1981.

Florey, Francesca A., and Avery M. Guest. "Coming of Age Among U.S. Farm Boys in the late 1800s: Occupational and Residential Choices." *Journal of Family History* 13, no. 2 (1988): 233–49.

Formanek-Brunell, Miriam. *Made to Play House: Dolls and the Commercialization of American Girlhood, 1830–1930*. New Haven: Yale University Press, 1993.

Frank, Stephen M. *Life with Father: Parenthood and Masculinity in the Nineteenth-Century American North*. Baltimore: Johns Hopkins University Press, 1998.

Fuller, Wayne. "Making Better Farmers: The Study of Agriculture in Midwestern Country Schools, 1900–1923." *Agricultural History* 60, no. 2 (spring 1986): 154–68.

———. *The Old Country School: The Story of Rural Education in the Middle West*. Chicago: University of Chicago Press, 1982.

Gjerde, Jon. *The Minds of the West: Ethnocultural Evolution in the Rural Middle West, 1830–1917*. Chapel Hill: University of North Carolina Press, 1997.

Grossberg, Michael. "Changing Conceptions of Child Welfare in the United States, 1820–1935." In *A Century of Juvenile Justice*, edited by Margaret Rosenheim et al., 3–41. Chicago: University of Chicago Press, 2002.

Hampsten, Elizabeth. *Settler's Children: Growing Up on the Great Plains*. Norman: University of Oklahoma Press, 1991.

Hanawalt, Barbara. *Growing Up in Medieval London: The Experience of Childhood in History.* Oxford: Oxford University Press, 1993.

Hawes, Joseph M., and N. Ray Hiner, eds. *Children in Historical and Comparative Perspective: An International Handbook and Research Guide.* Westport, CT: Greenwood Press, 1991.

Haynes, Fred E. *Child Labor Legislation in Iowa.* Iowa City: State Historical Society of Iowa, 1914.

Haywood, C. Robert, and Sandra Jarvis. *"A Funnie Place, No Fences": Teenagers' Views of Kansas, 1867–1900.* Lawrence: Division of Continuing Education, University of Kansas, 1992.

Hindman, Hugh D. *Child Labor: An American History.* Armonk, NY: M. E. Sharp, 2002.

Hiner, N. Ray, and Joseph M. Hawes. *Growing Up in America: Children in Historical Perspective.* Urbana: University of Illinois Press, 1985.

History of Olmsted County, Together with Biographical Matter, Statistics, Etc. Chicago: H. H. Hill, 1883.

Hoffbeck, Steven R. *The Haymakers: A Chronicle of Five Farm Families.* St. Paul: Minnesota Historical Society Press, 2000.

Holt, Marilyn Irvin. *Children of the Western Plains: The Nineteenth Century Experience.* Chicago: Ivan R. Dee, 2003.

———. *Orphan Trains: Placing Out in America.* Lincoln: Bison Books, 1992.

Hostetler, John. *Amish Society.* Baltimore: Johns Hopkins University Press, 1993.

Hunter, Kathryn M. *Father's Right-Hand Man: Women on Australia's Family Farms in the Age of Federation, 1880s–1920s.* Melbourne: Australian Scholarly Publishing, 2004.

Hunter, Kathryn, and Pamela Riney-Kehrberg. "Rural Daughters in Australia, New Zealand and the United States: An Historical Perspective." *Journal of Rural Studies* 18 (2002): 135–43.

Illick, Joseph E. *American Childhoods.* Philadelphia: University of Pennsylvania Press, 2002.

Jellison, Katherine. *Entitled to Power: Farm Women and Technology, 1913–1963.* Chapel Hill: University of North Carolina Press, 1993.

Jensen, Joan. "The Death of Rosa: Sexuality in Rural America." *Agricultural History* 67, no. 4 (fall 1993): 1–12.

———. "Out of Wisconsin: Country Daughters in the City, 1910–1925." *Minnesota History* 59, no. 2 (summer 2004): 48–61.

Johnson, Keach. "Elementary and Secondary Education in Iowa, 1890–1900: A Time of Awakening," Parts 1 and 2. *Annals of Iowa* 45, no. 2–3 (fall 1979/winter 1980): 87–109, 171–95.

Jones, Lu Ann, and Nancy Grey Osterud. "Breaking New Ground: Oral History and Agricultural History." *Journal of American History* 76, no. 2 (September 1989): 551–64.

Katzman, David M. *Seven Days a Week: Women and Domestic Service in Industrializing America.* Urbana: University of Illinois Press, 1981.

King, Charles R. *Children's Health in America: A History.* New York: Twayne, 1993.

Kusmer, Kenneth L. *Down and Out, on the Road: The Homeless in American History.* Oxford: Oxford University Press, 2002.

Landale, Nancy S. "Opportunity, Movement, and Marriage: U.S. Farm Sons at the Turn of the Century." *Journal of Family History* 14, no. 4 (1989): 365–86.

Lindenmeyer, Kriste. *"A Right to Childhood": The U.S. Children's Bureau and Child Welfare, 1912–1946.* Urbana: University of Illinois Press, 1997.

Lowenthal, David. *The Past Is a Foreign Country.* Cambridge: Cambridge University Press, 1985.

MacLeod, David I. *Building Character in the American Boy: The Boy Scouts, YMCA, and Their Forerunners, 1870–1920.* Madison: University of Wisconsin Press, 1983.

Marten, James. *The Children's Civil War.* Chapel Hill: University of North Carolina Press, 1998.

McClellan, Marjorie L. *Six Generations Here: A Farm Family Remembers.* Madison: State Historical Society of Wisconsin, 1997.

Mergen, Bernard. "The Discovery of Children's Play," *American Quarterly* 27, no. 4 (October 1975): 399–420.

Mintz, Steven, and Susan Kellogg. *Domestic Revolutions: A Social History of American Family Life.* New York: Free Press, 1989.

Neth, Mary. "Leisure and Generational Change: Farm Youths in the Midwest, 1910–1940." *Agricultural History* 67, no. 2 (spring 1993): 182–83.

———. *Preserving the Family Farm: Women, Community, and the Foundations of Agribusiness in the Midwest, 1900–1940.* Baltimore: Johns Hopkins University Press, 1995.

Odem, Mary E. *Delinquent Daughters: Protecting and Policing Adolescent Female Sexuality in the United States, 1885–1920.* Chapel Hill: University of North Carolina Press, 1995.

Ostergren, Robert. *A Community Transplanted: The Trans-Atlantic Experience of a Swedish Immigrant Settlement in the Upper Middle West, 1835–1915.* Madison: University of Wisconsin Press, 1988.

Osterud, Nancy Grey. *Bonds of Community: The Lives of Farm Women in Nineteenth-Century New York.* Ithaca: Cornell University Press, 1991.

Oxford Companion to Children's Literature. New York: Oxford University Press, 1984.

Patzer, Conrad E. *Public Education in Wisconsin.* Madison, WI: State Superintendent of Schools, 1924.

Peavy, Linda, and Ursula Smith. *Frontier Children.* Norman: University of Oklahoma Press, 1999.

Pederson, Jane M. *Between Memory and Reality: Family and Community in Rural Wisconsin, 1870–1970.* Madison: University of Wisconsin Press, 1992.

Peiss, Kathy. *Cheap Amusements: Working Women and Leisure in Turn-of-the-Century New York.* Philadelphia: Temple University Press, 1986.

Plakans, Andrejs. "Intergenerational Ambivalences in the Past—A Social-Historical Assessment." In *Intergenerational Ambivalences: New Perspectives* on *Parent-Child Relations in Later Life,* edited by Karl Pillemer and Kurt Luscher, 63–82. Amsterdam: Elsevier, 2004.

Pleck, Elizabeth. *Domestic Tyranny: The Making of American Social Policy Against Family Violence from Colonial Times to the Present.* New York: Oxford University Press, 1987.

Pollock, Linda. *Forgotten Children: Parent-Child Relations from 1500 to 1900.* Cambridge: Cambridge University Press, 1983.

Reinier, Jacqueline S. *From Virtue to Character: American Childhood, 1775–1850.* New York: Twayne, 1996.

Reynolds, David R. *There Goes the Neighborhood: Rural School Consolidation at the Grass Roots in Early Twentieth-Century Iowa.* Iowa City: University of Iowa Press, 1999.

Riney-Kehrberg, Pamela. "Alice Churned, Kathleen Washed, Hugh Milked: Daughters and Sons on New Zealand's Turn-of-the-Century Farms." *Turnbull Library Record* 33 (2000): 63–80.

———. "'But What Kind of Work Do the Rest of You Do?' Child Labor on Nebraska's Farms, 1870–1920." *Nebraska History* 82, no. 1 (spring 2001): 2–10.

———. "Farm Boys." *Boyhood in America: An Encyclopedia,* vol. 1. Edited by Priscilla Ferguson Clement and Jacqueline S. Reinier, 237–41. Santa Barbara, CA: ABC-CLIO, 2001.

———. "Growing Up in Kansas." *Kansas History: A Journal of the Central Plains* 26 (spring 2003): 50–65.

———. "Helping Ma and Helping Pa: Iowa's Turn-of-the-Century Farm Children." *Annals of Iowa* 59, no. 2 (spring 2000): 115–40.

———. "The Limits of Policy: Rural Children and Work in the United States and New Zealand, 1870–1920." *History of the Family* 6 (2001): 51–67.

———. "Women in Wheat Country." *Kansas History: A Journal of the Central Plains* 23, no. 1–2 (spring–summer 2000): 56–71.

Rotundo, E. Anthony. "Boy Culture: Middle-Class Boyhood in Nineteenth-Century America." In *Meanings for Manhood: Constructions of Masculinity in Victorian America,* edited by Mark C. Carnes and Clyde Griffen, 15–36. Chicago: University of Chicago Press, 1990.

Rugh, Susan Sessions. "American Pastoral: The Family Farm and the Making of the Nation." Presented at the Organization of American Historians Midwestern Regional Conference, Ames, Iowa, August 3–6, 2000.

Ryan, Mary P. *Womanhood in America: From Colonial Times to the Present.* 2nd ed. New York: New Viewpoints, 1979.

Schob, David E. *Hired Hands and Plowboys: Farm Labor in the Midwest, 1815–60.* Urbana: University of Illinois Press, 1975.

Schrumpf, Ellen. "From Full-Time to Part-Time: Working Children in Norway from the Nineteenth to the Twentieth Century." In de Coninck-Smith, Sandin, and Schrumpf, *Industrious Children,* 47–78.

Schwieder, Dorothy. *Iowa: The Middle Land.* Ames: Iowa State University Press, 1996.

Schwieder, Dorothy and Elmer. *A Peculiar People: Iowa's Old Order Amish*. Ames: Iowa State University Press, 1975.

Sherman, Arloc. *Falling by the Wayside: Children in Rural America*. Washington, DC: Children's Defense Fund, 1992.

Sjoberg, Mats. "Working Rural Children: Herding, Child Labour and Childhood in the Swedish Rural Environment, 1850–1950." In de Coninck-Smith, Sandin, and Schrumpf, *Industrious Children*, 106–28.

Smith, Michael. "And They Say We'll Have Some Fun When It Stops Raining: A History of Summer Camp in America." PhD diss., Department of History, Indiana University, 2002.

Sutton-Smith, Brian. *A History of Children's Play: New Zealand, 1840–1950*. Philadelphia: University of Pennsylvania Press, 1981.

Thelen, David. "Memory and American History." *Journal of American History* 75, no. 4 (March 1989): 1117–29.

Theobald, Paul. *Call School: Rural Education in the Midwest to 1918*. Carbondale: Southern Illinois University Press, 1995.

Tinsley, Katherine Ann. "Continuing Ties: Relations Between Middle Class Parents and Their Children in Midwestern Families, 1870–1920." PhD diss., University of Wisconsin–Madison, 1995.

Toynbee, Claire. *Her Work and His: Family, Kin and Community in New Zealand, 1900–1930*. Wellington, New Zealand: Victoria University Press, 1995.

Walker, Barbara M. *The Little House Cookbook: Frontier Foods from Laura Ingalls Wilder's Classic Stories*. New York: HarperCollins, 1995.

West, Elliott. *Growing Up in Twentieth Century America: A History and Reference Guide*. New York: Garland, 1996.

———. *Growing Up with the Country: Childhood on the Far Western Frontier*. Albuquerque: University of New Mexico Press, 1989.

West, Elliott, and Paula Petrik. *Small Worlds: Children and Adolescents in America: 1850–1950*. Lawrence: University Press of Kansas, 1992.

Wohl, Richard. "The 'Country Boy' Myth and Its Place in American Urban Culture: The Nineteenth-Century Contribution." *Perspectives in American History* 3 (1969): 77–158.

Zelizer, Viviana. *Pricing the Priceless Child: The Changing Social Value of Children*. Princeton: Princeton University Press, 1994.

Index

Masculinity, 24–25
Maturity, achievement of, 6–7, 89,
  94–95, 189–190
  awareness of, 183
  farm life and, 183
  measured by marriage, 197
McCormick Company, 42
McLary, Norman, 56
Measles, 74
Mechanization, 3, 227
  boys' labor and, 42
  dangers of, 227
Memoirs
  contradictions of, 223–224
  purpose of, 212
  as sources, 8, 211–212, 224–225,
    229
Memory, 7, 210–233
Menstruation, 220
Methodist Church, 148
Michigan, 26, 68, 161
Midvale, Nebraska, 156
Midwest, definition of, 3
Migration, rural-urban, 1, 3, 7, 109–111,
    123, 197–211, 227–228
  delinquency and, 193, 264n16,
    265n34
  education and, 20–21, 25, 80–81
  play and, 29–32
Miles, Floyd, 49–50
Miles, Leslie, 50
Milk, processing, 45
Miller, William S., 210, 218, 220, 225
Milwaukee, Wisconsin, 123, 195
Minneapolis, Minnesota, 105
Minnesota, 6, 40, 53, 60, 78, 135–137,
    145–146, 186–187, 214
  distribution of population, 2, 211
Minor, Maurice, 130, 212–213, 217–218,
    225–226
Modesty, 220–221
Montgomery Ward, 136
Moon, Minnie Mae, 135, 145, 148
Moore, Frances, 218
Morrison family, 170–171
Mortgages, 263n2
Mothers
  abusive, 163
  death of, 47–48, 173
  family roles, 11
  illness of, 47
  labor of sons and, 44–45
  play and, 30

unmarried, 160–161, 167, 170,
    192–193, 196
  work, in relation to childbirth, 37
Moulton, Frank, 153
Moulton, Lewis, 153
Movies, 28, 152, 187, 204
Munson, Ralph, 141
Murder, 163
Music, 30–31, 152, 207–208
Myres, Oliver Perry, 54, 64, 84, 149
Mythology, 7–9

National Child Labor Committee, 28
Native Americans, 4
Nature, 210
  educational value of, 21
  impact on male development, 24–25
  memoirs and, 216–218
  play and, 136
  study, 21, 25
Navajo puberty rituals, 184
Nebraska, 46, 49–52, 55–59, 77, 82, 126,
    136, 138, 141, 143, 156, 190, 205–206
  compulsory attendance laws, 2
  distribution of population, 2, 211
Nebraska City, Nebraska, 126
Nebraska Farmer, 29, 52–53, 79, 81, 133,
    156
  as source, 8
Neglect, of children, 158, 163, 170,
    173–174
Neighborliness, 251n29
Neighbors, and child care, 172
Neth, Mary, 15, 51
Neurasthenia, 24–25
New Richmond, Wisconsin, 167
New Year's Eve, 145
New York City, 150, 159
New Zealand, 15–16, 34, 247n47
Normal, Illinois, 135, 148
Normal schools, 105–106, 135
North Dakota, 72, 193
North Des Moines, Iowa, 65
North Liberty School, 73
Norton, Curtis (Curtie), 43–44, 137,
    185–186
Norton, Henry, 43–44
Norton, John, 43–44, 186
Norton, Lottie, 40–41
Norton, Mary, 149
Norton, Will, 43–44, 152, 186
Norwegian-Americans, 4, 134–135, 148,
    215–216